The Book of the
Ivatt 4MTs
The LMS Class 4 2-6-0s
43000-43161

By Ian Sixsmith

The appearance of the first fifty 4MTs was marred by a hideous double chimney which proved ineffective and quickly led to complaints from enginemen about poor steaming. 43027 was tested with its original double chimney between Crewe and Holyhead in April 1949. The main conclusion of the tests was that 'some modification to the draughting arrangement will be necessary, and further trials will be carried out with one of these engines fitted with a single blastpipe and chimney'. 43027 is pictured with the single chimney used for the second series of tests carried out between Crewe and Holyhead in May 1949. Unfortunately the results were inconclusive. However the use of the smaller chimney coupled with the application of the lined mixed traffic livery improved the appearance considerably.

Irwell Press Ltd.

Copyright IRWELL PRESS LIMITED

ISBN 978-1-906919-45-0

First published in the United Kingdom in 2012
by Irwell Press Limited, 59A, High Street, Clophill,
Bedfordshire MK45 4BE
Printed by Konway Press.

Contents

For some reason lost in the mists of time, the attractive single chimney of 43027 was replaced in 1950 by a stovepipe example which, while not as bad as the horrendous double chimney, did nothing for the engine's appearance as shown in this picture taken at St Pancras.

The 4MTs had a striking appearance with everything on view. They were designed for ease of maintenance and operation, hence the very high running plate attached to the boiler, leaving the wheels fully exposed and therefore completely accessible. The side window cab had angled weather boards which added a modern touch. The tender was similar to that of the 2MT 2-6-0 having open frame steps up to the footplate which was enclosed by folding doors; the spectacle plates were angled to minimise unwanted reflections at night. The tender cab was appreciated by footplatemen who had suffered from exposure to the elements on the primitive cabs on many older engines. However there was one drawback; when the engines became run down and sat onto their springs a gap opened up between the cab roof and the tender canopy through which howling gales whistled and created a deafening din. On this official Doncaster portrait of 43108, taken in May 1951, the tablet catcher has not yet been fitted. The first Doncaster and Darlington engines were delivered in unlined black, but the LNWR style mixed traffic lining which suited these engines was used from 43097 onwards. Unlike those built at Horwich, there was no lining on the cylinders or the edge of the footplate.

1. Introduction and Acknowledgements

When a class of engine is christened by enthusiasts 'Doodlebugs' or 'Flying Pigs', amongst a number of other less than admiring nicknames, there is an implication that the LMS Ivatt Class 4 2-6-0s were not the most admired of locomotives. Little has been written about them compared with their more glamorous brethren and it seems that in their early days there was some confusion about their purpose. They were the last steam design produced by the LMS and intended as a replacement for the 4F freight engines, but much of their time was spent on passenger work.

They were quickly re-designated mixed traffic engines by their new British Railways owners and this book uses '4MTs' as an appropriate short-hand for these 2-6-0s.

In their early days the 4MTs had something of a Jekyll and Hyde existence: although fitted with all the post-war labour-saving fixtures and equipped with well-intended creature comforts for the enginemen, there was obviously something amiss in their proportions because they were often chronically short of steam. It took several years and some Swindon magic to make a few simple but transformational changes to put them right. After that, they settled down and became widely travelled and generally well regarded, at least by railwaymen if not by enthusiasts.

As is now standard in the *Book of* series a large chunk of the material by volume comes from the Engine History Cards and Engine Record Cards aided and abetted by information begged and borrowed from a number of sources, and backed up by a large number of photographs. Thanks particularly go to Paul Chancellor, Rail-Online and The Transport Treasury for the use of their pictures.

I am indebted to Allan C. Baker for help on matters technical and to Michael Back for his help on the chapter about the work of the class on the Midland & Great Northern line during the 1950s and for making the accompanying photo captions much more informative than otherwise they would have been.

Thanks also go to the Brassmasters team (purveyors of exquisite etched kits of LMS prototypes including an excellent finescale chassis kit for the Ivatt 4MT – PO Box 1137, Sutton Coldfield, West Midlands, B76 1FU www.brassmasters.co.uk for the use their notes on the detail differences between the various batches.

3000 did not appear so different from its LMS contemporaries such as the Black Five when seen at this angle, and the cut-off running board was similar to the so-called 'utility' front end of the de-streamlined Coronations.

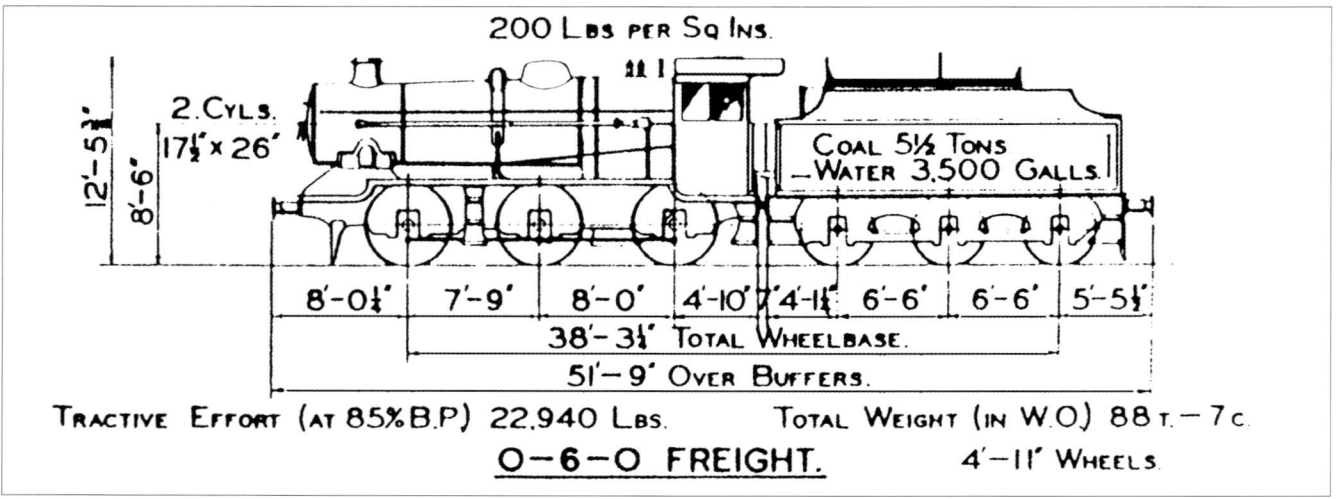

200 Lbs per Sq Ins.

2.Cyls.
17½" x 26"

12'-5"
8'-6"

Coal 5½ Tons
Water 3,500 Galls.

8'-0¼' | 7'-9' | 8'-0' | 4'-10' | 4'-1½' | 6'-6' | 6'-6' | 5'-5½'

38'-3½' Total Wheelbase.

51'-9' Over Buffers.

Tractive Effort (at 85% B.P.) 22,940 Lbs.   Total Weight (in W.O.) 88 t.—7 c.

0-6-0 FREIGHT.   4'-11" Wheels.

A modernised 4F with a taper boiler was included in T.F. Coleman's design proposals dated 24 April 1942 for a range of LMS standard types for the post-war years. It appeared in various forms over the next year or two before the decision to opt for a 2-6-0 was taken.

A sketch showing an early 1944 incarnation of the 2-6-0, effectively a tender version of the Fairburn 2-6-4T, with 5ft 9in driving wheels and a tender based on that being developed for the Ivatt 2MT.

Letter from Ivatt to the Chief Civil Engineer dated 27 November 1945 which confirmed that a replacement for the 4F 0-6-0 had been under discussion since 1937.

KZZ.14/
T.3/9

Encl:

W.K. Wallace, Esq.,   512
Chief Civil Engineer,
WATFORD. H.W.   27th November,   45

        Proposed 2-6-0 Class 4 Freight Engines.

        As far back as 1937 the question of providing
a No.4 class freight engine of the 2-6-0 wheel arrangement
was under discussion. At that time you suggested certain
axle weights which would be acceptable for an engine of this
type which would enable it to run over all the routes available
to the existing standard No. 4 class 0-6-0 freight engines. These
particulars were given in your letter and enclosures of the
2/7/37, reference 26749/C, and have been borne in mind in
preparing the present proposals.

        I attach three copies of Drawing No. DE.514 and
also three of profile diagram DE.515: these give the
particulars and throw-over on 5 chain curve for the engine
now proposed.

        I shall be glad if you will look into this
question and advise me of the suitability of the engine
shewn on these drawings for the routes indicated.

                H.G. Ivatt,
                Acting C.M. & E.E.

1. FROM 4F TO DOODLEBUG

The LMS had been contemplating a successor to the Fowler 4F 0-6-0 since the early 1930s, but it was to be only a few weeks before the company was nationalised in December 1947 that it eventually appeared. Over seven hundred 4Fs had been built up to 1932 when William Stanier became CME. One of the earliest schemes under his new regime was to assess whether taper boilers could be fitted to existing designs, and an outline diagram for an 'updated' 4F was produced in December 1932. When in 1936 the Traffic Department needed more 4Fs to replace old locomotives that were to be withdrawn, it was surprising that another fifteen of the 1911 Fowler design were sanctioned. The reasons for this are not officially documented, but it seems likely that it was expedient to order more of a numerous type known to have low running costs and that were familiar to maintenance staff and footplatemen all over the railway.

Even more surprising was the authorisation of another thirty 4Fs in May 1937, although the Mechanical and Electrical Engineering Committee noted that there was 'a possibility that they will be built as a modified 2-6-0 type'. In fact several schemes based on the Stanier 2-6-4T had been produced, but these came to nothing and more 0-6-0s were built, the last one not appearing until March 1941.

During the war thoughts reverted back to a modernised 0-6-0 with various schemes for a taper-boilered replacement for the 4F. These culminated in one with bar frames, a wide firebox, Allen valve gear, single side-window cab and a stove pipe chimney which had more than a passing resemblance to the WD Austerity 2-8-0. The silly season ended in 1944 with a more conventional 2-6-0 proposal based on the Fairburn 2-6-4T,

but this was superseded by several what might be described as 'mongrel' designs using various parts from existing designs.

In October 1945 the Chief Locomotive Draughtsman at Derby, Tom Coleman, told Eric Langridge in the development section 'to get out a scheme for a No.4 Goods engine. In fact I think we might consider two or three schemes'. The introduction to the first

Alternative proposals to replace the Fowler 4F 0-6-0

Date	Wheel Arrangement	Cylinders Diameter & stroke	Coupled wheel Diameter	Boiler Pressure (pounds per sq.in)	
12/32	0-6-0	19 x 26	5'3"	200	Taper boiler version of existing 4F
5/37	2-6-0	18 ½ x 28	5'6"	225	Modified version of 2-6-4T
5/37	2-6-0	18 ½ x 28	5'6"	200	Modified version of 2-6-4T
1937	2-6-0	19 ⅝ x 26	5'9"	200	Direct adaptation from 2-6-4T
1941	0-6-0	18 ¼ x 26	4'11"	200	Taper boiler version of existing 4F with raised footplate over rods
1943	0-6-0	18 ½ x 26	4'11"	200	Taper boiler version of existing 4F Simplified footplate
1943	0-6-0	17 ½ x 26	4'11"	225	Bar frames, wide firebox, Allen Valve Gear, stovepipe chimney
1944	2-6-0	19 ⅝ x 26	5'9"	200	Tender version of Fairburn 2-6-4T. Straight footplate
1947	2-6-0	17 ½ x 26	5'3"	225	3000 as built

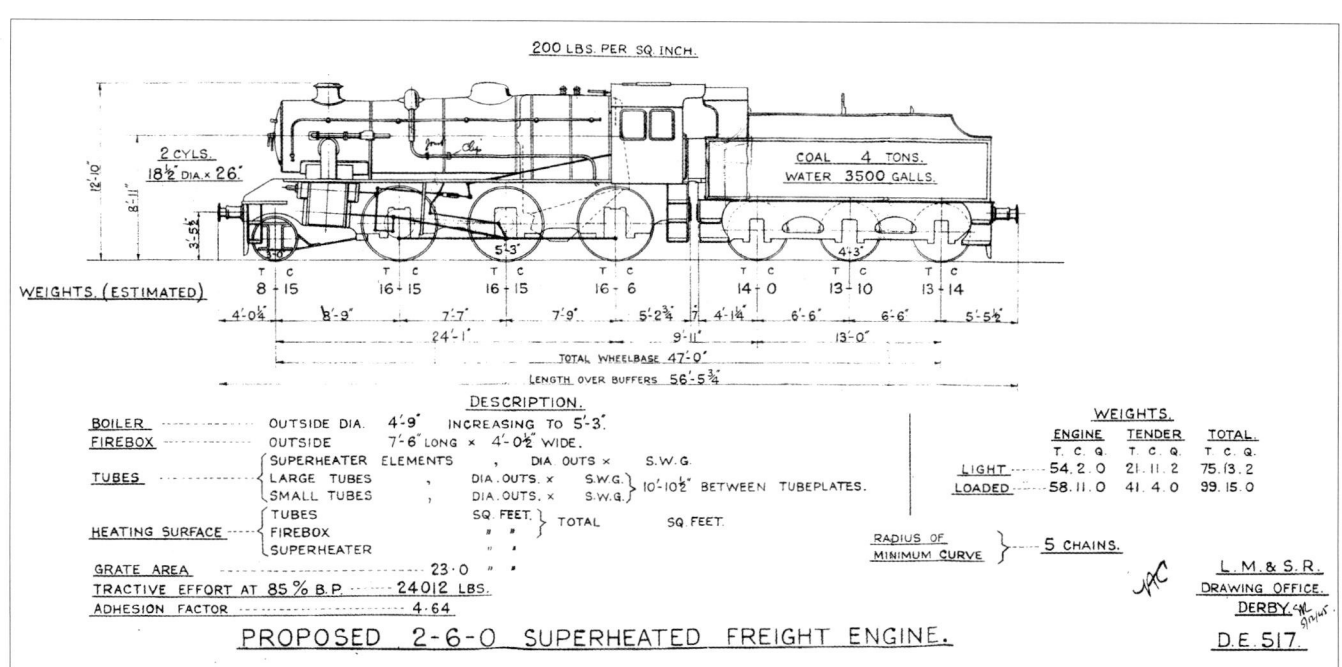

Diagram D.E 517 dated 5/12/45, used in the LMS 1947 Locomotive Renewal Programme submission. The main dimensions were as finally built, but with a 200 pounds per square inch boiler and single chimney. It was visually similar to a Stanier 2-6-0 with a conventional running plate and cab, and a standard Fowler type tender with tender cab.

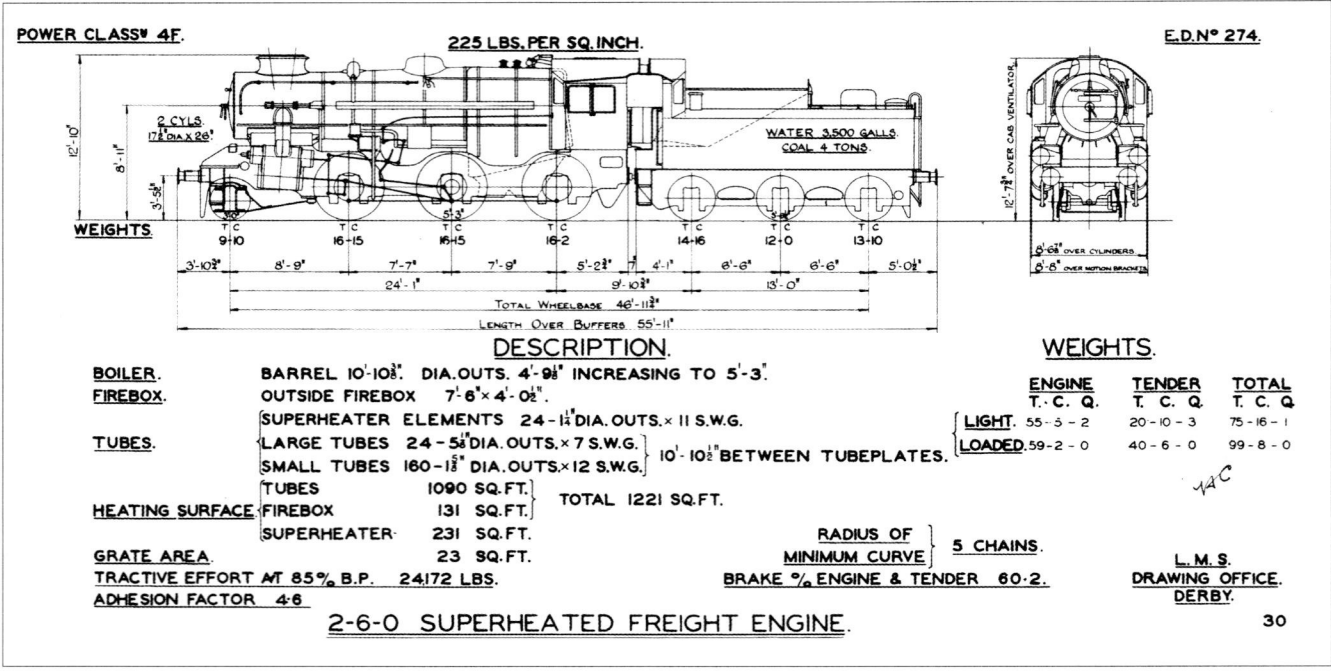

POWER CLASS 4F.
225 LBS. PER SQ. INCH.
E.D. N° 274.
2 CYLS. 17½" DIA x 26"
WATER 3,500 GALLS.
COAL 4 TONS.
WEIGHTS.
TOTAL WHEELBASE 46'-11¾"
LENGTH OVER BUFFERS 55'-11"
DESCRIPTION.
BOILER. BARREL 10'-10⅜". DIA. OUTS. 4'-9⅛" INCREASING TO 5'-3".
FIREBOX. OUTSIDE FIREBOX 7'-6" x 4'-0½".
TUBES. SUPERHEATER ELEMENTS 24-1¼" DIA. OUTS. x 11 S.W.G.
LARGE TUBES 24-5⅛" DIA. OUTS. x 7 S.W.G.
SMALL TUBES 160-1⅝" DIA. OUTS. x 12 S.W.G.
10'-10½" BETWEEN TUBEPLATES.
HEATING SURFACE. TUBES 1090 SQ. FT. FIREBOX 131 SQ. FT. TOTAL 1221 SQ. FT.
SUPERHEATER 231 SQ. FT.
GRATE AREA. 23 SQ. FT.
TRACTIVE EFFORT AT 85% B.P. 24172 LBS.
ADHESION FACTOR 4·6
WEIGHTS.
ENGINE T. C. Q. TENDER T. C. Q. TOTAL T. C. Q.
LIGHT. 55-5-2 20-10-3 75-16-1
LOADED. 59-2-0 40-6-0 99-8-0
RADIUS OF MINIMUM CURVE 5 CHAINS.
BRAKE % ENGINE & TENDER 60·2.
L. M. S. DRAWING OFFICE. DERBY.
2-6-0 SUPERHEATED FREIGHT ENGINE.
30

The final form - as built with the double chimney, high running plate, angled cab and an Ivatt pattern tender.

Fig 1 - the cause of all the trouble; and the designers had held out such high hopes for it. 'The double blast pipe and chimney arrangement has been found by experience to give the desired degree of vacuum in the smokebox with a lower back pressure in the cylinders than is the case with a single blast pipe. This has the advantage of increasing the cylinder efficiency and giving a more powerful engine'. It took several years before the engines reached anything like their potential and only after the boffins at Swindon worked their magic on 43094 and prescribed new chimney and blastpipe proportions.

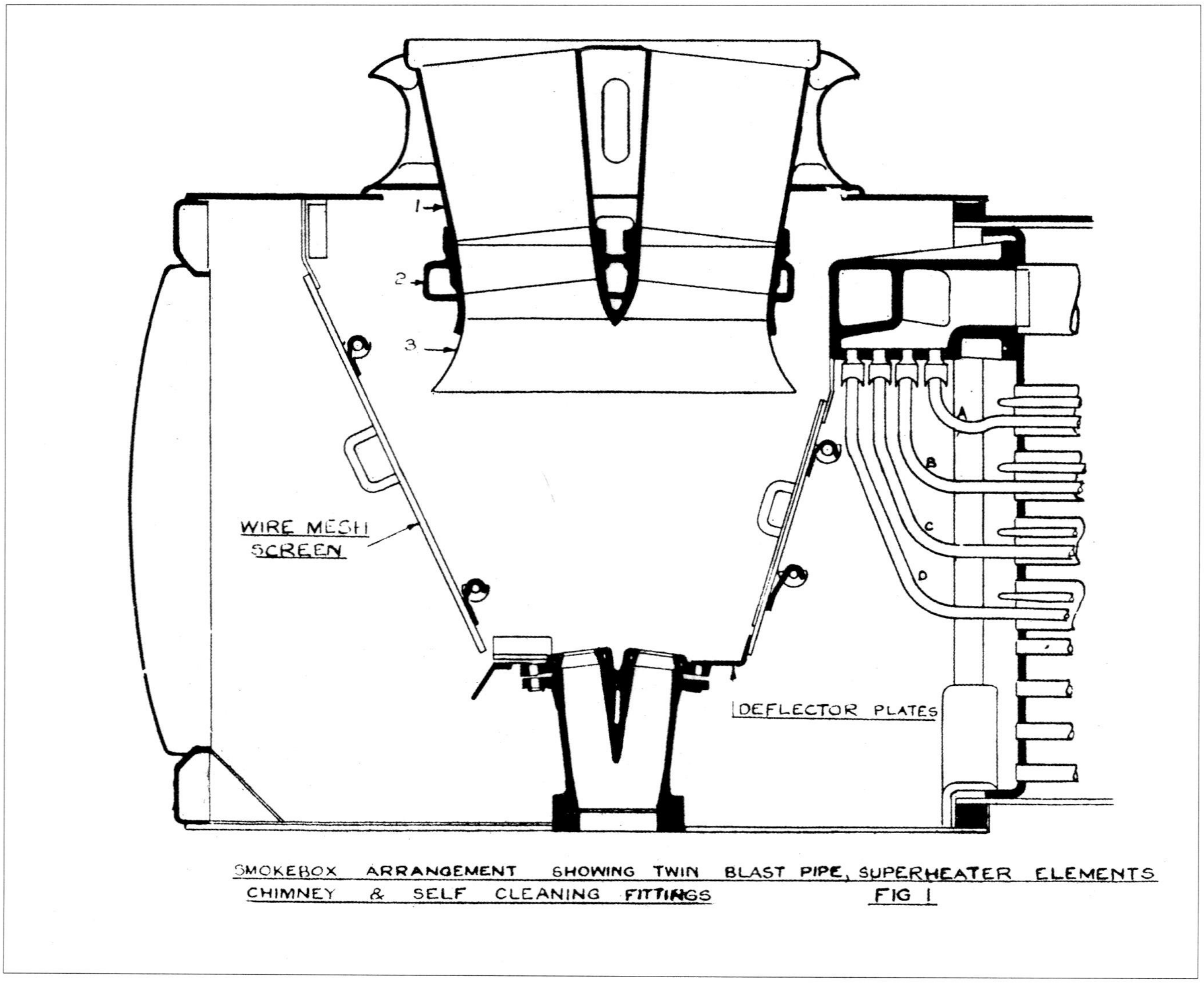

1
2
3
WIRE MESH SCREEN
DEFLECTOR PLATES
A
B
C
D
SMOKEBOX ARRANGEMENT SHOWING TWIN BLAST PIPE, SUPERHEATER ELEMENTS
CHIMNEY & SELF CLEANING FITTINGS
FIG 1

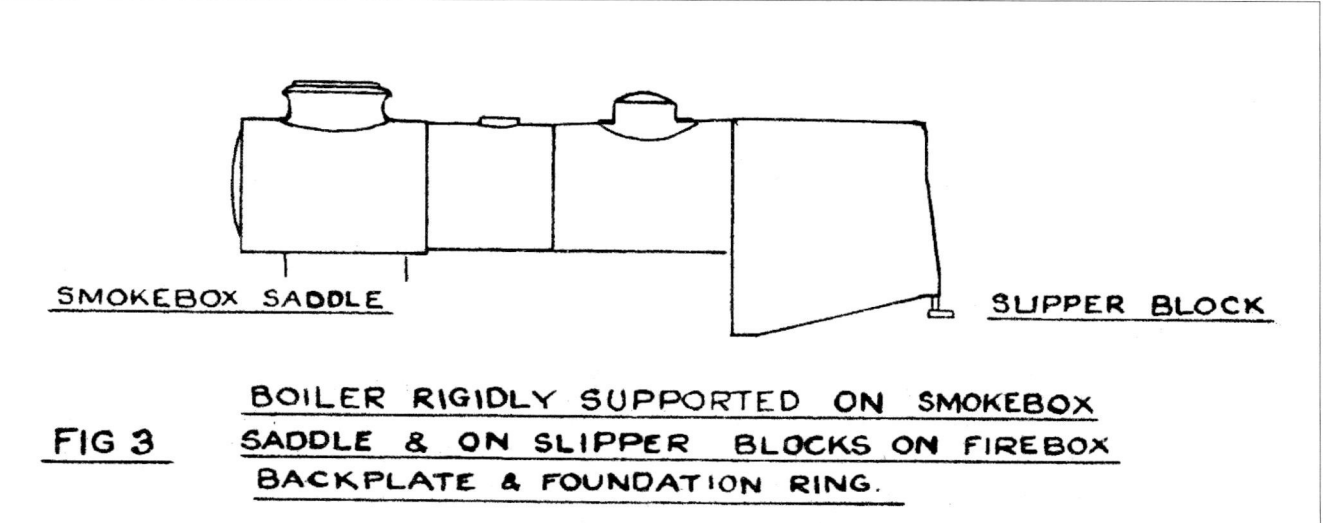

SMOKEBOX SADDLE   SUPPER BLOCK

FIG 3   BOILER RIGIDLY SUPPORTED ON SMOKEBOX
SADDLE & ON SLIPPER BLOCKS ON FIREBOX
BACKPLATE & FOUNDATION RING.

Fig 3 The so-called 'floating' boiler was supported on two steel supports riveted to the foundation ring which rested on brass rubbing plates fitted on the hind dragbox. This allowed longitudinal movement of the boiler due to expansion. Rectangular section side rubbing blocks were incorporated in the support design to retain the boiler in a central position, and provision was made to hold the boiler down.

two schemes, which were produced within the following month, stated 'that there are two possible ways of designing the engine details:-

Scheme (1) – Bringing in the maximum numbers of [existing] patterns and parts.

Scheme (2) – Using new parts designed in accordance with latest ideas'.

The two schemes had the same basic dimensions using a modified version of the taper boiler fitted to the 2-6-4 tank engines with an increased working pressure of 225 pounds per square inch

which produced a tractive effort of 24,172lb. The barrel and firebox were both shortened to keep the weight within limits acceptable to the Civil Engineer because the engine was intended to have as wide a route availability as possible, and for the same reason the safety valves and domes were reduced in height. The frames, axles, coupling rods, crankpins and brake gear were the same as those on the 2-6-4Ts with a shortened wheelbase; the wheels, radius rods and expansion links were from the 2-6-2 class 3 tank

engines, and the pony trucks from the 2-6-0 class 2Fs. There were some new parts in both proposals including the piston rods and connecting rods; the second scheme had new cylinders, pistons and crossheads.

George Ivatt, who became Acting Chief Mechanical Engineer in 1945 following the death of Charles Fairburn, wrote to the Chief Civil Engineer on 27 November: 'As far back as 1937', he noted, 'the question of providing a No.4 class freight engine of the 2-6-0 wheel arrangement was under discussion'. The

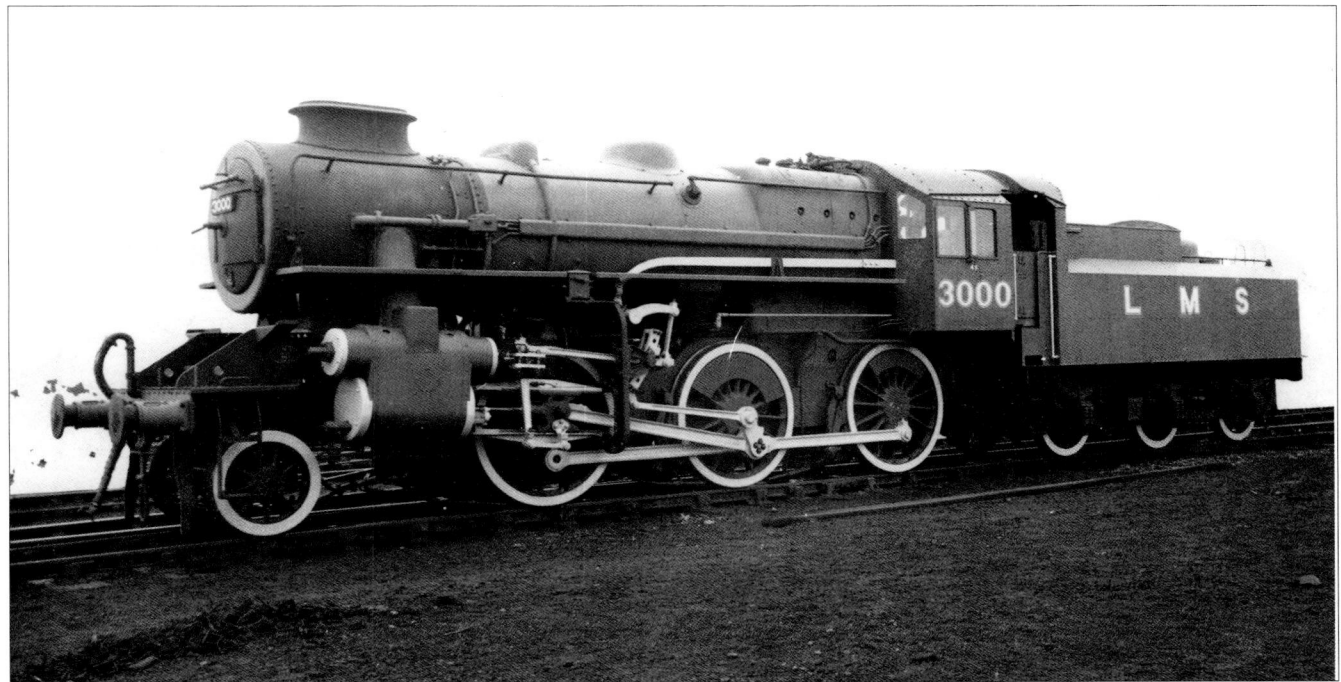

For the official photo 3001 was painted grey with white rods and temporarily renumbered as 3000 because 3000 had been sent to Derby for trials. It usefully highlights a number of features starting with the external rodding which connected the regulator handle running from the front of the cab alongside the boiler to a point just below the dome. The steam manifold was positioned over the firebox outside the cab with the steam supply pipes running externally to the injectors mounted below the cab on the fireman's side. Feed water from these entered the boiler via top clack valves located forward of the dome. Mechanical lubricators were attached on either side to extensions of the motion brackets with their tops flush with the running plate.

What have we done now? 3001 under inspection by the men in hats at Crewe.

43037 at Horwich in June 1949. The lined out cylinders and the absence of the red lining band on the footplate edge are clear in this picture.

The other side of 43037 posed at Horwich.

engine was to 'run over all the routes available to the existing standard No.4 class 0-6-0 freight engine' and the two design proposals took account of the Civil Engineer's 1937 requirements.

There then followed much discussion about whether or not to adopt a sloping cab front plate. The minimum angle of 45 degrees would prevent the use of sliding cab windows in the length of side plate available and it would be almost impossible to give sufficient knee room for the driver between the cab seat and the reversing screw. The rear plate on the tender would have to be sloped to match which would push back the coal space and would either reduce the self-trimming properties or decrease the accommodation for oil feeders, lamps, etc alongside the tool boxes. By enclosing more boiler within the cab 'it might be worthwhile arranging for the manifold to be outside the cab front plate'.

Ivatt was appointed Chief Mechanical Engineer on 1 January 1946 and by the 7th the essentials of the final proposal included in the 1947 Locomotive Renewal Programme, which was approved on 19 December 1945, had emerged. The engine would have a shortened version of the 4C boiler used on the 2-6-4T operating at a pressure of 200 pounds per square inch, with 'steam manifold outside the cab front if possible', and 5ft 3in coupled wheels. The 1[!in thick frames were to be 'cut down as much as possible between coupled wheels and at the front end'. There were new pattern cylinders and

cylinder covers – 17½in x 26in in the final version – and pistons with Ivatt type fixing, the same crosshead as the Class 5, the 2-6-4 tank coupling rod, and the pony truck from the 2-6-0 No.2 freight engines. The connecting rods, axlebox guides, hornblocks and frame ties would be new. The 3,000 gallon tender was a modified version of the Fowler 3,500 gallon type carrying 4 tons of coal with a tender cab and reduced width bunker to provide protection and a good look-out when running tender first. Final details were added; 'Mr Ivatt agreed' for instance, 'that two live steam injectors should be fitted … and no sandgun would be required'. A mock-up of the cab fittings and arrangement was ordered in March 1946 using fittings from the 2-6-2T. More fundamental was the addition of a double chimney, of which more anon, and the replacement of the traditional running plate on the top of the frames with one much higher up attached to the boiler.

The final design, labelled '2-6-0 Superheated Freight Engine' as shown in Engine Diagram 274, had the boiler pressure increased to 225 pounds per square inch and a new 3,500 gallon tender.

Description

When the 2-6-0 appeared in late 1947, the obligatory LMS press release emphasised the modernity of the new design…

The requirement for an intermediate size of general purpose freight engine, capable of almost universal use over the lines of the former L.M.S. railway, has for many years been met by Sir Henry Fowler's 0-6-0 Class 4 freight locomotive of which no fewer than 772 are in service.

The design of this class dates from as long ago as 1911, when the Midland Railway brought out No.3835, and includes the simple straightforward features of the conventional English goods engine with inside cylinders and Stephenson's valve gear.

Whilst these locomotives have given excellent service, experience under modern conditions, and in competition with later designs, has revealed that with inside cylinders far more trouble with hot axleboxes has to be reckoned with. Further, as must of course be the case with an old design, many other features which are not in accordance with the latest practices leave something to be desired in the matter of maintenance, availability and effectiveness in service.

Due to the breaking up of many of the older engines of comparable power, mainly of types taken over by the L.M.S. from its constituent companies, the necessity has now arisen for further units of this power and the opportunity has been taken to produce an entirely new design, incorporating all the latest features of L.M.S. practice. The design has been prepared by Mr. H. G. Ivatt, M.I.Mech.E., Chief Mechanical Engineer.

The new engine has outside cylinders and Walschaerts valve gear, and a leading pony truck has been provided to assist in making the engine a good one from the riding and track aspect. The boiler carries a pressure of 225lb. per sq. inch and the flange plates

A staged photograph with the Horwich production line in full flow and an engine being wheeled. The pony truck is not yet in place showing clearly the guard irons attached to the frames.

for this are made from the same blocks as are used for the 2-6-4 tank engine boiler, the fire box and barrel plates being slightly shorter. A particularly tidy arrangement of the boiler backplate and fittings has been achieved by placing the steam collector for supplying steam to the various auxiliaries, on the boiler top outside the cab. This enables the various pipes to be carried outside and permits of a dust-tight connection between the footplate and the boiler. It also prevents excessive heat in the cab and any slight steam leaks do not cause the windows to be steamed up.

A vertical grid type regulator is fitted having the operating rod outside the boiler from a gland on the boiler side. The regulator handles are duplicated and work in a fore and aft direction, being attached to a shaft running across the firebox backplate. An inclined indicator plate is provided on the reversing gear to enable the driver to read the cut-off comfortably from his sitting position and all the controls have been located in such a manner as to be as convenient as possible. The brake handle is also duplicated on the fireman's side so that the engine can be controlled equally well from either side. Two Davies & Metcalfe vertical live steam injectors with Monitor type cones are fitted under the cab on the fireman's side.

A cab backplate and roof is mounted on the tender giving complete protection to the crew from the weather and the fire-irons are carried in a tunnel fixed to the platform in front of the cab on the fireman's side. A rocking grate and self-emptying ashpan are fitted.

The platform alongside the boiler is carried on brackets attached to the boiler at a height which enables the fitting staff to deal easily with cocks and joints of pipes on the boiler top. The sandboxes have been collected together into one central box mounted across the main frames. The cylinders, which are steel castings made in Crewe Locomotive Works, have a bore of 17½ in. diameter whilst the piston valves have the relatively large diameter of 10 in. in order to make the engine

Principal dimensions

Boiler (225 lbs per Sq.Inch)	Barrel 10'-10⅜" Diameter outside 4'9 ½" increasing to 5'3"
Firebox	Outside firebox 7'6" x 4'0½"
Tubes	Superheater elements 24 – 1¼"Dia.Outs x 11 S.W.G.
	Large tubes 24 – 5⅛" Dia.Outs x 11 S.W.G.
	Small tubes 160 - 1⅝" Dia.Outs x 12 S.W.G.
Heating Surface	Tubes 1090 Sq.Ft.
	Firebox 131 Sq.Ft.
	Superheater 231 Sq.Ft.
	Total 1221 Sq.Ft.
Grate Area	23 Sq.Ft.
Tractive Effort	24172 lbs. At 85% B.P.
Driving wheels	5'3"
Weight	Engine 55 T 5C 2Q Tender 20T 16C 1Q

The frames for the first Doncaster built engines were cut in late 1949 and by the time this picture was taken on 17 March 1950 construction of 43050 was well advanced. It eventually emerged on 20 July, just a few weeks ahead of 43070, the first 4MT from Darlington. M.N. Bland, www.transporttreasury.co.uk

The 3,500 gallon tender had an inset bunker carrying four tons of coal and apart from the tender cab was arranged as the standard LMS 4,000 gallon type with brake and water scoop handles either side of the shovelling plate.

The back of the tender showing the long rear ladder fitted only to the first fifty tenders. The sloping tank tops, although giving a good view when working tender first/setting back onto stock, proved distinctly more hazardous to firemen than the earlier flat tops of the Fowler and Stanier types.

The cab, showing the two regulator handles, one either side attached to a common transverse rod, provided to allow the engine to be operated from whichever position the driver chose. The vacuum controlled steam brake is similarly interlinked, but this was removed at an early stage. The second regulator handle was retained despite presenting the obvious danger to the fireman of a heavy metal bar making sudden, unexpected movements in the darkness of the cab. The positioning of the main steam manifold outside the cab gave a neat and uncluttered boiler face. The fire-irons were housed conveniently in a tunnel running at framing level alongside the firebox on the fireman's side. The sliding firedoors were positioned at a convenient height and below these were the rocking grate levers and catches. On the fireman's side are the two water level gauge glasses (LMS standard pattern not Klinger type) with combined shut off cocks, the boiler and carriage warming apparatus and pressure gauges, with the vacuum gauge at the other side in front of the driver. The large sliding ventilator in the roof helped to keep temperatures bearable in the almost totally enclosed cab, although it naturally let rain in as effectively as it let heat out.

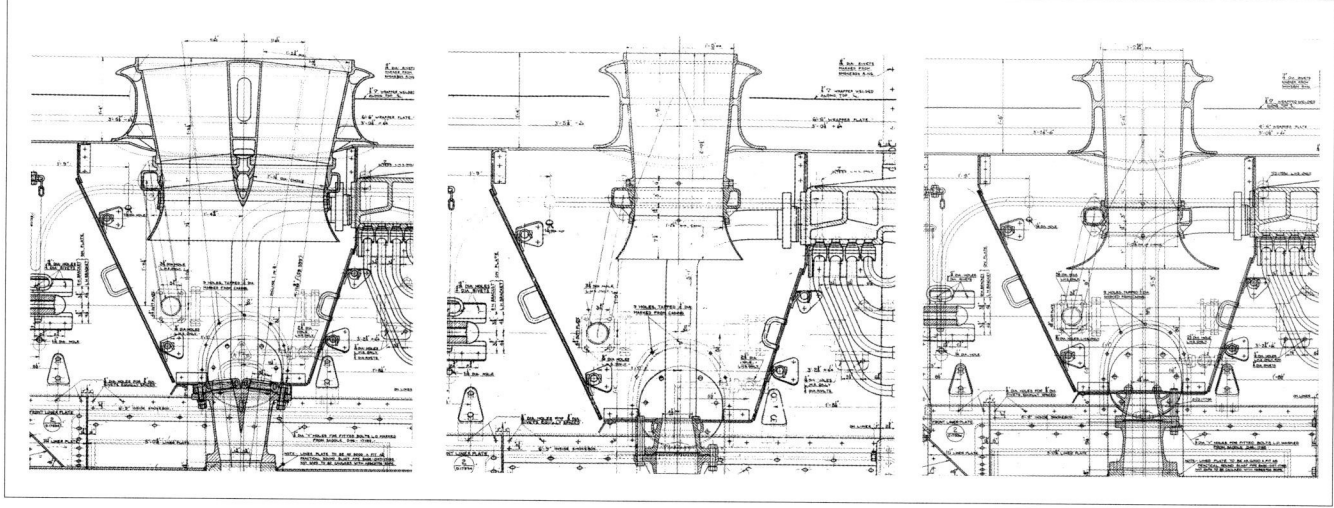

Three chimneys — or what a difference a fraction of an inch makes. From left to right: the original double chimney, the Black 5 type and the final version.

a free running one. The valve gear has a maximum cut-off of 75%, and a valve lap of 1½ in. A double blast pipe and chimney are fitted and these are of a novel type in which the twin jets instead of being vertical and parallel are divergent, in order to give a freer passage to the exhaust steam. The smokebox is also provided with the standard self-cleaning arrangement.

The Bissel Truck is similar to that used on the Class 2 freight and tank locomotives recently built. The design includes manganese steel liners on the coupled wheel axle boxes and guides, and the axleboxes are lubricated by means of an underkeep pad fed by a mechanical lubricator.

The tender is slightly larger but otherwise very similar to that fitted to the Class 2, 2-6-0 freight locomotives and water pick-up is fitted.

Special Features
A booklet for staff was produced soon after the class was introduced 'to summarise, and illustrate where necessary, special features of the 2-6-0 Class 4 mixed traffic engines built in Horwich Locomotive Works. The features selected for description are mainly those in which a departure has been made from what has previously been standard practice'. Note that the engines were already being described as mixed traffic instead of freight, reflecting the duties on which the first few had been put to use. The text ran as follows:

General details
Whilst the design is simple and straightforward, the appearance of the locomotives is somewhat unorthodox, and this is largely due to the height of the platforms alongside the boiler. This has been done for the convenience of maintenance staff in order to make the fittings on the top of the boiler as accessible as possible, and to give free access to the motion parts.

Another point of interest, although this does not affect the maintenance or operation of the locomotive from the Motive Power

angle, is the use of cylinders in cast steel, fitted with renewable cast iron liners. The casing on the top of cylinders houses the air relief valve.

All steam, water and lubrication pipes are made of steel on these engines, in place of the more usual copper, and to improve accessibility, no pipes are run under the boiler clothing.

Double Blast Pipe and Chimney
The design of the "front end" is one of the main factors governing the steaming qualities of a boiler and the performance of the locomotive as a whole.

The double blast pipe and chimney arrangement has been found by experience to give the desired degree of vacuum in the smokebox with a lower back pressure in the cylinders than is the case with a single blast pipe. This has the advantage of increasing the cylinder efficiency and giving a more powerful engine. Adequate vacuum can be obtained at all cut-offs to produce the steam required.

In previous designs of double blast pipe and chimney, the practice has been to arrange the orifices parallel with a vertical centre line with the chimney; to enable this to be done, it has been necessary to introduce two sharp bends in the blast pipes, thereby offering some resistance to the flow of exhaust steam.

Bearing the foregoing points in mind, an attempt has been made on this class of engine, to reduce the resistance to steam flow by arranging the blast pipe orifices divergent and symmetrical about a vertical centre line, the steam thereby passing with the least possible deviation from a straight line through the blast pipe to the chimney.

The layout of the double blast pipe and chimney fitted on the 2-6-0 class 4 is shown in fig.1. The blast pipe orifices are in one casting, but separate caps incorporating jet rings are provided.

The chimney assembly is built up of (1) twin chimney casting, (2) ejector exhaust ring, and (3) petticoat.

The self cleaning feature of conventional design is provided in the smokebox.

Arrangement of Regulator
To facilitate driving of the engine from either side of the cab, there are two regulator handles coupled together by a cross shaft, and fitted one on either side of the boiler back plate.

The regulator is of the vertical grid type and housed in the boiler dome. It consists of the top casting, the main valve and the pilot valve.

(1) Regulator top casting is of conventional design.

(2) Main slide valve differs from standard in that there are two shapes of port. The main ports are of standard shape, but those for the pilot valve are triangular, the apex pointing vertically downwards, as shown at b.

(3) Pilot valve. The ports of this valve are identical with the triangular ports in the main valve.

The main object of the triangular ports in the pilot valve is to obtain a more gradual admission of steam to the cylinders when the regulator is opened, and thereby reduce any tendency to slip when starting.

Operation: Fore and aft movement of the regulator handle in the cab is transmitted through the long rod, situated on the left hand side of the boiler to an arm on a transverse shaft, which in turn passes through a standard stuffing box and gland on the boiler shell and partially rotates in a bearing cast integrally with the regulator bottom casting. Movement of the regulator valves is then effected through a rod pinpointed at one end to the valves and at the other to lugs on the cross shaft.

Boiler Supports
The method of supporting the boiler is shown in fig. 3. The boiler is constrained at the smokebox end in the usual way, but the alteration in frame design has necessitated a change in the type of support to be fitted at the firebox end. Accordingly the expansion angles on the firebox wrapper plate have been dispensed with, and the boiler is supported on two steel supports riveted to the foundation ring. These supports rest on brass rubbing plates fitted on the hind

15

dragbox and permit longitudinal movement of the boiler due to expansion. Rectangular section side rubbing blocks have been incorporated in the support design to retain the boiler in a central position, and provision is made to hold the boiler down.

Rocking Grate and Self-emptying Ashpan

The object of this arrangement is principally to facilitate the disposal of engines at Sheds, but the rocking grate also provides mechanical means for agitating the fire to eliminate ash and break up the formation of the clinker while running.

The grate is composed of firebars that have end trunnions and can be rocked by means of connecting linkage to a lever above the footplate.

The front half of the grate is rocked independently of the back, the lever on the left hand side in the cab operating the front half and the right hand side operating the back.

Each lever is provided with a two way stop and locking clip. With the stop in one position, the movement of the lever is limited by a bracket only and the bars can be rocked through a wide angle (about 40 degrees each way) for dropping the fire. In a second position, with the locking clip raised, the movement is restricted by the stop and only a limited rocking movement is effected for breaking up clinker when running. To agitate the firebar sections, it is only necessary to raise the locking clip, which can be done by hand. Except in an emergency, the stop (which is provided with a squared end to fit a standard ½" spanner) must only be released for full rocking of the grate when the engine is standing at a fire-cleaning or disposal point, and the ashpan doors must be fully open before operations are commenced.

The self-emptying ashpan has two butterfly type doors which are opened by means of a lever on the left hand side of the ashpan. A catch is provided for locking the doors in the closed position and care should be taken to ensure the catch is dropped back into position and the locking key inserted immediately after the doors have been operated. The same detachable handle is used for operating either the rocking grate or the ashpan doors and means have been provided in the cab for stowing the handle when not in use.

Coupled Wheel Springs

The spring link arrangement comprises a flat tension link which is anchored to the main spring at the top end and to an auxiliary rubber spring at the bottom by means of cotters bearing on case-hardened pads. The design is such that the whole spring and hanger assembly can drop straight through the brackets when the wheels are dropped without disconnection of the cotters being necessary. It is first necessary, of course, to remove the safety pins, one of which is situated in each bracket below the spring ends.

Water Feed Valve

In addition to the perforated plate over the tender sump, two combined water feed valves which incorporate a sieve for trapping any particles of dirt present in the water from the tender to the injectors, are fitted one on each side of the main frame. The feed valve chamber is provided with a simple drop down hinged base and quick release screw to facilitate removal of the sieve for cleaning. It should be emphasised that the feed stop valve must normally be kept fully open.

Klinger Water Gauges

Klinger water gauges are to be fitted to the Class 4 2-6-0 engines to determine if improved reliability can be obtained compared with standard water gauge fittings.

Monitor Injector

The injector is a Davies and Metcalfe live steam Monitor type. TWO of these are fitted on the right hand side of the engine below the footplate. This type of injector is designed to be as simple as feasible in construction and operation, and is fitted with cones specially suitable for working with high pressure steam. The injector consists of a casing containing the cones, back pressure and overflow valves, and also a water regulator feed valve.

Steam Manifold

Steam for the various boiler mountings is taken from a manifold fitted to the firebox top outside the cab, behind the safety valves. The manifold comprises :

(1)	The manifold casting.
(2)	Injector steam valves.
(3)	Stop valve for driver's brake steam pipe.
(4)	Atomiser steam pipe stop valve.
(5)	Sanders steam pipe stop valve.
(6)	Master stop valve.
(7)	Elbow casting supplying steam to blower valve.
(8)	Stop valve - carriage warming apparatus.
(9)	Whistle valve.
(10)	Whistle.

The object of this arrangement is to prevent steam from any leaking joints condensing in the cab and impairing the driver's vision. It has enabled a much neater arrangement of the controls and mountings on the boiler back plate to be made, and will lead to the cab remaining cooler in hot weather. It also renders the fittings more accessible for attention.

Interior of Cab

The arrangement of the cab on this engine includes several new features compared with previous standard practice.

The brake and regulator are both provided with duplicate handles, one on either side of the boiler back plate, to enable the driver to work the engine from both sides of the footplate. It will be noticed that the regulator also varies from previous practice in that it is opened and shut by a fore and aft movement.

The reversing screw cut-off indicator is arranged to work in a sloping position to permit more comfortable observation by the driver from his sitting position.

Both injectors are fitted on to the fireman's

side of the engine. It is intended that each injector will be used in turn so as to share the work of feeding the boiler between them, and avoid complaints arising through lack of use, which occur with the left hand injector in the usual arrangement.

The spindles of the injector steam valve on the manifold are extended through the cab front and through a bearing plate studded to the firebox back plate, and fitted with hand wheels.

The steam sanding valve is situated on the left hand side of the cab forward of the driver's seat.

The pressure reducing valve for the carriage warming apparatus is located in the cab front plate on the right hand side. Fire irons are housed in a tunnel running along the platform on the right hand side. Vertically above this tunnel is a handle to operate the manual blowdown valve.

The cylinder cock operating lever is situated on the left hand cab side plate forward of the driver's seat. Provision is made to increase the stroke of the lever by lowering the quadrant when motion is lost due to wear in the operating rods and pins.

Authorisation and Building

Ivatt, as Acting CME following the death of Fairburn, presented the 1947 Locomotive Renewal Programme to the LMS Mechanical & Electrical Engineering

Committee on 19 December 1945 for the first twenty locomotives, Nos.3000-43019, under lot 188 at an estimated cost of £157,500 'to replace a large number of non-standard locomotives which are due for breaking-up'. The following year, 43020-43039 were approved on 23 October 1946 in the 1948 Programme at an estimated cost of £150,000, and 43040-43049 were authorised in the 1949 Programme on 29 October 1947 at £107,500.

The first twenty engines were delivered from Horwich in a little over six months, with only the first three appearing before nationalisation. Then there was a gap of six months before the next batch and a further break of over a year after 43049 entered traffic and before the first of the final Horwich batch, 43112, was delivered in March 1951.

In the meantime, British Railways had selected the design for use on the Eastern and North Eastern Regions in preference to a new small 2-6-0 designed by Peppercorn at Doncaster. Construction took place in parallel between Doncaster and Darlington Works, the former pipping the latter with the first engine in July 1950 by only a month. The ex-LNER works delivered their engines more or less simultaneously up to July

1951, and two more orders were placed with them while the first lots were being delivered. 43107, the first of these, emerged from Doncaster in May 1951, although in fact 43107-43111 were originally planned to be built at Darlington. However, they were diverted to Doncaster and completed before the second Doncaster lot, although these had been ordered first. The class was completed in September

1952 with 43161, although there had been a six months delay between 43156 in January and 43157 in July 1952. New construction was concentrated on the BR Standard types and the 76000 Class 4MT 2-6-0, which was based on the Ivatt engines, emerged by the end of the year.

The shortened 2-6-4T tank boiler used on the class was designated 4D and 170 were built, giving eight spares. The LMS

Lot	Nos.		Works nos.	Built at	Dates
188	3000	43019			Dec 1947 – Jun 1948
193	43020	43039		Horwich	Dec 1948 - Jul 1949
200	43040	43049			Jul 1949 – Nov 1949
1276	43050	43069	2057-2076	Doncaster	Jul 1950 - Dec 1950
1278	43070	43106	4720-4756	Darlington	Aug 1950 – Apr 1951
1352	43107	43111	2077-2081	Doncaster	May 1951 – Jul 1951
223	43112	43136		Horwich	Mar 1951 – Jan 1952
1308	43137	43161	2082-2106	Doncaster	Jul 1951 – Sep1952

43094 on 27 June 1951 running at 25mph and then stationary with smokebox door open on the Swindon Test Plant. 'The initial tests on the stationary plant indicated that the capacity of the boiler was severely limited by the designed single chimney draught arrangement for it was found impossible to produce continuously more than 9,000lb of steam per hour'. These were followed by tests on the road using the Controlled Road Testing System to validate the results.

had concentrated boiler production at Crewe Works prior to the war and so all the boilers for the Horwich engines came from there. In addition three spare boilers were made at Crewe: in November 1948, January 1949 and one as late as January 1959. Darlington made 62 boilers for its own construction (43070-43106) and the first two Doncaster batches (43050-43069, 43107-43111) plus five spares (built between August 1952 and February 1953). These were numbered 13656-13717 for 43050-43111 and 14088-92 for the spares). Finally, 25 boilers were built at Doncaster for the last batch of locomotives constructed there (nos. 13758-82 for 43137-43161).

It was not only boilers that were sub-contracted from other works; the tender bodies for the Darlington engines were constructed at Gorton and the frames at Gateshead before joining up for final assembly at Darlington.

Short of steam
It did not take long before enginemen realised that their brand new modern 2-6-0s were a major disappointment in terms of their steaming capability. The anticipated benefits from the carefully designed double chimney arrangement failed to materialise as the engines with their small cylinders were unable to achieve the same relative improved results as the double-chimneyed Pacifics

and 4-6-0s. One ex-fireman wryly commented 'that the double chimney quite achieved the objective of economical running – it made it impossible to burn the coal!'

Messrs Cox and Kinder in their *Covered Wagon Case Book* article suggested that there was a another factor which contributed to the poor steaming. 'The bottom two or three rows of tubes were originally obstructed by the brick arch and, as the bottom rows of tubes contribute most to the output of the firebox/combustion chamber, this must have affected performance. The reason why the brick arch was so unfavourably located initially is not known. Perhaps the original intention had been to fit a concrete arch which would have been much thinner. Whatever, the position of the arch was subsequently lowered a few inches, thereby eliminating that particular problem'.

It was, however, to be almost four years from the introduction of 3000 before the root cause of the steaming problem had been identified and a solution produced. The LMS had, since before the war, carried out extensive tests on its newer engines in order to investigate problems, often related to poor steaming, with the 'Jubilees' being one of the worst cases. When the Ivatt designs emerged after the war, it was natural that they were put through the same procedures and so the Class 2MT

2-6-0 was put though its paces in April 1947. No.6419 was tested on the Crewe-Holyhead route with a load of 270 tons and it received a glowing report. *Running times were maintained without difficulty, and the engine was exceptionally free steaming. The boiler pressure was maintained at 195-200 lbs. per square inch practically throughout the test. The riding of the engine was very good, and at the highest speeds there was no undue vibration or discomfort in the cab.*

In spite of the steaming troubles it was not until April 1949, almost 18 months after 3000 first appeared, that the 4MT went through the same process. The aim was *to ascertain the coal and water consumption and general performance... when working a special empty stock train to Class 4 passenger timings*. It was noted that *when these engines were first put into traffic it was reported that there was a tendency to pull the fire under the brick arch, particularly when working heavily. In order to overcome this trouble the centre bridge plate in the ashpan was increased in height and the twin blastpipe caps were opened out from 3½" diameter to 3¾" diameter*. The problem stemmed from the steep slope of the grate – approximately 1 in 4 and ironically much the same as the Fowler 4F 0-6-0 grate – which was subject to some criticism. Great care had to be taken to put the coal just inside the door and in the back corners, otherwise gravity and vibration quickly piled it all up in a great mound under the brick arch.

The engine used in these tests, 43027, had been built at Horwich in February 1949 and had received this modification. Two runs were made in each direction between Crewe and Holyhead, with the 8.40am Crewe to Holyhead on April 5 and at 10.15am Holyhead to Crewe on April 6. This was repeated on April 7 and 8, using the same crew as earlier. The train was loaded to 394 tons, including the dynamometer car, and was scheduled to run non-stop at an average speed of 46.2 mph in both directions.

On the first run to Holyhead steaming was very poor and time was lost on several sections, and after sustained periods of working – following a coasting period or signal check – the boiler pressure dropped almost invariably to 160 to 175 pounds per square inch. On the return trip sectional timings were kept and the steaming was rather better but still unsatisfactory. An examination of the smokebox and firebox did not reveal anything to account for the poor steaming, though it was noted that poor quality coal was a contributory factor. The normal test coal, Barnboro No.5 – Barnsley Hards, had been supplied but was 'not up to the usual standard' and the grate was heavily clinkered at the end of each run. So, for the second test, the 3¾in diameter blastpipe caps were replaced by 3]!in diameter caps and 'there was some improvement in the steaming, but it was still not entirely satisfactory'.

One notable feature was the method of working the engine. On the first three trips it was mainly worked at 20-25% cut-off with one third to one half regulator but, fortuitously, on the last two runs, because of strong cross winds, it was worked harder than the first two and produced 'some improvement in the steaming'. On the final run 43027 was worked mainly with full regulator and 17-20% cut-off, which gave much better steaming and overall performance. It was also noted that coal and water consumption on the second test was particularly satisfactory (39.6lb and 28.3 gallons per mile respectively). Maximum sustained outputs of 750-800 DBHP were recorded and steam chest temperatures of 680-690F sustained for comparatively long periods when the 3]!in caps had been fitted.

One of the few bright spots was a vindication of the self-cleaning smokebox – 'The smokebox was not emptied during this series of tests, and there were only three to four buckets of ash in the smokebox at the conclusion of the trials'. However, the main conclusion of the tests was that 'some modification to the draughting arrangement will be necessary, and further trials will be carried out with one of these engines fitted with a single blastpipe and chimney'.Less than a month later 43027 was fitted with a

single blast pipe and the tests were re-run over the same route with the same load. It was tested with three different chimney and blast pipe arrangements between 17 and 25 May. The first attempt used a Class 5 4-6-0 chimney with a 4½in diameter blast pipe which gave little improvement over the double chimney – 'steaming was poor, and the water level in the boiler was not maintained satisfactorily. The average pressure was 180-190lbs/sq.inch'. The blast pipe diameter was reduced to 4¼in for the next day's run and the results were 'steaming very good. Full working pressure and water level maintained without difficulty. Very little clinker'.

A week later, a new combination was tried using a 4½in diameter blast pipe and a Class 4P 2-6-4T chimney which had the same choke diameter and taper but was 3½in higher. Steaming was still good, 'but not quite as free as with the 4¼in diameter blast pipe cap orifice. The coal clinkered badly on this test'.

The overall verdict on coal and water consumption demonstrated the 'marked economy of the engine', but the variable quality of the coal used 'made it difficult to assess the comparative efficiency of the various blast pipe and chimney modifications'. In other words they still had not got to the bottom of the problem. The next batches built at Doncaster and Darlington the following year were fitted with Class 5 4-6-0 pattern chimneys though the effect was somewhat exaggerated by E.S. Cox, recording in *Chronicles of Steam* that the substitution of the single chimney 'improved matters considerably'. By December 1950, 43027 was observed with a stovepipe chimney which was narrow at the bottom and much wider at the top, though whether this was the chimney fitted for the previous year's trials or a replacement is not clear. Cox and Kinder again 'At that time it was sent to Nuneaton; it stayed there until March 1951 and is recorded as regularly working the 1.10pm stopping passenger to Stafford. It is still remembered by Nuneaton men, along with the considerably improved performance that the new stovepipe chimney made possible'. (The stovepipe was finally replaced by the new standard chimney and draughting arrangements described below, in January 1955).

Testing at Swindon
Next it was the turn of the Ivatt 2MT 2-6-0s to go under the spotlight again after 46413 was loaned to the Western Region in July 1949. This time it was a different story. It was found that the locomotive was 'less suitable than the obsolescent W.R. 2301 Class on certain duties demanding relatively high efforts at low speeds and high rates of evaporation at higher speeds from locomotives of limited axle loads'. The 'Dean Goods' tested was 2579, then just over 50 years old! After this unfortunate verdict, 46413 was summoned to

Swindon in early 1950 to be scrutinised by Sam Ell and his team under the auspices of the BR Locomotive Testing Committee. The declared objective was to 'find what alterations to this Class were necessary to enable them to work to best advantage under conditions of Welsh coal'. Ell's team put 46413 through their standard regime, firstly on the stationary testing plant followed by tests on the road using the Controlled Road Testing System. In its original condition with self-cleaning plates 46413 achieved an evaporation rate of 9,050 lb/hour compared with the Dean Goods at 13,700 lb/hour. Reducing the blast pipe orifice and removing the self-cleaning plates improved the position to 11,600 lb/hour. The original blastpipe was restored and the chimney remodelled on the 'obviously superior proportions of the W.R. engine' which produced a slightly better output – 12,300 lb/hour with Bedwas coal and 14,000 lb/hour with Blidworth, both without the self-cleaning plates, and 10,600 lb/hour and 11,200 lb/hour with them. The report noted 'the most economical working range of the Class 2 corresponds to steaming rates between 8,000 and 11,000 lb/hour' so that while keeping the self-cleaning plates the improved chimney proportions made it possible to work freely 'to the upper limit of this range'.

The tests demonstrated the necessity of improving the draughting arrangements, 'to make available a higher proportion of the potential capacity of its boiler'. The report's primary conclusion was that the existing chimney should be modified 'so that by improvement in draughting efficiency, a higher proportion of the potential capacity is made available and rates of evaporation are made possible that will cover the whole of the useful and efficient operating range of the locomotive'.

It should not therefore have been a surprise to the London Midland authorities when the 4MT went to Swindon for the same treatment that the result would be similar, although why it took so long to be put through its paces is unknown. It was after all not uncommon for such developments to undergo lengthy delay, or even to be put to one side altogether over large parts of BR. Darlington-built 43094 was sent from South Lynn to the Swindon Locomotive Testing Plan at the end of February 1951. It had run some 6,000 miles since entering service in December 1950 and since that date it had received neither piston and valve exam nor had it been into shops for repairs or any special preparation. By the end of the tests its mileage had increased by 3,240.

The introduction to Swindon's report noted that 'Road tests carried out by that railway [the LMS] had indicated no advantage of this [double chimney] arrangement for the duties normally undertaken, in comparison with a single chimney, and this single chimney was

fitted to later built engines including a series completed after nationalisation for the Eastern and North Eastern Regions'. The report noted 'It was intended that this class of engine should form the basis of one of the 12 Standard types of steam locomotives for British Railways, and the tests were, therefore, undertaken in successive stages. First of all it was desired to ascertain what changes if any were necessary in fundamental design'. Then data were obtained 'on the level of efficiency of the engine.... and on the price in terms of coal and water of working at all the different rates of which the engine is capable'.

The boiler and cylinder performance and efficiency were established in the first instance by tests on the stationary testing plant where also the draughting arrangements were examined, modified and proved. The stationary testing plant tests were followed by tests on the road; on these, the boiler and cylinder performances which had been established on the stationary plant were reproduced and their efficiencies confirmed, and the coal and steam rates were related to horsepower at the drawbar.

The initial tests on the stationary plant indicated that the capacity of the boiler was severely limited by the designed single chimney draught arrangement for

it was found impossible to produce continuously more than 9,000lb of steam per hour. (It is interesting to speculate quite how low was the steaming rate with the double chimney – it is not surprising that they were so maligned in this form). The chimney dimensions were duly modified by fitting a liner within the existing chimney, although no alteration was made to the existing blastpipe orifice, at 4½in diameter. The special liner reduced the choke diameter of the chimney from 14¼in to 12¾in and made the taper of the sides 1 in 14, with a minimum height above of 2ft 4in. The trials proper were all carried out with this modification, and observations made showed that the draught at the choke invariably exceeded twice the final smokebox vacuum.

The maximum continuous rate of evaporation that could be maintained for the stipulated test period, with the self-cleaning smoke box plates in position, was raised to 17,000lb per hour on each of the three coals tested, 'this being about 1500-2000lb/hr less than the limit imposed by the size of the grate'. (The three coals used were Bedwas, Blidworth and Lilleshall; the latter, it was noted, had proved troublesome in service). The stationary tests were followed by Controlled Road Tests

between Wantage Road and Filton during which 'the boiler and cylinder performances that had been established on the Stationary Plant were reproduced and their efficiencies confirmed'. 43094 was observed on September 25 1951, with indicator shelter fitted at the front, passing Swindon at mid-day on a test train of eleven coaches and the dynamometer car. These tests continued into October and on October 17 the engine was seen working the 1.30pm Westbury to Swindon pick-up. 43094 returned to South Lynn by the end of the month.

In addition to examining the steaming problems, the tests were also to provide data on which the most economic working of the loco could be based, consistent with traffic requirements, and it would be of interest to mention three other modifications/findings. Perhaps the most important was the experimental fitting of a back damper. A more even air distribution over the grate was obtainable when the experimentally fitted back damper was used instead of the original front damper. Whether this back damper was left in situ after the tests is not known but it seems unlikely. Certainly no other engines seem to have been modified. Indeed, there were potential hazards to a back damper on these engines because, if the back of the firegrate had been cleaned by rocking the rear bars and any of the fire had gone through the back damper, the flexible oil pipes to the rear axleboxes would have been in direct line.

The controlled road tests were conducted at rates of evaporation ranging between 8,000 and 16,800lb/hr with loads up to 534 tons behind the tender. The speed range covered was 15-50 mph, the upper limit being imposed by the effect of 'mechanical disturbing forces' on the fire, a major factor in which was considered to be the 1 in 4 slope of the grate. (This had also happened during tests on the Stationary Plant.) This effect was successfully overcome for testing purposes 'by allowing the brakes to drag on some down grades while the steam rate to the cylinders was maintained'. Violent oscillations were recorded when speeds reached 60mph and above, although the report noted that this 'did not accord with the general reputation of this class of engine in respect to riding qualities' and the various defects noted in the course of the tests were 'primarily connected with standards of construction and maintenance and are not, other than the slope of the firegrate, inherent in the design'. The final comment was that the 'test results are 'representative of a locomotive of this class in somewhat less than first class condition'.

The principal conclusion, an astonishing one, was that certain *simple* modifications to blast pipe, chimney and ashpan *improved the maximum continuous steam production rate by 89%*. In fairness to the London Midland it must be realised that draughting arrangements and the associated chimney proportions were still very much a black art even at this time, so late in the day for the steam locomotive in general, despite the work of Andre Chapelon in France during the 1930s. There were some notable exceptions, in particular at Swindon, but there still seemed to be an inexplicable and obstinate reluctance to improving chimney arrangements. For example, it took the Eastern Region until 1957 to have Kylchap chimneys fitted to the

thirty A4s which were not built with them. There were no career advantages in being associated with steam developments...

43027 was involved in yet another round of tests, albeit very brief, shortly afterwards. In accordance with Minute 456 of the Locomotive Testing Committee, a timing exercise was proposed on three Regions. A Hall and a B1 were the other two engines involved and these, along with 43094, had already been tested to find their most economical range of operation. 'The object of the tests was to examine representative rosters to ascertain how far coal economy could result from variation in loads and speeds' and, on April 22 1952, a suggested programme was agreed at Marylebone Road.

43027 was monitored on the 6.45am Chaddesden-Hunslet freight on April 29 and May 1 1952 and the 9.50am stopping passenger Leicester-London and 3.22pm return on May 6, 7 and 8. The objective was to study only the 'free running under power' parts of the journey which was something of a contradiction in terms. These were isolated by obtaining the amount of coal burnt and time taken for all the other purposes; that is, standing, initial acceleration, signals and permanent way slacks, coasting and braking, shunting and fire cleaning, although quite what was left after this is open to question. There are perhaps a couple of important observations, so far as we are concerned here. The engine was fired at the rate of eight shovelfuls at a time throughout and steamed very well on all the trains. The riding was adjudged 'good, but a certain amount of vertical roughness was experienced at speeds above 60mph'.

The workings on the freight trains were virtually ruined for test purposes by severe signal checks and so produced few worthwhile conclusions. The most useful was that the 28 minutes allowed between Ambergate and Stretton for a train of 666 tons would have led to an inefficiently low steaming rate. It was the actual time taken each day, 20 minutes, which gave a steam rate in the economical range of working – 10,000lb/hr and above. Similarly, on the passenger workings, the graphs revealed 'that any saving of time should be made on the up gradients, as this could be done with the least increase in coal consumption. For example, a minute off the booked time from Kettering to Wellingborough would cost an extra 35lbs of coal, whilst on the steeply graded Wellingborough to Sharnbrook section the same extra expenditure of coal would show a saving of almost four minutes'. If only freight train operation was so precise!

The report ended fairly obviously by advising that: *When considering any increase in load for freight trains, it can be seen that the coal consumption would increase accordingly. For present timings, however, it is desirable to work with the*

highest permissible loads in order to operate the engine at the highest efficiency on a coal/ton mile basis. Unfortunately other variables such as the weather, the coal quality, the condition of the engine and above all the attitude of the crews were in practice much more important. For example, on the first day of the passenger tests, the working was not entirely satisfactory 'since the driver on the first stage of the journey worked the engine rather high in the gear for the train requirements. This resulted in considerable time gained over certain sections but at the expense of heavy fuel consumption'. In the words of one old driver: Time keeping is one thing and coal saving is another and you can't do both unless you have an engine and a fireman in the best of condition. In bad conditions or even ordinary ones you have enough to do in keeping time without bothering about anything else!

And finally...
Four years after their introduction, Job no.5658 under BR Financial Authority WO/R2204 was finally issued in April 1952 to modify the class, both single and double chimney varieties, with a 'New chimney arrangement'. This was the taller chimney fitted to the BR Standard 76000 class which had been designed to incorporate Swindon's recommended dimensions. Even then, there is no record of the work being started until 43040 went into Horwich in April 1953. The modification was carried out at both Light and Heavy overhauls and appears to have been done at Darlington and Stratford as well as Horwich and Doncaster, although the surviving records are silent on the subject for over half of the class. No attempt seems to have been made to fit liners in the existing single chimneys, as was done on 43094 at Swindon, as an interim measure and presumably 43094 kept its liner until its chimney was replaced. The last recorded work was in late 1955 although photographic evidence shows that 43001 was not treated until mid-1956, when it finally lost its double chimney. Whether this was the last engine to be dealt with is unknown, although the Job itself remained open until October 1957. It seems therefore there was no great urgency to apply the changes which perhaps reflects the non-taxing nature of the duties on which many of the class were employed.

Carlisle on 14 July 1966, and 43000 starts away on the down 'Joint' with wagons for the south. Cowans Sheldon works — from which so many railway cranes and turntables emerged — to left. The first of the class spent time at each of the three Carlisle sheds after transfer from Nuneaton in 1961. It left for North Blyth in August 1966 and was withdrawn in September 1967. D. Forsyth, colourrail.co.uk

The first six engines were sent to Bletchley where they worked mainly on local and branch passenger services. 43001, departing from there for Banbury Merton Street on 2 October 1948, had already been renumbered from M3001 in August. Contemporary reports observed 'After one or two failures, 3000-3005 have settled down on the three branches from Bletchley, though their running is described as dull'. B.W.L Brooksbank, Initial Photographics.

The early 4MTs did actually do some of the freight work for which they had been designed as 4F replacements. M3010 passes through Derby in 1950.

2. HERE, THERE AND EVERYWHERE

Early Days

The initial fifty engines all went to London Midland Region sheds since they had been ordered under the LMS Locomotive Renewal Programmes, with Bletchley and Workington deemed most in need of the new locomotives. The remainder were spread around the country from the south west through the Midlands and into Yorkshire, most recipients getting three or more engines. The deliveries of the first orders from Doncaster and Darlington were naturally to Eastern Region and North Eastern Region sheds and were concentrated at New England and South Lynn on the Eastern and at half a dozen sheds on the North Eastern, with the largest number at Hull Dairycoates. It was originally intended to send 43066-43069 and 43090-43095 to the Scottish Region but this was changed and they went to the Eastern Region instead, with a similar number of K2 2-6-0s going north in their place.

The allocations for the 1951 engines were intended to be 43112-43121: London Midland, 43122-43126: North Eastern, 43127-43136: Scottish Region, and 43137-43161: Eastern Region. The first ten from the final Horwich batch went to the London Midland, mainly to depots with an existing allocation although Skipton and Cricklewood received their first allocations. The remainder went to the North Eastern, eight of their ten going to Dairycoates, and the last five to Scotland, at Eastfield.

Apart from the first five which went to the Scottish Region, the last two lots from Doncaster were used to complete the virtual takeover by the class of the Midland & Great Northern, allocated to South Lynn, Melton Constable and Yarmouth Beach.

Original Allocations

In the full list below, engines which went to Crewe South, New England or Darlington for a few days during their 'running-in' period are shown under their first 'proper' shed.

London Midland Region

Bletchley	3000-3006
Workington	3007-3009
Derby	3010-43011, 43019, 43031, 43048-43049
Bristol	43012-43013, 43036, 43046-43047
Sheffield	43014-43015, 43032, 43037-43038, 43041-43042, 43114-43115
Holbeck	43016-43017, 43030, 43039, 43116-43117
Nottingham	43018, 43033, 43040, 43118-43119
Nuneaton	43020-43025
Sutton Oak	43026-43029
Lancaster	43034-43035
Saltley	43043-43044
Leicester	43045
Skipton	43112-43113
Cricklewood	43120-43121

Eastern Region

New England	43058-43069, 43080-43089
South Lynn	43090-43095, 43104-43111, 43137, 43142-43145
Melton Const'le	43146-43156
Yarmouth Beach	43157-43161

North Eastern Region

Middlesbrough	43050-43051, 43054
Scarborough	43052
Heaton	43070, 43129
Darlington	43055-43057, 43071-43075
Dairycoates	43053, 43076-43079, 43099-43103, 43122, 43124-43128, 43130-43131
Selby	43096-43098, 43123

Scottish Region

Eastfield	43132-43136, 43138
Carlisle Canal	43139
Polmont	43140-43141

London Midland Region

No.3000 was completed at Horwich and put into service during the first week of December 1947. It was first observed running trials on 15 and 16 December

M3007-3009 went to Workington from new and although their early duties were not well recorded they were noted as gradually taking over from 4F 0-6-0s the through goods workings from Workington to Carnforth. Soon afterwards it was reported that they seemed to be spending most of their time working passenger trains between Whitehaven and Carlisle as illustrated by M3007 arriving at Carlisle with a train from Maryport in 1948.

43012 with a train of SR stock in its original unlined livery with large LMS pattern hand-painted cab numbers. Note the tablet catcher fitted to the tender for working over the SDJR; later engines so fitted had a recess cut out of the tender tank to accommodate these. 43012 went new to Bristol and was observed frequently at Bournemouth West in late July/early August 1948; it was loaned to Bath from January 1949 until April 1950.

Like the animals in Noah's Ark, the first 4MTs went in pairs to various sheds across the London Midland. Sheffield received 43014 and 43015 and the latter is seen there in 1949/50. The white staining caused by leakage from the top feed can be observed in many 4MT photographs. www.rail-online.co.uk

with the 11.28pm Chaddesden-Leicester freight returning on a similar working from Leicester at 3-25am. It continued on these duties for the next few weeks, moving to Rowsley for a short time.

The first real indication of the future role of the class came when 3002-3006 were delivered to Bletchley where they replaced the ancient ex-LNWR Webb 'Cauliflower' 0-6-0s on the depot's three branch line passenger workings. 3006 was noted on Banbury trains during week ending 7 February 1948 and 3002 on the 2.5pm Cambridge-Bletchley on 9 and 12 February. The latter engine also worked the 1.20pm and 5.28pm passenger trains to Oxford and was recorded on a Bletchley-Cambridge train a week later. It reached a maximum of 66mph with its four coach load on the six-mile stretch from Millbrook to Bedford and arrived at Cambridge two minutes early, averaging nearly 30mph despite encountering a severe snowstorm en route. The London Midland Region duties at Cambridge were transferred to the Eastern Region on 1 October 1950, and several of the Bletchley 4MTs were loaned there until Eastern Region engines took over in December.

Before its official move to Bletchley, 3005 was at Newton Heath on 12 February 1948 and on 14th was seen on banking duties at Manchester Victoria, temporarily replacing the shed's two Class 2MT 2-6-0s which normally spent their time on pilot duty at the station. 3001 did not reach Bletchley until the first week of March; this allowed 3006 to move to Workington two weeks later to join 3007-3009 which had gone there from new. Their early duties were not recorded in the contemporary press except for a comment that they were gradually taking over from 4F 0-6-0s on the through goods workings from Workington to Carnforth. This did not last long and it was reported that they seemed to be spending most of their time working passenger trains between Whitehaven and Carlisle, leaving 4Fs on the Carnforth goods turns once again.

The next batch went two by two, in numerical order, to the Midland Division: 3010 and 43011 (Derby), 43012 and 43013 (Bristol Barrow Road), 43014 and 43015 (Sheffield Grimesthorpe), 43016/43017 (Leeds Holbeck) and 43018/43019 (Nottingham). Their wider role had already been recognised on their Engine History Cards as the Freight description used up to 3009 was changed to Mixed Traffic beginning with 3010.

43012 was observed frequently at Bournemouth West in late July/early August 1948 and was loaned to Bath from January 1949 until April 1950; 43013 followed from August 1949 until February 1952. They were joined by newly built 43036 in June 1949, while 43017 transferred from Saltley in December 1949. 43013 went to Derby in February 1952 and the other three had moved away to Saltley by the end

of 1953. The south western contingent also worked on local goods, such as the Yate and Mangotsfield short trips, as well as on longer distance freights to the Midlands and North West.

Following subsidence during December 1948 which resulted in the closure of Arley tunnel (between Birmingham and Nuneaton) Birmingham-Leicester workings were diverted via Rugby where reversal was necessary. M3010, 43014, 43017 and 43019 were transferred to Saltley, initially for these workings, but remained there after the tunnel re-opened in April 1949. Saltley received two more of the class in June when newly built 43043 and 43044 arrived from Horwich. They became a common sight on the Midland Division side of Birmingham New Street on station pilot duties and worked local passenger services and empty stock trains. They were regulars on the Redditch-Ashchurch branch, working the passenger services right up to closure in June 1963 and on the daily goods from Washwood Heath to Redditch. One interesting working to the Midlands was recorded in the *Railway Observer* during 1960, a new Monday-Friday working from Yarmouth to Birmingham Curzon Street conveying containers of Birds Eye frozen foods begun on 4 July. It was hauled by Eastern Region B1s and Ivatt 2-6-0s throughout, although no details were given of which depot the engines came from.

Nuneaton received the first six of the second batch (43020-43025) in January 1949, beginning a long association with the class and over twenty of the London Midland Region allocated engines were based there at one time or another. (Chapter 6 covers some of their exploits at that depot). Sutton Oak shed at St Helens received the next four, 43026-43029, and the final twenty (43030-43049) were sent to the Midland Division, fifteen to the five sheds which had the earlier engines, and the others to Saltley, Lancaster, and Leicester.

In January 1951 Devons Road acquired 3000 and 3001 from Bletchley and 43020-43024 from Nuneaton (43023 was returned within two weeks) and employed them on cross-London freight duties along the old North London line to the Southern marshalling yards at Feltham and also to Hither Green. They remained there until late 1957/early 1958 when Devons Road became the first fully dieselised depot in the country. The only other London Midland Region engines based in the London area were at Cricklewood, which had two of the new engines built in summer 1951, 43120 and 43121. These were joined in November 1952 by 43019 and 43118. They were also used on transfer freight work but turned their hand to passenger duties when required and often hauled boat trains from St Pancras to Tilbury (Riverside). 43119 later followed 43118 from Nottingham, going to St Albans in October 1955 where it took over the

Johnson 3F 0-6-0 duty on the freight-only Harpenden to Hemel Hempstead branch, 'The Nickey Line', until January 1960 when it moved to Cricklewood. 43121 even turned up at Liverpool Street on 16 May 1961 with a Tilbury boat train when it was diverted because the usual route was blocked.

The 4MTs on the London Midland maintained a low profile for the next few years as far as the enthusiast press was concerned as they operated on the unglamorous freight and secondary passenger duties. They continued on workings to Cambridge; in 1956 Leicester engines were on a two day round diagram, which covered journeys to Cambridge and Bletchley as well as Leicester and Birmingham. 43089, the solitary Cambridge 4MT for several years, was regularly used on the mid-day Cambridge-Oxford passenger duty up to its transfer to Kings Lynn in late-1957.

There was a re-shuffling in January 1957 when all engines at sheds in the Wakefield and Leeds Districts, except Skipton and Hellifield, were transferred to the North Eastern Region; this involved 43039 and 43117 at Holbeck, 43014 and 43144 at Stourton and 43114 and 43116 at Normanton. Also in that month the Sutton Oak engines were ousted by BR Standard 76000s, 43025, 43026 and 43028 going to Workington and 43029 and 43035 to Tebay. The 4MTs displaced at Devons Road moved to Nuneaton in October; 43000, 43001 and 43024 joined in March 1958 by 43020 when 43021 and 43022 went to Sutton Oak. Shortly before it left Devons Road, 43001 was noted on ECS workings at Euston during September.

In February 1962 43007, 43021, 43052, 43112, 43113 and 43115 were transferred from Lancaster to Nuneaton, where they were put to use on goods workings to Northampton and Market Harborough and two daily parcels trains to and from Leicester. They also replaced 2-6-2Ts on the morning and evening Coventry workmen's trains. However for most of them their stay was brief and in June 43052, 43112 and 43115 were moved on again to Northampton as Nuneaton acquired eleven more Stanier 2-6-0s, and 43007 and 43021 went to Watford.

There was a big re-shuffle in late-1962 as dieselisation started to make an impact on the class. In September Wellingborough received 43019, 43031 and 43118-43021 from Cricklewood, leaving none at the London shed. They were joined there by 43012, 43013 and 43047 from Saltley, which also lost 43033, 43036, 43040, 43041 and 43046 to Trafford Park and 43049 and 43063 to Heaton Mersey, reducing its allocation to just two, 43017 and 43122. Heaton Mersey also took 43042 and 43048 from Kettering, giving the Manchester shed its first permanent allocation of the class. Amongst the routes on which they were used was the former Cheshire Lines

43020 tops up its water tank at Broad Street on 21 February 1951. It had been transferred from Nuneaton to Devons Road the previous month along with 43000 and 43001 from Bletchley and 43021-43024 from Nuneaton. Their duties included the cross-London freights along the old North London line to the Southern marshalling yards at Feltham and also to Hither Green. They left Devons Road in late 1957/early 1958 when it became the first fully dieselised depot in the country.

Derby allocated 43010 on 7 June 1952 at Ambergate with the type of secondary passenger duty the 4MTs were frequently employed on. E.R. Morten.

Committee to Liverpool. In the following month, October 1962, Nuneaton lost all of its remaining 4MTs; 43020, 43022, 43024, 43034 and 43113 went to Crewe South and 43001, 43002, 43003 and 43005 to Bescot. Northampton also lost its allocation with 43026 and 43052 going to Crewe South and 43112 and 43115 to Bescot. Most of those sent to the Midlands shed moved on the following year to Stoke or Crewe South leaving only 43002 and 43005 which were both seen in use during June 1965 on electrification PW trains in the Coventry area. They were also employed at Coventry on the thrice-daily Leamington parcels, the remaining goods yard shunt and trip workings to Nuneaton until October of that year. 43005 was withdrawn the next month while 43002 stayed on until March 1966, when it followed the others to Stoke.

After barely a mention in the railway press the work done by the Carlisle 4MTs began to be noted as steam came to an end. In 1964 the 2-6-0s became regular station pilots at Carlisle, at both north and south ends (Kingmoor providing the former and Upperby the latter) taking over from the tank engines which were previously used. They were also seen on the Silloth branch and the Langholm branch stalwart 43139 worked the last passenger train there on 6 September 1964. By 1966 their activities were reported more frequently as they were found on duties such as the Carlisle-Appleby local passenger and with pick-up freights on the Maryport & Carlisle line.

In February 1966 Lostock Hall received its first 4MTs when 43019, 43041, 43046, 430118 and 43119 were transferred from Lower Darwen after that shed closed. One of their regular jobs was as bankers, stationed all day at Whalley, assisting freights to Wilpshire, north of Blackburn. The Tebay engines were also occasionally used up to Shap, although the shed's 2-6-4Ts were much more common. They also sometimes worked as pilots, for example on 9 June 43029 assisted 44669 from Oxenholme to Shap. Although most of the time was spent on freight work they were seen on the odd passenger turn such as the 12.44 and 20.45 Preston-Blackpool South during October.

In 1967 the arrival of more 4MTs at Lostock Hall from Carnforth and Tebay meant the withdrawal of the remaining 2-6-4Ts, and the Preston station pilot duties were then shared by them with the BR Standard 75000 4-6-0s, along with the various Skipton and Colne parcels workings which the tanks also worked. The 4MTs were seen regularly double heading the 09.45 Farington Junction-Chorley which usually loaded to over 60 wagons. They also appeared frequently on the 02.50 Colne parcels, returning with the 19.14 ex-Colne, and on the 20.20 Chorley-Wigan parcels. One was used regularly to heat sleeping cars in Preston station whilst the others continued on the Whalley banking duties with Black 5s and 8Fs, the assistance of trains to Wilpshire still being required by diesels on the Long Meg turns. At Christmas, only two of the Lostock Hall engines remained in use, 43019 and 43088 having been taken out of service, the latter with nothing worse

than a hot box, but three more arrived from Workington in January; 43006, 43008 and 43027.

The continuing onset of dieselisation saw the demise during 1967 at Crewe South of 43151 in February, 43024 in May, 43034 in June and 43001, 43003, 43007, 43021 and 43112 in September; 43088 was also recorded as withdrawn from there in December, although the shed was closed the previous month. Those further north also succumbed: by the autumn, the Kingmoor 4MTs had given way to Clayton Type 1 diesels on local freight turns both around Carlisle and in West Cumberland and all were withdrawn, with the exception of 43106 which went to Lostock Hall. As 1968 dawned the six remaining engines were all now allocated to the Preston shed. Apart from the final survivor 43106, which lasted until June, the others had been built to LMS orders in 1948/9; 43006, 43008 and 43033 were withdrawn in March and 43019 and 43027 in May.

Eastern Region
As early as June 1948 43011 arrived at Stratford for trials which lasted until the end of July. At the same time 43018 was sent to Colwick, Annesley and New England, all in the space of six weeks. It was seen in the Vale of Belvoir on an iron ore train and at Derby Friargate on freight workings and on 12 July worked to Grimsby on the 9.52am from Peterborough, returning on the 3.4pm stopping passenger. Two days later it even ventured onto the GN main line when it worked a No.1 express goods from Kings Cross to Peterborough and the 11.35pm up No.3 goods from New

The 4MTs were a common sight on the Midland Division side of Birmingham New Street on station pilot duties and worked local passenger services and empty stock trains. 43048, a Derby engine at the time, has one of these, the 5.25pm from Malvern Wells on 16 August 1955 at Halesowen Junction. T.J. Edgington.

43035 returning to Tebay with coke empties from Barrow, on Tebay troughs on 8 July 1958. It had been transferred from Sutton Oak to Tebay in January 1957 and remained there until withdrawn in November 1965. J.E. Wilkinson.

No 4MTs were based at Crewe until 1962 when seven were transferred from Nuneaton and Northampton. Among them was 43034 seen here on station pilot duties at Crewe. www.rail-online.co.uk

One of the many 4MTs which gravitated to Barrow Hill as steam was eliminated further south on the Eastern Region; 43067 at Beeston with a local passenger train in 1964. www.rail-online.co.uk

43000 on one of its visits to Horwich, in the early 1960s. It doesn't look bedraggled enough to be awaiting imminent overhaul, but neither is it so sparkling that it can definitely be said to have already undergone works attention. D. Forsyth, colourrail.co.uk

England to East Goods Yard. It was September 1950 before the first engine, 43058, arrived at New England from Doncaster and by the end of the year it had been joined by 43059-43069 and 43080-43089. 43090-43096 went to the Midland & Great Northern shed at South Lynn and some eight or ten of them from New England were normally outshedded at Spalding and Bourne, mainly for M&GN work. Their exploits on the M&GN are covered in detail in the next chapter.

The 4MTs do not seem to have been particularly well received; drivers reckoned the new engines rode 'rough' and they did not work especially far. Besides local journeys and duties, they normally worked only to Barford, Grantham, Bourne, Spalding and South Lynn. They did appear on the main line from time to time; for example 43080 worked the 5.5 pm Peterborough to Kings Cross slow train on 4 August 1951, and again on the 8th, this time returning home with the rubbish train from Ashburton Grove, the 'Ashburton Pullman'. A more typical working was that of 43083 which in May and June made itself at home with the two coaches of the Essendine-Bourne branch service, an ex-GNR articulated twin still in LNER livery. One of the regular freight duties since the 4MTs arrived at New England was to Barford Power Station (near Tempsford) but this was taken over by Austerity 2-8-0s when four of the class were transferred to New England in 1953. The Great Central section had received its first 4MTs when

43069 and 43089 were moved from New England to Neasden in April 1951, where they operated on local freight and pick-up duties to Harrow-on-the-Hill and points north previously worked by Robinson J11 0-6-0s, L3 2-6-4Ts and N5 0-6-2Ts. They also appeared on local passenger trains including services out of Marylebone to High Wycombe. On 20 July two successive London Transport trains from Aylesbury were hauled by the two Neasden engines, the 8.6am to Liverpool Street by 43089 (running tender first), and the 8.20am by 43069.

Seven more of the class arrived at Neasden at the end of February 1953, 43065-43068 from New England, 43107 and 43144 from South Lynn and 43161 from Yarmouth Beach, as part of the introduction of 'Reserved Group' freight engine workings. This was the nomination of a number of engines to work exclusively on a selected group of freight diagrams and involved close co-operation between the Operating and Motive Power Departments. Naturally this wasn't as exclusive an arrangement as the title implied and 43107 and 43161 were soon spotted working out of Aylesbury on trains from Baker Street deputising for the regular L1. They also found their way onto the six-coach Marylebone-Princess Risborough-Aylesbury trains when the usual Neasden A5s were unavailable. The 2-6-0s stayed at Neasden for just over twelve months, all nine returning to the sheds whence they came, so presumably the experiment was not a

great success. Only one other member of the class was ever allocated there again, 43010 which came from Saltley in October 1959 but soon left for Wellingborough in the following April. The only representatives of the class on the Great Central for a number of years were 43063 and 43106 which went to Woodford Halse in mid-1956 until March 1962.

A few more odd appearances by New England engines on the Great Northern main line were recorded in later years. On 23 July 1955 43059 hauled the 5.0pm from Kings Cross to Cambridge. 43086 was on Hitchin shed on 25 May 1957 after working the 7.5am Peterborough-Kings Cross parcels, and the next week 43066 worked the 7.35pm Welwyn Garden City-Colwick freight three times in succession.

In December 1957 eight New England engines (43059, 43061, 43062, 43064, 43065, 43080, 43083 and 43085) were transferred to Boston when the sub-shed at Spalding was moved into the Lincoln District; they were followed in June 1958 by another three (43058, 43060 and 43066). When the M&GN was closed in February 1959 sixteen of its 4MTs joined them, giving the Lincolnshire shed a total of no less than 28. Seven went to Norwich Thorpe, six to Stratford, and two each to Colchester and Kings Lynn. One of the latter merited a report in the *Railway Observer* when it arrived at Liverpool Street with a train from Kings Lynn on 26 March. 43145, one of the Norwich allocation, moved north to the former GC shed at

When 4MT repairs were transferred from Horwich to Swindon in 1964, the engines were frequently observed at Westbury running in before returning to their home sheds. 43047 from Heaton Mersey was there on 15 August 1964 following a Heavy Intermediate completed on 15 July. www.rail-online.co.uk

Staveley In March 1960 and was joined two weeks later by 43087 from Cambridge; they were immediately noted on a former D11 diagram which took the engine down the GC line to Leicester in the evening. The drift northwards continued with Stratford losing its final 4MT in August while Retford gained its first 4MTs in early 1961, 43158 from Lincoln in February, quickly followed by 43142 and 43157 from Boston in April and 43127 from New England in May. The Boston contingent drifted away over the next few years; they went mainly to Colwick – eight in December 1962 and two a year later in December 1963 when the shed was closed and Sleaford became a sub-shed of Colwick. Of the others remaining at that date three moved to New England and five, 43068, 43083, 43107, 43110 and 43142, were withdrawn.

Barrow Hill, the ex-Midland Railway shed at Staveley transferred to the Eastern Region on 1 February 1958, had around half a dozen 4MTs on its books from 1960 onwards when 43087, 43089, 43090, 43145, 43160 and 43161 arrived from Norwich and Cambridge, although 43087, 43111 and 43159 were

The 4MTs were occasionally chosen for use on railtours such as 43002 on 12 February 1966 in a snowy Sutton Park with the Warwickshire Railway Society 'Midlander' Tour. It worked from Birmingham Snow Hill to Rugby Midland via Old Hill, Dudley, Aldridge, Water Orton, Nuneaton Abbey Street, Measham, Burton-on-Trent, Trent, Ambergate, Gresley, Wigston and Market Harborough. BR Sulzer Type 2 D5011 was added as a pilot engine at Rugby because 43002 was low on coal and together they took the train to Leamington Spa, handing over to Black Five 45031 for the return to Snow Hill. www.rail-online.co.uk

Above. 43009 on a PW Department ballast train at Long Meg on 12 July 1966 with a Shark leading the rake of ballast hoppers ready to spread their load. The 4MTs were a favourite on this type of duty, especially in the winter, as their cabs were warm and comfortable. GNSRA (Murdoch)/ www.transporttreasury.co.uk

Middle. Before the 4MTs were introduced on the ex-LNER lines they were sent to the Eastern Region for trials in mid-1948. 43011 is an object of some curiosity at Stratford, where it worked from June until the end of July; at the same time 43018 was sent to Colwick, Annesley and New England.

Bottom. The Eastern Region 4MTs immediately went into fleet service on the former Midland & Great Northern Joint lines, operating initially from New England shed at Peterborough. 43083 heads a mix of coaching stock on 14 September 1951 at Peterborough North, the westerly terminus for the M&GN 'main line' from Yarmouth. The exploits of the Doodlebugs on the M&GN are covered in some detail in the next chapter. E. Sawford/ www.transporttreasury.co.uk

New England's 4MTs did appear on the East Coast main line from time to time. 43059 is at Hadley Wood on 23 July 1955 with a train to Kings Cross. It returned with the 5.0pm from Kings Cross to Cambridge.

sent to Grantham in November 1962 to replace L1s which were going to Colwick. However they soon returned and in the following May 1963 joined 43088, 43151 and 43161 which had been transferred in March. 43127 also arrived in May, 43062 and 43153 in September, 43067, 43082, 43085, 43109, 43143 and 43148 in November, 43059, 43084 and 43089 in June 1964, and 43080, 43092 and 43108 in January 1965 by which time the allocation had reached nineteen. Almost all of them were withdrawn from

there later in the year with just a handful escaping; 43109 in March to Canklow followed by 43082 and 43084 to Stourton in July.

When New England shed closed to steam at the end of 1964 only five 4MTs remained; 43092 was transferred to Barrow Hill and the others, 43081, 43086, 43147 and 43150 were withdrawn. 43081 was the only Eastern Region engine to remain at one shed throughout its career; it went straight to New England in October 1950 and

stayed there until the end. Colwick's allocation averaged around sixteen 4MTs during 1963/64, but all had gone by the start of 1965. By the middle of that year most of the remaining Eastern allocation had been withdrawn, with a handful transferred to the North Eastern Region and a few staying on at Barrow Hill and Canklow. The final five survivors were withdrawn from Langwith Junction in November 1965 after being transferred the previous month; they were 43082, 43089 and 43149 from Barrow Hill plus

43146 at Brundall in the early 1950s, before it had a replacement chimney, shows that the M&GN engines were not restricted to operating purely on that system's lines. The Melton Constable 4MT heads a long train of decidedly mixed ex-LNER coaches on the ex-Great Eastern Norwich-Great Yarmouth/Lowestoft line. R.K. Blencowe.

43161 at Rickmansworth on 12 March 1954. It was one of the 4MTs transferred from M&GN sheds to Neasden in 1953 for the introduction of Reserved Group freight engine workings, whereby a number of engines were nominated to work exclusively on a selected group of freight diagrams. The 2-6-0s stayed at Neasden for just over twelve months, all nine returning to the sheds whence they came, so presumably the experiment was not deemed a great success.

43108 and 43109 ex-Canklow. Whether they ever turned a wheel there, or this was merely a paper housekeeping transaction is not known.

North Eastern Region
The first 4MT to come to the North Eastern Region was 43050, from Doncaster in July 1950, quickly followed by 43051-43057. By the end of October the Region had nearly twenty in service as simultaneous deliveries were also made from its own works at Darlington (43070-43079) and another eight arrived in the first quarter of 1951, 43096-43103. The North Eastern also received ten, 43122-43131, from the final Horwich

batch before the year was out, and in February/March 1952 43014, 43015, 43016, 43030, 43038, 43043 and 43044 were transferred from the London Midland Region sheds at Sheffield, Leeds and Saltley.

Little is recorded of their early activities in the enthusiast press although the *Railway Observer* had a regular correspondent in Scarborough – Bill Hoole it is thought – who provided numerous observations of the new engines starting with the arrival on 18 August 1950 of the local shed's own 43052 ex-Doncaster. The next day it was station pilot. This was not the first of the class to appear there, 43015 having

turned up in 1949 on a through working from the London Midland.

43052 spent its first weeks at Scarborough on the early morning mineral empties to Gascoigne Wood near Selby, returning with a full load before taking the 2.40pm slow to Hull. On 21 August it brought back from York a 17-coach empty stock train and was in difficulties when it arrived in Scarborough. 43053 and 43054 started working in from Hull during September and soon after 43076-43079 were also noted at Scarborough on Hull turns. Further 4MTs on Hull workings in March 1951 were Dairycoates' latest acquisitions, 43099-43103, arriving on a morning goods and returning at 7.0pm; in between the engine was used by Scarborough on a goods to York and back, a working that continued into the 1960s. Details of other workings of the large Dairycoates allocation are scarce since they were primarily employed on freights. On 25 September 1951 43122 was recorded on the 9.45pm Hull-Mottram freight and after visiting Gorton it returned the following day with the 1.30pm Dewsnap-Hull. 43053 worked the 6.0pm Leeds Neville Hill-Hull goods on 17 March 1953. Scarborough on a summer Saturday hosted a variety of 'foreign' engines from many different sheds and the 4MTs were no exception: on 13 August 1960 three of the class arrived on passenger trains, 43014 of York on a private excursion from Earswick, 43063 of Woodford Halse on the 9.42am arrival from Grantham and 43146 of Grimesthorpe on the 12.32pm arrival

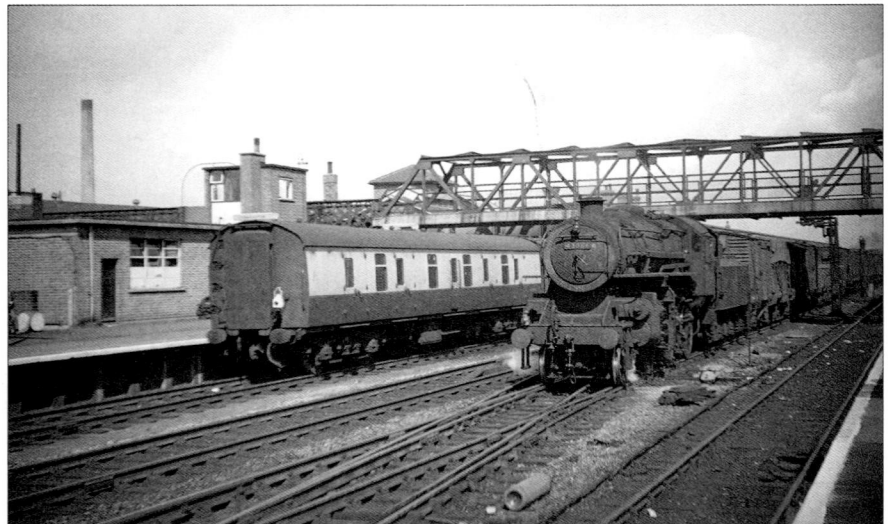

Boston's 43066 passing through Doncaster with a freight in the early 1960s. It was transferred from New England in June 1958 and left for Colwick at the end of 1962. www.rail-online.co.uk

43127 pulls out of the yard on 22 June 1960 at Stamford Town with one of those long gone pick-up freights. Although originally a North Eastern Region engine at Dairycoates it had reached New England earlier in the year. www.colourrail.co.uk

from Chesterfield. Selby had several 4MTs on its books from new (43096-43098, 43123) and 43052 from Scarborough in July 1951. Their passenger duties were occasionally reported, such as on the double headed Saturdays Only trains running from the West Riding and Lancashire to Scarborough in July 1952 where they were paired with D20 or D49 4-4-0s from the same shed. On Sunday 24 August when the East Coast mainline was closed between Selby and York for relaying work, 43123 hauled the Wakefield-York

from Selby. One of their regular duties was the 6.30pm York-Harrogate.

Selby had nine by 1959, but all had gone by the end of that year when 43051, 43053 and 43054 were transferred away to Leeds Neville Hill in May and in September 43057, 43071 and 43096 went to York, 43097, 43098 and 43125 to Goole, and 43123 to Dairycoates. The Hull shed, which received eighteen of the class from new, lost its final four when 43076-43079 went to Royston in October 1965. 43131 was unusual in remaining at Dairycoates throughout,

arriving new in November 1951 and withdrawn in December 1963.

The engines in the north of the Region also were little-known, with only occasional sightings recorded. 43072 worked on Saltburn-Darlington services in April/May 1952 and a few months later several of the Middlesbrough allocation were loaned to Saltburn to cover for their absent 4-6-2Ts. The 4MTs usually worked tender first from Saltburn to Darlington. 43101 and 43102, transferred from Dairycoates in June 1952, were working from Middlesbrough on mineral and iron ore trains along with 43050, 43051, 43054, 43072, 43073 and 43074. On 9 September Middlesbrough provided 43102 for the 5.23pm train to Newcastle, possibly the first occasion one had appeared on these trains. Amongst the many freight duties covered by the depot were those on the Wensleydale branch from the various quarries to Tees-side. In June 1953 Heaton sent two of its 4MTs to work on the Alston branch, running southwards from Haltwhistle on the Newcastle-Carlisle line.

Probably the most arduous freight duty undertaken by the 4MTs concerned the 1,370 feet high Stainmore summit. Following the completion of bridge strengthening work, trials with mineral trains of 32 twenty ton coke wagons took place in April 1955 between West Auckland and Tebay, with a banking engine to the summit in each direction. Three 4MTs were involved, 43056, 43057 and 43071, two double heading the train and a third as the banker. The trials were successful and the class began regular work over the line the following month,

43052, the only 4MT allocated to Scarborough, at Bridlington on 10 January 1953. During its first weeks there it was employed on the early morning mineral empties to Gascoigne Wood near Selby, returning with a full load before taking the 2.40pm slow to Hull. 43052 had been transferred to Selby over a year before this picture was taken. A.G. Forsyth, Initial Photographics.

Above. Ex-London Midland Region engine 43030 with a mixed freight at Manningham on 24 June 1959. It moved to the shed there from Heaton in June 1957 and stayed until withdrawn in October 1966.
www.transporttreasury.co.uk

Middle. 43015 in March 1963 at West Hartlepool on a typical freight working in the North East. Originally a Sheffield engine it moved to the North Eastern Region at Dairycoates in February 1952 and to West Hartlepool in June 1955.
J.A.C. Kirke,
www.transporttreasury.co.uk

Bottom. 43123 pours out smoke on 25 August 1962 at its home shed, West Hartlepool. A number of 4MTs had gathered on Tyneside by the summer of 1966 with transfers from the London Midland Region and York adding to the existing allocations; by November North Blyth had fourteen including 43123 and West Hartlepool three. All except one were withdrawn by the end of June 1967.
www.rail-online.co.uk

43057 at Newcastle on 29 September 1963 was one of two 4MTs taking part in a marathon tour around the North East organised jointly by the SLS and RCTS, which began on 27 September and ended on 1 October. 43057 worked the train to Percy Main where it was taken over by 43129, and then took over again at Tyne Commission Quay to Morpeth via South and North Blyth. www.rail-online.co.uk

43129 at Newcastle Tyne Commission Quay after bringing the tour train from Percy Main before handing back to 43057 for the next leg to Morpeth. 43129 completed the final stage from there back to Newcastle. G. Harrop.

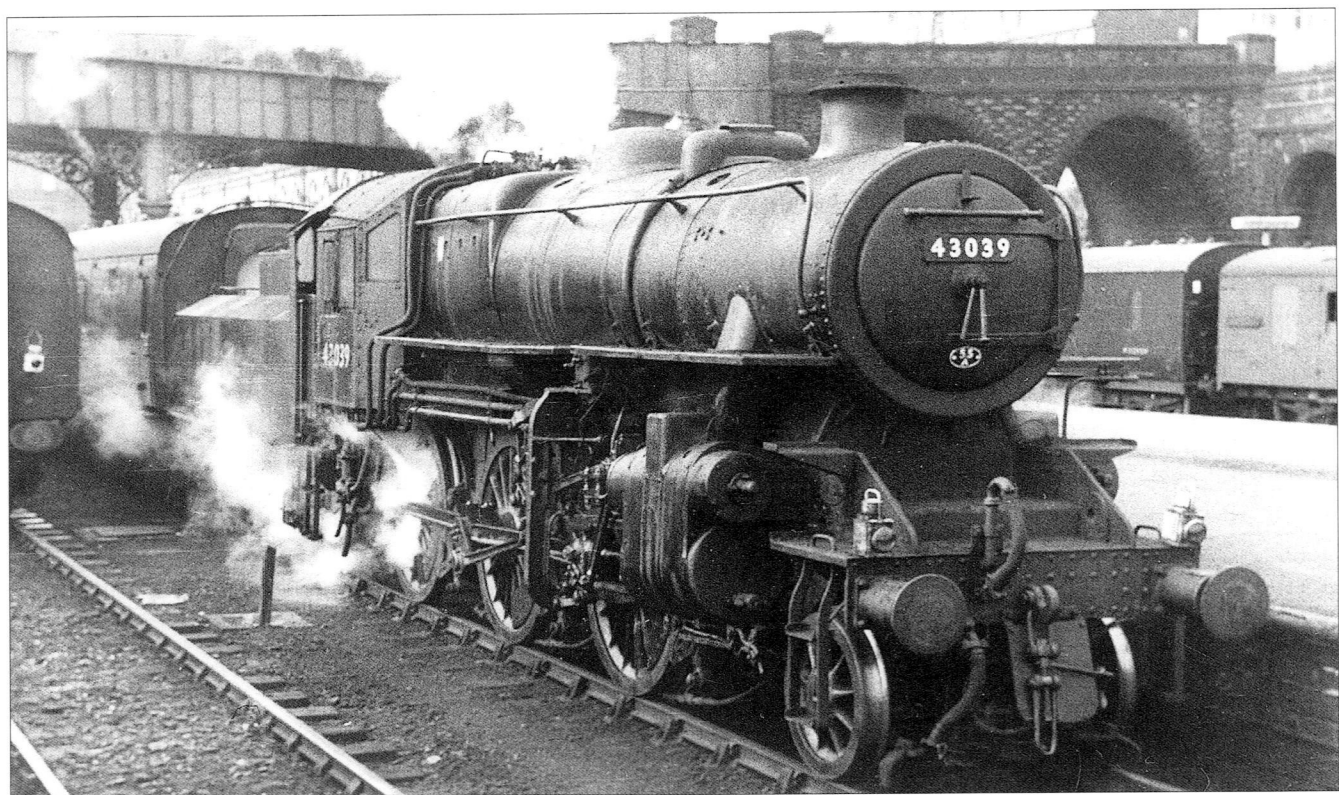

43039, which remained at Holbeck for its whole career, waits at Leeds City on 7 May 1966 with the 07.02 to Bradford. It was withdrawn by the end of the year after just over sixteen years at the Leeds shed.

with six engines transferred to Kirkby Stephen. These were 43038, 43122, 43124 and 43130 from Dairycoates, 43055 from West Hartlepool and 43128 from Alston. Five went to West Auckland; 43056, 43057, 43071 and 43075 from Darlington and 43125 from Selby. As was often the case their stay was short-lived and by May 1956 they began to be displaced by the BR Standard equivalents. 43038 had already left for Middlesbrough in November 1955 and in June 1956 the remainder were transferred away to other sheds in the Region, mainly on Tyneside, apart from 43130 which lingered on until September. The North Eastern 4MTs continued to work across Stainmore until closure, particularly on passenger trains – usually excursions.

After the shed passed to the London Midland on 1 February 1958, 4MTs returned to Kirkby Stephen when its eight BR standard 76000 2-6-0s were transferred away to be replaced by 43018, 43023, 43027, 43045 and 43103 and two 2MTs. In just over two years the 4MTs were to be moved once again. In view of the proposed closure of the ex-NER lines in the Kirkby Stephen district including the line from Barnard Castle over Stainmore and from Kirkby Stephen to Tebay, a trial re-routing of freight traffic began for a month from 4 July. Mineral traffic from Durham to the Barrow area was worked via the Newcastle and Carlisle line and thence via the Maryport & Carlisle between Workington and Whitehaven to the Furness line. The mineral traffic originating from Merrygill (east of Kirkby Stephen) and Warcup was

worked to Carlisle using the North Eastern to Appleby East and then after a double reversal on to the Midland. Two empty wagon trains a day were operated from Durran Hill for this traffic, one for Warcup which conveyed a double load and was double headed and one for Kirkby Stephen, both workings returning to Carlisle later in the day. Four of Kirkby Stephen's 4MTs (43018, 43023, 43027 and 43103) were transferred to Kingmoor for this work, leaving just 43045, which was noted on 12 July 'greased up' and out of use – it was presumably soon reinstated because it stayed there for several years until it joined 43139 at Carlisle Canal in November 1961.

Tebay shed was also affected by the changes as its engines formerly worked the mineral trains forward from Tebay to the Barrow District and two of their 4MTs, 43028 and 43029, were moved to Upperby in September, presumably for working the diverted trains via the M&C, as the new arrangements became permanent.

The work of the Leeds-based engines went virtually unrecorded until the early 1960s; Neville Hill had acquired 43051 and 43054 in May 1959 and the former was noted in 1962 as a frequent performer on the daily pick-up goods from Leeds which was a circular trip, outwards via Church Fenton and Tadcaster returning via Wetherby and Bardsey. Mirfield had the briefest acquaintance with the class when 43096 was allocated there between July and December 1962. During that time it was regularly used on the Huddersfield

Midland branch, having displaced 4F 44056.

The Holbeck allocation emerged from obscurity when in November 1965 a number of its 4MTs appeared at Huddersfield on parcels trains. They were often used at that time on express services between Bradford and Leeds and also on some of the Morecambe trains. More mundane local freight workings included the 06.20 Hunslet-Ilkley, returning at 10.00 and the 12.40 Stourton-Ilkley, returning at 15.15. Holbeck's 43039 was one of only three engines in the whole class to remain at one depot – it arrived in July 1949 and was withdrawn from there in December 1966.

By the end of 1965 the remaining North Eastern allocation was concentrated in a handful of sheds in Yorkshire and on Tyneside:
Normanton 43043, 43098, 43099, 43116, 43125, 43141
Royston 43076, 43077, 43078, 43079
Stourton 43044, 43084, 43096, 43102, 43117, 43135, 43140
York 43071, 43097, 43126, 43133, 43138
Manningham 43014, 43016, 43030, 43051, 43074
Holbeck 43039, 43069, 43124, 43130
Wakefield 43070, 43137
Neville Hill 43054

The Tyneside allocation was supplemented in July and August 1966 by five transfers from the London Midland and five from York when that shed lost its 4MTs; by November North Blyth had 43000, 43012, 43040, 43048, 43055, 43063, 43071, 43097, 43101, 43123,

43130 shunting at Idle on 29 March 1967. The station was on the ex-Great Northern line which ran north-east of Bradford from Laisterdyke through Eccleshill, Idle and Thackley to Shipley. It lost its passenger service but goods traffic continued on the whole line until October 1964 and between Shipley and Idle until 1968.

43047 at its home shed Saltley (rebuilt roundhouse in background) on 29 July 1961. Prodigious and sustained leakage from the regulator valve has splashed salt deposits even on the cab front and side. D. Forsyth, colourrail.co.uk

In May 1953 four of the Eastfield contingent, 43132, 43033, 43035 and 43037 were sent to Fort William for a few weeks in exchange for four K2s to work on the Mallaig line while the ashpits at Mallaig were being rebuilt and so their rocker grates and hopper ashpans came into their own. The turntable was also put out of use during this work and so the 4MT tender cabs also proved handy. '4MT' on bufferbeam. 43137 is at Arisaig on 4 June 1953 with the 4.40 Fort William-Mallaig. A.C. Gilbert.

43132, 43133, 43137 and 43138 and West Hartlepool 43015, 43056 and 43057. Apart from 43137 which lasted until September, all were withdrawn by the end of June 1967.

Scottish Region

The Scottish Region, having lost its original planned allocation to the Eastern in 1950, finally received its first 4MTs in August 1951 when 43137-43141 arrived from Doncaster, the first three after running in for a few weeks on the Eastern Region. 43137 and 43138 went to Glasgow Eastfield and 43140 and 43041 to Polmont. They soon caught the attention of the local enthusiasts who reported 43137 on a freight near Haymarket on 16 August and two days later working the 6.37pm Waverley-Queen Street. The other five to complete the promised ten, 43132-43136, were built at Horwich and were all delivered to Eastfield in December 1951.

One of the ten, 43139, was immediately despatched to Carlisle Canal and was noted on 14 August 1951 working the two coach train on the Langholm branch, which left the Waverley line at Riddings Junction to the north of Carlisle. It was to continue on this duty for more than ten years, usually working the afternoon and evening trains, until the line closed to passenger traffic on 15 June 1964. It

transferred to Kingmoor when Canal closed in June 1963. (Canal shed had come under London Midland Region control from 23 February 1958). Other Kingmoor 4MTs also appeared regularly on the branch including 43000; 43011 was noted on the penultimate day heading two coaches but naturally 43139 was used to work the last train.

Little was written about the 4MTs as they settled down to a mix of freight and passenger work – there was just so much steam to write about of course and these were, after all, humble successors to 0-6-0s. Reported sightings during 1952 included 43133 on the 7.18am Stirling to Glasgow Buchanan Street on 21 April and 8 May and 43137 on the Oakley coal trains in the Fife coalfield. On 18 May the Sunday service on the Milngavie-Hamilton trains was operated by 43132-43134, the first time the entire service had not had ex-LNER locos. 43136 of Eastfield worked the fortnightly 'provision' train of one coach from Blair Atholl to Aviemore and back on 9 August. This was the first appearance of the class as far north as this. On 17 September the 5.50am Perth to Struan local and 8.40am return was worked by 43132.

When they first arrived at Eastfield, there seems to have been some thought of using the 4MTs on the West Highland line in place of the K2s, but nothing

came of it because of their more limited coal and water capacity. Nevertheless, in May 1953 four of the Eastfield allocation, 43132, 43033, 43035 and 43037 were sent to Fort William for a few weeks. They were exchanged for K2s 61783, 61788, 61790 and 61791 for work on the Mallaig line, though this was only to satisfy a temporary local requirement. The ashpits at Mallaig were being rebuilt and since the 4MTs had rocker grates and hopper ashpans they were deemed ideal for the situation. Similarly, when the turntable was temporarily isolated as a result of this rebuilding, thus necessitating tender first working, the 4MTs with their tender cabs were again considered the best remedy. They appear to have been in a fairly deplorable condition, and were heartily disliked by the crews, perhaps also because they still had their original chimneys. They were returned to Eastfield at the end of June.

The Eastfield allocation was reduced in 1956 when 43132-43134 moved to Kipps, and again in July 1960 when 43135, 43036, 43040 and 43041 were transferred to Parkhead, although 43137 stayed there until February 1961 when it was moved to Grangemouth. Other sheds in the Region to have a 4MT on their books for a short time included Bathgate, Dawsholm, Greenock and Hurlford. Polmont based 43141 worked the last passenger trains from Polmont to Bo'ness on 5 May 1956 and then had two long spells at Hawick on the Waverley line between June 1958 and October 1963 where it worked on freight and passenger trains to both Edinburgh and Carlisle.

The local 4MTs were among the types brought in as replacements in December 1960 when the newly electrified Glasgow suburban service was suspended after a fire and numerous failures, and a replacement steam service improvised. The 4MTs continued until the end of September when the electrics finally returned.

In November 1963 the nine Scottish based engines were transferred to the North Eastern Region in exchange for Crabs and BR Class 4 2-6-0s as part of a scheme to ease and speed-up repairs and to reduce the range of spares carried at depots. 43132 and 43137 went to Wakefield, 43133, 43138, 43140 and 43141 to West Auckland, 43134 and 43136 to Ardsley, and 43135 to Thornaby.

Withdrawals and Preservation

The first 4MT to be withdrawn was Normanton's 43114 in November 1963; five others went in the same year, another fourteen in 1964 and then there was a steady attrition over the next three years, 42 in 1965, 34 in 1966 and 59 in 1967, leaving only six in service at the beginning of 1968. Interestingly, of the original fifty LMS-ordered engines

the only withdrawals up to mid-1965 were the two transferred to other Regions and also only one of the second Horwich batch. This was not a reflection on those built at the ex-LNER works but merely the result of the earlier elimination of steam traction on the Eastern and North Eastern Regions and the corralling of the last steam engines into the North West of England. The Ivatt 4MTs outlasted by several months the later BR Standard version, the 76000s, the last four of which were withdrawn from Springs Branch by the end of 1967, having been mostly in store for several months.

One came to a very sticky end; Ardsley's 43072 was cut up on site after falling into the main road at Laisterdyke in November 1964. The *Yorkshire Post* headline read 'A RUNAWAY locomotive and tender crashed 30ft into a Bradford street on November 10'. It then went onto describe the incident in typical journalistic prose:

The 150-ton train raced about a mile down the track from Laisterdyke and through the Adolphus Street goods yard at about 50mph.

It demolished a porter's mess room and then smashed through a 6ft wall onto Dryden Street, off Wakefield Road.

The driver, fireman and guard all jumped clear moments before the crash.

Driver Arthur Wilby, 60, of Sunnyview, East Ardsley, was treated for shock; fireman Edward Bedford, 26,

also of East Ardsley, suffered facial cuts and guard Arthur Wrightson, 50, of Morley, had arm injuries.

Several rail workers reported they came just feet from death as the runaway train thundered past them.

Only one 4MT escaped the cutter's torch, 43106 built at Darlington in April 1951. It spent its first few years on the M&GN at South Lynn before departing to Woodford Halse in July 1956, where it stayed until transferred to Saltley in March 1962. It then had short stays at East Midlands sheds Wellingborough and Kettering before moving to the North West in 1963, firstly to Trafford Park in August and then a few weeks later to Heaton Mersey. Its next stop was Carlisle Kingmoor in August 1966 before its final posting to Lostock Hall in September 1967. 43106 was withdrawn at the end of June and was purchased for preservation, moving to the Severn Valley Railway under its own steam on 3 August, where it remains to the present day. It has recently been restored and looks superb in its lined black livery.

43139 spent most of its life as the Langholm branch engine, allocated to the Canal shed at Carlisle for the purpose. The regular engine on the afternoon and evening trains, it is pictured waiting at the terminus on 16 June 1962 with the 3.23pm to Carlisle.

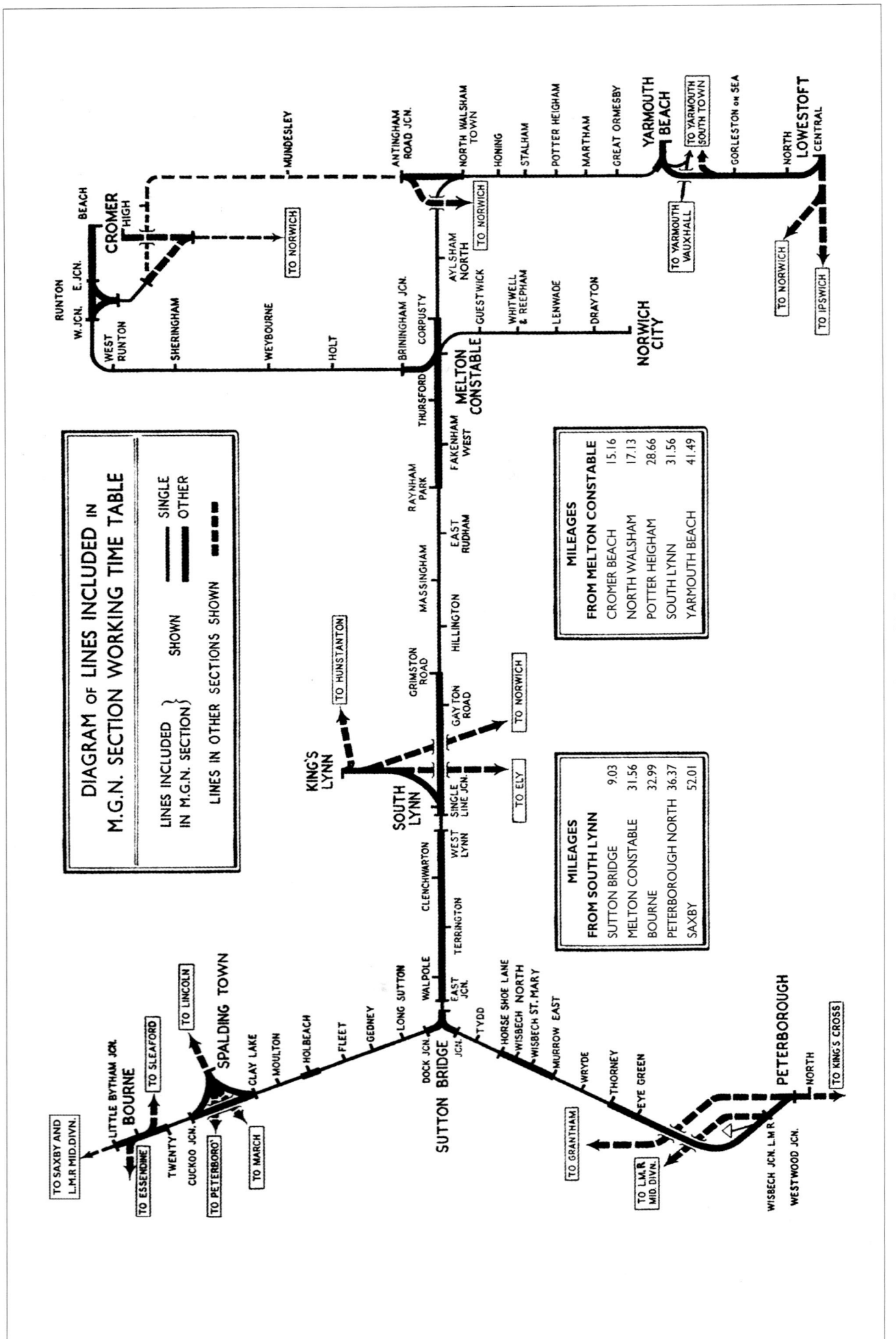

The sheer number of stations served by the M&GN in the early 1950s is readily appreciated from this diagram.

3. DOODLEBUGS LAND ON THE M&GN

If there was one part of the country that will always be associated with the 4MTs it is that served by the former Midland & Great Northern Joint Railway in East Anglia, principally Norfolk. The motive power on the line was transformed virtually overnight when over fifty 'Doodlebugs' (though the term would have been unknown) landed there between September 1950 and September 1952. A collection of pre-grouping Great Eastern and Great Northern relics with little hope of improvement was transformed into the newest engine stud in the country. The engines soon acquired another nickname, 'Mangles', which was something of a back-handed compliment to their modern, 'everything outside' appearance.

The line itself was a thing of contrasts; during the week it enjoyed the somewhat somnolent life of a rural railway, but at the weekend, at least in summer, it was transformed into a bustling route to the various seaside resorts, the principal of which was Great Yarmouth. Hordes of holidaymakers arrived from or departed to the Midlands and the North. The M&GN was incorporated in 1893 and took over a number of small independent concerns, some of which had been worked by the Midland Railway and others by the Midland jointly with the Great Northern. It escaped the 1923 Grouping and continued to provide its own locomotives and stock, nominally under the control of the LMS. In

October 1936 the LNER took responsibility these, although the 'M&GN' remained nominally independent until nationalised in 1948.

Most of the route was single track and hence Whitaker tablet exchange apparatus was fitted to the 4MTs. This had been developed by Mr Whitaker, the locomotive superintendent of the Somerset & Dorset Joint Railway and was introduced on the M&GN in May 1906. The fixed 'standard' stood parallel with the line, and when about to be used the upper portion was turned at right angles to face the approaching train. The ring of the tablet pouch to be collected was placed in its lower arm and the upper arm had a metal jaw shaped to catch the pouch's ring on the tender. The fitting on the tender was similar with a jaw to pick up the pouch, with the ring of the pouch to be collected held at a slightly higher level to correspond with the jaw on the lineside apparatus. When not in use, the catcher was turned flat against the tender but when an exchange was to be made the fireman turned it outwards at right angles, like the lineside apparatus. The momentum of a tablet pouch received from the passing train was sufficient to swing the lineside apparatus back parallel to the rails again, where it was then locked by a catch handle. The exchange could be carried out at speeds of 40-50mph rather than the 10mph laid down for the manual process, which made for more efficient utilisation of the single line sections. There was one drawback: if the

exchange was 'missed' the train had to stop and the fireman had to walk back along the line to the token apparatus, resulting in a long delay. Fortunately this was not a regular occurrence.

The M&GN was diagrammatically essentially an elongated 'H' with Bourne and Spalding to the north west, Peterborough in the south west, Cromer in the north east and Norwich and Yarmouth in the south east. The horizontal spine was from Sutton Bridge to Melton Constable, with the pivotal South Lynn between them. Although the 'main' line ran from Peterborough to Yarmouth, an important section branched off at Sutton Bridge and ran for thirty miles via Spalding and Bourne to Little Bytham Junction where it met the ex-Midland railway line from Saxby, thus forming the link for the traffic to and from the Midlands. Some M&GN trains continued for the next eleven miles down to Saxby, although others were handed over to the Midland further east at Bourne. At Spalding there were important connections to the ex-Great Northern Peterborough-Boston and the ex-Great Northern and Great Eastern Joint March-Doncaster lines.

Passenger workings were characterised by frequent engine changes and reversals for which the tender cabs of the 4MTs came into their own, keeping out those cold winds that came across the North Sea. For a rural railway, operations were complicated and not just as a result of the single line sections but also because the M&GN was

M&GN trains used the ECML station at Peterborough North which they reached by crossing over the main line near the entrance to New England shed and joining it at Westwood Junction. 43092 is coming off the M&GN on 10 January 1957 with the 11.45am from Kings Lynn. www.rail-online.co.uk

Many M&GN trains started from or terminated at Peterborough Westwood Sidings, which involved crossing over from the M&GN onto the ECML, then shunting back onto the Down Slow. On 10 January 1957 43091 is propelling its train, an M&GN down freight which is to terminate in the Sidings, backwards onto the Down Slow. www.rail-online.co.uk

arranged with a virtual Chinese Wall at South Lynn between its eastern and western sections, with only one regular through engine working unchanged between Yarmouth and Peterborough. Many trains thus had two and sometimes three different engines as they made their way along the line.

The M&GN had always been reluctant to allow its engines to work off the home patch and this continued until closure with only a handful of workings to Nottingham and Leicester as the exceptions to prove the rule. Even within its boundaries there was an unwritten rule that under normal circumstances New England engines remained to the west of South Lynn, and Yarmouth engines correspondingly stayed in the east; only those from Melton Constable and South Lynn worked to both extremities of the line. Partly because of this, generally the M&GN 4MTs enjoyed a pretty easy life, often working for less than ten hours each day although their modern labour saving features would have allowed them to remain in traffic for a large proportion of the full working day. The footplate staff took them to their hearts after a run down 0-6-0 or a rattling Gresley mogul; who wouldn't?

Freight workings had a life of their own and until the late-1950s the M&GN carried a large quantity of agricultural produce such as sugar beet, fresh fruit, cut flowers and potatoes from the area and brought in fuel and other supplies

in the other direction. Most of the trains spent a considerable proportion of their journey time picking up and setting down wagons at almost every station along their way, another indication of the importance of the line to the local economy.

Sadly, the fate of the line was sealed by the irresistible tide of the internal combustion engine which took away both freight and passenger traffic and led to inevitable closure in early 1959. However with the help of the Eastern Region 1952 Working Timetable (at the National Archive, Kew) and detail in W.S. Becket's *District Controller's View* (Xpress Publishing) it is possible to gain a good understanding of the weekday operation of the 4MTs at their zenith on the M&GN during 1951/52. The diagrams they worked from each of the sheds on the line provide a fascinating picture of a busy and extensive rural steam railway with much unnoticed nocturnal activity to deal with the goods trains. It should, however, be borne in mind that the freight timings shown can only be considered at best a guide given the vagaries of seasonal traffic and single line operation.

New England

The motive power for the western flank of the M&GN was provided by New England shed at Peterborough with some of the engines outstationed at Bourne and Spalding, and one lone 4MT based at the ex-Midland Spital Bridge

shed. The passenger services used Peterborough North station and the freight was handled at a number of locations, in particular Westwood and Crescent yards, with both outward and inbound traffic also processed through the Midland yard at Wisbech West Junction where the M&GN proper began.

New England received 22 new 4MTs in late-1950 when 43058-43069 and 43080-43089 arrived from Doncaster and Darlington respectively. The allocation remained intact until 43069 and 43089 moved to Neasden in April 1951, although 43089 did return to the M&GN in June 1957 at Melton Constable. 43084 went to Grantham for six months from May 1952, replaced by 43087 which itself only stayed there for two weeks before returning to Peterborough when 43058 took its place, this time staying until March 1954. The next departures were 43066 and 43067 which left for Neasden in March 1953, returning to the fold in August 1954 and 43063 which left for good in June 1956 to Woodford. 43086 was loaned to Melton for three months between June and September 1957.

The sub-shed at Spalding was transferred from the New England district to the Lincoln district as from 29th December 1957, becoming a subsidiary of Boston (40F). The engines which followed the transfer were 43059, 43061, 43062, 43064, 43065, 43080, 43083 and 43085 and they were joined by 43060 and 43066 in June 1958.

43067 at Bourne West about 1956, approaching from Saxby with a three coach train of LMS design stock. The severed line to Essendine bears off to the left in the distance, the trackbed now occupied by the goods yard shunting spur. www.transporttreasury.co.uk

An unusual view of 43109 in the summer of 1954, climbing away from Saxby with the through Birmingham to Yarmouth train, known to all on the M&GN as 'The Leicester', which also carried through coaches for Cromer and Norwich. The first coach is a LNER buffet car which, like the engine, only went as far as Leicester where they were prepared for the return working. During the week the buffet came off at South Lynn but from Friday to Monday it worked to Yarmouth. P.H. Groom.

43088 leaving Tydd on 31 August 1958 with the 9.55am Sunday train from Murrow East to Hunstanton which was loaded to nine coaches. The station was between Wisbech and the junction at Sutton Bridge and its all timber signalbox was of M&GN design, combining elements of both Melton and GN with distinctive 'bite and tongue' bargeboards. H. Ballantyne.

NE1

This began with an early start off shed at 4.50am for the 5.10am from Peterborough North to King's Lynn which was one of the M&GN's few express services, connecting with the 1.00am King's Cross-Edinburgh passenger and newspaper express. After a 6.30am arrival at King's Lynn, the engine ran round and took the ECS to South Lynn to form the 7.08am back to Peterborough. After going on shed for servicing, it was back to Peterborough North at 8.45am with the 7.30am from Melton Constable (taking over from a Melton 4MT on diagram MC9). Following a 10.21am arrival at Peterborough North, it took the ECS to Nene Carriage Sidings before visiting Peterborough North shed. Next came another trip back South Lynn with the 12.45pm to Yarmouth, arriving South Lynn at 2.11pm and handing over to a South Lynn 4MT on diagram SL8. It then returned east with the 2.45pm Parcels to Wisbech North (arr. 3.56pm), leaving there at 4.25pm on its final trip of the day back to Peterborough North (arr. 5.20pm), and then disposing of the stock to Nene Carriage Sidings before returning home to New England.

NE2

This was a night diagram, departing New England shed at 5.45pm and over to Crescent yard for the 6.10pm Goods to South Lynn, arriving there at 8.50pm. It returned with the 11.05pm Goods from South Lynn to Crescent yard, which was the only M&GN train

operating in the small hours, arriving at 1.00am and then back to New England.

NE3

Another early departure, off shed at 6.25am for the 6.45am from Peterborough North to Yarmouth as far as South Lynn (arr. 8.02am) handing over to a South Lynn 4MT on diagram SL11. It returned to Peterborough North at 9.55am with the 6.51am from Yarmouth, taking over from a Yarmouth B12 4-6-0. Arrival at Peterborough North was at 11.07am, before disposing of the ECS to Nene Carriage Sidings and an early finish on New England before midday.

NE4

Departure from the shed was at 6.25am to Westwood yard for the 6.50am Goods to South Lynn, which conveyed empties to Eye Green and the two Wisbech stations, arriving at Wisbech (Horse Shoe Lane) at 10.30am. It continued, after much shunting activity there, over three hours later at 1.47pm to South Lynn (arr. 3.15pm) following more shunting work at Tydd and Sutton Bridge. The 4MT returned home at 4.38pm with the 12.55pm Parcels from Yarmouth, taking over from a South Lynn Ivatt on diagram SL11, and arriving Peterborough North at 8.50pm, taking the ECS to Nene Carriage Sidings and then onto New England shed.

NE5

The 4MT left New England at 9.10am to go to Crescent yard for the 9.30am Goods to Wisbech (Horse Shoe Lane), which served all stations from Dogsthorpe onwards and took more empties for the next day's traffic. It arrived at 1.20pm, and returned with the 3.50pm Goods to Westwood sidings, reaching there at 7.22pm before ending the day back at New England.

NE6

Off shed at 11.25am to Westwood sidings for the 11.45am Goods to South Lynn arriving over seven hours later at 7.05pm and retiring for the night to South Lynn shed. The overall journey time masks the large number of stops en route, totalling almost five hours, including Eye Green (30 minutes), Thorney (15), Wryde (20), Murrow East (12), Wisbech St.Mary (58), Wisbech Horse Shoe Lane (128) and Sutton Bridge (25). The engine on this diagram alternated with the 4MT on South Lynn diagram SL10 which took even longer in the opposite direction.

Spalding

The small ex-Great Northern two road shed usually had around seven or eight New England 4MTs at any one time to cover five diagrams for the 2-6-0s. It had one diagram to Nottingham but apart from that its 4MTs did not stray very far from home. The short distances worked were due in no small part to the reversals necessary for passenger trains at Spalding.

43094 passing over the level crossing at Murrow West between the M&GN South Lynn-Peterborough and the ex-Great Eastern (GN&GE Joint) March-Spalding-Doncaster line. The signalbox there, which handled over 160 trains per day, was opened in November 1950 after an accident brought about the demolition of its predecessor. The lever frame was of GNR (Ireland) pattern and apparently one of a number purchased by the Eastern Region from the Railway Signalling Company after the GNR (I) cancelled an order. Dr Ian C. Allen, www.transporttreasury.co.uk

The Sutton Bridge East box signalman, Jack Mears, waits to collect the single line tablet pouch from 43159's fireman. The train is on the unique Cross Keys swing bridge which carried both road and rail traffic side by side. The first bridge at this location was originally opened just for road use but the Lynn & Sutton Bridge Railway managed to obtain authority to also use it for their new line in 1866. The bridge poved inadequate and had to be replaced in 1897, with one built by Handysides of Derby and operated hydraulically using two three-cylinder engines. The signalbox was a Midland Railway design in common with most of those on the Peterborough–South Lynn section of the M&GN. Dr Ian C. Allen, www.transporttreasury.co.uk

61530 passing 43142 and two other 4MTs in the new corrugated asbestos shed at South Lynn on Wednesday 17 December 1958. It replaced a four road wooden shed and the description 'airy' would be premature – the sidewalls have yet to be added. Dr Ian C. Allen, www.transporttreasury.co.uk

SP1

This diagram involved three return trips to Sutton Bridge starting with the 5.30am Goods which engaged in extensive shunting at Holbeach for half an hour and at the following intermediate stations, reaching its destination at 8.42am, before returning with the 9.15am to Spalding (arr. 9.58am). After a two hour break it then took the 12.20pm to Sutton Bridge (arr. 1.05pm), returning on the 1.35pm to Spalding (arr. 2.20pm). Another rest followed there until the 4pm to Sutton Bridge (arr. 4.40pm) followed by the 5.30pm Goods which took empties for the local stations, exchanging them en route for loaded traffic routed via Spalding. Arrival there was due at 8.10pm, thence on to the shed. The 42 foot turntable at Sutton Bridge was too short for the 4MTs and the enginemen would certainly have appreciated the tender cabs on these workings.

SP2

The day began with the 6.27am Goods to Bourne (arr. 6.55am), returning to Spalding with the 8.30am Goods (arr. 9.14am) then retiring to the shed until 3.00pm when it left Light Engine for Long Sutton, shunting at Holbeach, Fleet and Gedney as needed on the way. Arriving at around 5pm the engine then took over the 1.50pm Goods from South Lynn which the 4MT on the *SP4* diagram

had delivered to Long Sutton at 3.05pm, departing at 5.44pm, and going far as Bourne (arr. 8.16pm), where it would hand over to a Nottingham 4F which took it forward to Saxby and beyond. The 4MT then worked as the pilot on the 7.42pm from Nottingham (together with the 4MT on the *SP8* diagram) departing at 9.07pm back to Spalding (arr. 9.26pm) where it went on shed.

SP4

The first duty was to take over the 9.55am from Saxby to King's Lynn from a Bourne 4MT on diagram *BN1*, leaving at 11.15am and arriving at 12.40pm. It then worked Light Engine tender first back to South Lynn and after turning there headed the 1.50pm through Goods to the Midland, taking it as far as Long Sutton (arr. 3.05pm,) where it was held so that it could pick-up the late afternoon westbound traffic from the intermediate stations between Gedney and Spalding. Next for the 4MT was the 3.30pm parcels to Moulton (arr. 4.43pm) before its final duty on the 6.00pm Goods back to Spalding (arr. 6.15pm) whereupon it retired to shed.

SP5

This was the shortest Spalding diagram beginning with the 1.15pm Goods to Sutton Bridge (arr. 3.48pm) then running Light Engine to Long Sutton for the 4.45pm Goods back to Spalding

(arr. 6.51pm) retiring to shed after less than six hours work.

SP8

The 4MT on this diagram went off the M&GN for most of the day working the 4.08pm to Nottingham, arriving at 6.06pm. It was piloted by another Ivatt on diagram *BN1* as far as Bourne. It disposed of the ECS to Nottingham carriage sidings before returning to the M&GN with the 7.42pm from Nottingham to Spalding, arriving 9.26pm. It was again piloted, this time by the *SP2* engine from Bourne, and was back in Spalding shed before 10pm.

Bourne

The stationing of two 4MTs at Bourne, less than ten miles from Spalding, seems strange and was no doubt rooted in ancient M&GN tradition. The pair were constrained within the small area bounded by Spalding and Saxby, although the parent shed at New England did rotate those outstationed there each week.

BN1

Off shed for the 7.40am to King's Lynn as far as Spalding arriving 8.00am, and exchanging trains there with the South Lynn 4MT on diagram *SL7* which had arrived with the 6.50am King's Lynn-Nottingham. Departure from Spalding was at 8.30am to Saxby arriving there

A small band of Ivatts gathered at South Lynn in 1958. Both 43091 and 43095 went there from new in 1950 until its closure in 1959.

An everyday scene at Melton Constable looking towards Yarmouth with the station in the background. The 70ft turntable was moved there from Grantham in 1953 and was then transferred to Kings Cross after closure. 43145 is turning while 43146 waits and two other 4MTs are in the background. The M&GN workshops which closed in 1936 were to the right of the shed. The flower tubs visible to the left of 43145's tender are an interesting touch, not found at many other steam sheds! Dr Ian C. Allen, transporttreasury.co.uk

43158 arrives at Melton West on the Fakenham line with a nine coach train. The other two 4MTs will be taking part in the usual engine changing and train splitting manoeuvres which were a feature of operation at this junction. On the right, the Cromer portion is waiting to back down and the engine for the Norwich coaches is waiting on the left. This photograph was taken from the bridge which crossed the end of the platforms, the junction pointwork being part of the station area. Dr Ian C. Allen, www.transporttreasury.co.uk

A busy weekday scene at Melton Constable West. On the right 43068 arrives off the Cromer Beach branch with the morning goods from Holt which appears to consist mainly of sugar beet. The Yarmouth D16/3 runs clear of the station after arriving with the 12.42pm Yarmouth-Peterborough while the 4MT on the left which has replaced it, takes it forward to Peterborough. Dr Ian C. Allen, www.transporttreasury.co.uk

43150 waits in the Goods Yard at Melton Constable on 5 August 1955 with the 10.35am Peterborough-Yarmouth as a train arrives in the down platform hauled by a pair of 4MTs. The station had an island platform which could accommodate twelve coaches at either side. The up platform had an intermediate loco release crossover and thus could handle two trains simultaneously.

at 9.36am and then back again with the 9.55am to King's Lynn, arriving Spalding at 10.59am where a Spalding 4MT on *SP4* took over the train. Next it left on the 11.45am to Saxby as far as Bourne (arr. 12.06pm), and handing over to *BN2*. It spent the next couple of hours as Goods pilot before taking over from *BN2* the 2.26pm (1.45pm ex-Saxby) to Spalding arriving 2.46pm. Then it piloted *SP8* on the 4.08pm to Nottingham as far as Bourne, arriving 4.29pm. Departure was at 6.10pm (on the 4.20pm ex-Nottingham which arrived with a Nottingham engine, usually a 2-6-4T) to Spalding arriving 6.35pm (and handing over to a D16 to take onto its destination at King's Lynn). Finally 8.36pm from Spalding arriving Bourne at 8.57pm stabling the stock for the 7.40am the following day.

BN2
A late start beginning with the 12.38pm to Saxby, the 11.45am ex-Spalding brought in by its shedmate on diagram *BN1*, arriving at 1.18pm and returning with the 1.45pm to Spalding, arriving Bourne at 2.22pm and swapping for the second time in the day with diagram *BN1*. Next was the 4.35pm to Spalding (arr. 4.56pm), departing from there at 6.05pm with the 4.21pm King's Lynn-

Nottingham (taking over from a South Lynn D16 4-4-0) as far as Bourne (arr. 6.29pm). There it handed over to the Nottingham engine which had brought in the 4.20pm before retiring to Bourne shed before 7pm.

Spital Bridge
One engine was allocated to the ex-Midland Railway shed at Peterborough Spital Bridge to cover a single M&GN diagram. 43064 was there from November 1950 until February 1954 when it was exchanged with New England's 43084, which in turn was swapped for 43127 from New England in August that year; 43127 stayed for more than five years until it returned to New England at the end of January 1960 when Spital Bridge shed was closed.

SB 18
Left Spital Bridge shed Light Engine to Wisbech Sidings for the 2.50pm Goods to Eye Green (arr. 4.20pm). Unlike most of the services which conveyed agricultural and general goods this train mainly carried bricks from Dogsthorpe sidings where it shunted for over an hour, before repeating the exercise at Eye Green, which had extensive sidings for the Northam works of the London Brick Company. The 4MT marshalled

the wagons in to up and down trains, with the up road traffic forming its return working to Peterborough at 8.52pm and the down road wagons going to South Lynn for remarshalling by the 6.10pm Peterborough-South Lynn Goods (diagram *NE2*). The 4MT arrived back at Westwood Sidings at 9.53pm and went to Spital Bridge for stabling.

South Lynn
South Lynn received nineteen 4MTs from new between December 1950 and September 1951: 43090-43095, 43104-43111, 43137 and 43142-43145, although 43137 stayed only for a month before going to Scotland. 43145 moved on after less than two weeks, initially to Yarmouth Beach, before settling down from January 1952 at Melton Constable. 43107 and 43144 went to Neasden in March 1953, returning in July 1954 to South Lynn along with 43068 which had originally been at New England for three years before going to Neasden. The only other departure before closure was 43106 which left in February 1958 for Woodford Halse, a move which saved its bacon because it ultimately led to its preservation.

As was often the case, British Railways embarked on a major piece of

43156 waits at Drayton with two coaches for Norwich in the 1950s. A pair of ex-LMS corridor coaches formed the daily through working from Birmingham, a journey lasting over six hours. They were combined at Melton with similar vehicles providing a through service from Lowestoft and Cromer, to form 'The Leicester'. Drayton was the final station before Norwich City and the most important intermediate station on the Norwich line with a grain warehouse as well as an ordinary goods shed, with sidings to match. The signalbox is an Eastern & Midlands Railway type on a brick base.

capital expenditure at South Lynn not long before the line's closure when it decided to rebuild the shed. It had originally had two roads and was later doubled in size, and these were swept away by a new corrugated asbestos construction completed in early 1958. The *Observer* described it as 'a roomy and spacious building', and it was intended that the ex-Great Eastern shed a couple of miles down the road at Kings Lynn station, which had lost all of its steam workings, would be closed and its remaining engines transferred across.

South Lynn was the focal point for the M&GN freight operations and its two yards, suitably labelled East and West, each dealt with and remarshalled nearly twenty trains every day including trip workings to and from the Great Eastern at nearby King's Lynn. The volume of traffic was such that the yard at Sutton Bridge, nine miles down the line to the east, helped out by handling almost as many trains each day. Hence the shed's 4MTs spent much of their time on both longer distance and trip Goods workings, although they did partake fully in the engine changing ritual on the through passenger services, working both eastwards to Yarmouth and westwards to Peterborough and on to the Midland to Nottingham.

SL2
A very early start in the middle of the night for a return trip to King's Lynn on the 4.03am Goods (arr. 4.10am) and back with the 5.30am Goods arriving South Lynn 5.40am. Next was the 6.30am Cromer Goods as far as Melton Constable (handing over to a D16 4-4-0) arriving at 8.21am. After a short wait it then worked the 9.35am to Cromer Beach (arr. 10.15am) whereupon is was on Beach shed until the early afternoon, returning to Melton Constable with the 2.10pm Goods arriving at 4.50pm. Finally back to its home shed on the 7.05pm Goods to South Lynn (arr. 8.42pm).

SL3
Off shed at the crack of dawn for the 5.32am Express Goods from West Yard to Norwich City arriving 8.05am. Then 10.30am back to Melton Constable (arr. 11.19am). After a long refuelling and rest break the engine returned to Norwich taking over the 12.45pm Goods from South Lynn from one of that shed's 4MTs on diagram SL15A, departing at 2.46pm and reaching Norwich at 4.08pm. Its final working of the day was the 7.45pm Goods back home to South Lynn (arr. 10.46pm), which carried traffic for onward

workings to Peterborough and King's Lynn.

SL5
Another early riser for the 5.55am Goods to Spalding, taking no less than seven hours for a journey of just 25 miles, which collected empty wagons and distributed them as it meandered up the line arriving at 12.42pm. Over five hours were scheduled to be spent shunting, beginning with over an hour on the dock line at Sutton Bridge before attending to the stations on the Spalding line, pausing at Long Sutton (109 minutes), Gedney (15), Fleet (33), Holbeach (28) and Moulton (62). After a decent period of recovery on Spalding shed the 4MT departed with the 5.45pm to Sutton Bridge (arr. 6.25pm) before finishing with the 7.35pm Goods to South Lynn arriving at 8.42pm, fifteen hours after it left there.

SL6
Off shed for the 6.02am Goods to Sutton Bridge (arr. 7.40am) followed by the 8.00am to Spalding (arr. 8.41am) and then back to South Lynn on the 10.00am Goods (arr. 12.22pm). A brief trip to King's Lynn on the 1.20pm Goods (arr. 1.30pm) then followed, returning with the 2.28pm Goods (arr. 2.40pm) and

The angled cab of 43146 catches the sun as it waits to depart from Norwich City on Saturday 26 May 1956. The line to Norwich was effectively one of two branch lines off the Yarmouth main line at Melton, the other going to Cromer. N.E. Preedy.

The distinctive braced girder footbridge at Aylsham North is in the background as 43151 waits to depart with the 10.05am Yarmouth-Peterborough on Friday 29 August 1958. The crossing loop could hold fifteen bogie vehicles and on summer Saturdays a porter had to help the signalman with the exchange of tablets because the tall signalbox had 21 steps up to the box. Hugh Ballantyne.

Two shunters proudly posing in front of 43156 for Dr Allen's camera at Aylsham North as it shunts beet wagons in the up goods yard. The M&GN 4MTs spent a good part of their lives engaged in this activity because the daily goods trains stopped to drop off and pick up wagons at the numerous and closely spaced stations en route. There is a nice Marriott reinforced concrete loading gauge in front of the engine. The M&GN produced a large amount of lineside furniture using this material between 1916 and 1925, ranging from signal posts to station nameboards and posts of all types. Dr Ian C. Allen, www.transporttreasury.co.uk

another local working on the 3.15pm Goods to Gayton Road (arr. 3.30pm) returning with the 4.20pm Goods to South Lynn (arr. 4.55pm) and to shed.

SL7

Off shed at 6.10am to run Light Engine to King's Lynn for the 6.40am to Nottingham taking it as far as Spalding (arr. 7.56am), handing it over to the Bourne 4MT on diagram *BN1*. Next was the 8.15am to King's Lynn (arr. 9.25am), working the ECS at 10.13am to South Lynn (arr. 10.18am) and then back to King's Lynn with the 10.30am Goods. Another short trip to South Lynn on the 11.13am to Peterborough, handing over to a Melton D16, arriving 11.18am and then to South Lynn shed for a couple of hours. Next was the 1.40pm ECS to Sutton Bridge arriving at 2.02pm, the 2.15pm Goods to Dock Junction (arr. 2.20pm) and back with a Goods for Sutton Bridge (arr. 2.35pm) returning later to South Lynn on the 5.08pm Goods (arr. 6.04pm) before finally another visit to King's Lynn with the 8.05pm Goods returning Light Engine to South Lynn shed.

SL8

This was the one of only two 4MT diagrams with visits to both extremities

of the line on the same day, beginning with the 7.08am to Peterborough North (arr. 8.26am), disposing of the ECS to Nene carriage sidings and on to Spital Bridge shed for a couple of hours. The 4MT then worked the 10.33am from Peterborough North-Yarmouth as far as South Lynn (arr. 12.01pm) handing over to a Yarmouth B12. After a brief trip to the shed before taking over the 12.45pm Peterborough to Yarmouth from the new England 4MT on diagram *NE1*, it departed South Lynn at 2.19pm for arrival at Yarmouth Beach 5.20pm. The return westwards began on the 6.15pm to Cromer, handing over to a Melton D16 at Melton (arr. 8.0pm) followed at 8.10pm by the 7.15pm from Norwich to King's Lynn, taking over from another Melton D16. Arrival back at South Lynn was at 9.18pm (with its shedmate on diagram *SL16* taking over for the final leg to King's Lynn) and on to the shed.

SL10

The diagram covered only a single working, the 7.50am Goods to Peterborough Westwood Yard with the 4MT completing the 38 mile journey in a little over eleven hours at 6.58pm before retiring to New England for the night. It worked back on the paired *NE6*

diagram the next day, the almost express 11.45am Goods which took a mere seven and a quarter hours to South Lynn. In fairness, the 7.50am was booked to spend over seven hours shunting and waiting during the course of its journey, with stops at Clenchwarton (24 minutes), Terrington (51), Walpole (53), Sutton Bridge (39), Wisbech Horse Shoe Lane (62), Wisbech St.Mary (25), Murrow East (38), Wryde (82), Thorney (36) and Eye Green (30). The South Lynn crew only worked to Horse Shoe Lane where they were relieved by a set of New England men who had travelled out passenger on the 12.45pm from Peterborough.

SL11

The day began by taking over from the New England 4MT on diagram *NE3* the 8.18am (6.45am ex-Peterborough) to Yarmouth Beach, arrival 11.05am. The return to South Lynn was on the 12.55pm Parcels to Peterborough (handing over to a New England 4MT on diagram *NE4*) arriving at 4.30pm and thence to South Lynn shed.

SL13

One of the shortest diagrams worked by a M&GN 4MT, comprising the 10.30am Goods to Fakenham West (arr.

43157 at North Walsham Town on Thursday 27 May 1954 with a typical LNER three coach train for Yarmouth. During the week most M&GN services were made up of either three or four coach sets but Saturdays saw the through trains from the Midlands loading to nine or ten vehicles. www.rail-online.co.uk

43161 leaving North Walsham Town with an eastbound train in the 1950s. The timber built goods shed and attractive 'gallows' loading gauge can be seen. The main signal ahead applied to the single line and the disc below it to the yard headshunt. The first vehicle, brake third corridor E16869 built at Doncaster in 1950, outlived the M&GN by 8½ years. Dr Ian C. Allen, www.transporttreasury.co.uk

43161 at North Walsham, photographed from the footbridge. The line to South Lynn curved away to the left while the trackbed of the former line to Mundesley and Cromer went off to the right in the background. Dr Ian C. Allen, www.transporttreasury.co.uk

43090 departing from Potter Heigham with an up train from Yarmouth. The tablet exchange apparatus is still extended after picking up the token for the next section of single line. Note the crossing gates and gate cabin right at the end of the platform – there were over 140 level crossings on the M&GN, more than one per route mile on average. Dr Ian C. Allen, www.transporttreasury.co.uk

43094 crossing the River Thurne at Potter Heigham on bridge no.155, one of several lattice girder bridges on the M&GN. Repair costs of this and the one at West Lynn were part of the justification for closure of the line. Intriguingly the lamps signify a Class E freight although the 4MT is clearly on a passenger train. The check rails either side of the running rails are a nice feature for the modeller. The footpath on the left leads up to Potter Heigham Bridge Halt. Dr Ian C. Allen, www.transporttreasury.co.uk

1.20pm) returning to South Lynn with the 2.50pm Goods (arr. 5.21pm).

SL15A

Off shed for the 12.45pm Goods to Norwich, arriving 2.23pm at Melton Constable and handing over to another South Lynn 4MT on diagram *SL3*. It then departed at 5.34pm after taking over from the Melton 4MT on diagram *MC2* with the 2.35pm Goods from South Lynn to Yarmouth Beach (arr. 8.23pm). It then went to shed for no less than seventeen hours – the next turn the following day was at 2.00pm on diagram *SL15B*.

SL15B

The diagram began with the 2.00pm local trip Goods to Yarmouth's White Swan yard arriving 2.05pm, returning at 2.30pm to Yarmouth Beach (arr. 2.35pm). Then the 4MT took charge of the M&GN's premier Goods train, the 4.00pm to Peterborough, which conveyed all manner of goodies including potato crisps, frozen food and fizzy drinks. It was also the only through working over the 112 miles from east to west on the system, and reached Westwood Yard in the very creditable time of 8.57pm and going onto Spital Bridge shed. Its day was not over and

it went to Crescent Yard for the 11.45pm Goods back to its home shed, arriving South Lynn at 3.22am.

SL16

An afternoon start on the 10.05am ex-Yarmouth, taking over from a Yarmouth B12 and departing at 1pm to Peterborough (arr. 2.08pm), disposing of the ECS to Nene carriage sidings then on to Spital Bridge. After a break of three hours it picked up the stock at Nene Sidings for its next working, the 5.55pm to King's Lynn (arr. 7.27pm). The 4MT spent the rest of the day shuffling backwards and forwards at Lynn, firstly working Light Engine over to King's Lynn for the 8.25pm local Goods to South Lynn (arr. 8.35pm) and next taking over the 7.15pm from Norwich to King's Lynn from a South Lynn 4MT on diagram *SL8*, departing at 9.25pm for the five minute run before working Light engine back to South Lynn. There followed another trip working, the 10.45pm Goods to King's Lynn (arr. 10.55pm) and then back to South Lynn with another Goods at 11.25pm (arr. 11.35pm) and onto South Lynn shed just before midnight.

SL17

Off shed to take over from a Melton

D16 the 3.40pm Peterborough to King's Lynn, departing South Lynn at 5.11pm (arr. 5.18pm). Then a trip to Peterborough on the 5.55pm arriving there at 7.38pm, and working the stock to Nene sidings and then onto Spital Bridge shed. After a two hour break it was back to Nene carriage sidings to pick up the ECS for the 10.45pm to King's Lynn (arr. 11.59pm). Then it was Light Engine to South Lynn shed.

Melton Constable

As the 4MT influx continued to spread eastwards, Melton Constable was next in line and eleven new 4MTs 43146-43156 were delivered there between September 1951 and January 1952. 43145 joined them in that month from Yarmouth Beach where it had been flying the flag until that shed's own engines were delivered. All then stayed until March 1959 except 43156 which took over from 43145 at Yarmouth Beach until returned in September. The only other change was New England's 43086 which arrived for three months from June until September 1957. Melton was the junction for the two branch lines to Cromer and Norwich and its two goods yards played an important role in M&GN freight working.

The photographer was up very early to record 43108 departing from Yarmouth Beach on Monday 28 August 1958 with the 6.02am to South Lynn. The four coaches include a BR mark 1 which were definitely not normally part of the weekday trains on the M&GN. H. Ballantyne.

MC1

The first working was the 5.40am Goods to South Lynn (arr. 7.28am) and then the 9.10am Goods to Norwich (arr. 1.51pm) followed by the 3.26pm Goods back to Melton (arr. 4.39pm). Next was the 6.24pm departure with the 5.30pm from Norwich to Fakenham West (taking over from a Norwich D16) arriving at 6.52pm and then working the ECS back to Melton and on shed by 7.25pm.

MC2

Off shed for the 5.50am Goods to South Lynn arriving there five hours later at 10.58am, after shunting and waiting for a total of over three hours at Thursford (26 minutes), Fakenham West (20), Raynham Park (15), East Rudham (28), Massingham (51), Hillington (30)and Grimston Road (15). The 4MT then returned to Melton Constable with the 2.35pm Goods to Yarmouth handing over to a South Lynn 4MT on diagram *SL15A* at Melton (arr. 4.29pm) before proceeding to the shed.

MC4

A very light duty leaving with the 6.36am to Norwich, arriving 7.25am and back with the 9.42am Goods arriving at Melton 12.55pm and on to shed for the rest of the day.

MC5

This diagram was paired with next day's Yarmouth *YB1*, starting with the 6.45am Goods to Yarmouth arriving almost 7 hours later at 1.22pm and then to Yarmouth Beach shed arriving 2.50pm after some shunting. The 42 mile journey included over four hours of scheduled stops at Corpusty (39 minutes), Aylsham North (9), North Walsham (99), Stalham (20), Potter Heigham (15), Martham (20), Hemsby (10) and Great Ormesby (33). There was a crew change at Stalham, with Yarmouth Beach men taking over after arriving on the 7.02am Goods from Yarmouth.

MC9

An early start on the 7.30am to Peterborough arriving South Lynn at 8.35am and handing over to a New England 4MT on diagram *NE1* and then back to Melton with the 9.40am Goods, arriving at 1.16pm. Then a second visit to South Lynn with the 4.20pm Goods arriving at 6.32pm and returning to Melton with another Goods at 7.45pm (arr. 9.36pm) and on to shed.

Yarmouth Beach

The eastern end of the line was the last to receive the new engines. The first Yarmouth 4MT was 43145 which was

transferred from South Lynn in September 1951 and stayed until exchanged in January 1952 for Melton Constable's 43156. This engine was required for diagram *YB1* paired with Melton's *MC5* and therefore the same class of locomotive was desirable. 43156 left In September 1952 after the last of the shed's own five engines, 43157-43161, had arrived. As with the other M&GN 4MTs there was a transfer to Neasden in March 1953, with 43161 moving to London and returning in June 1954. Yarmouth's 4MTs took over from the shed's D16 4-4-0s and the two diagrams *YB2* and *YB7* were some of the least exacting duties, although they did have to exert themselves on summer weekends with the heavily loaded holiday trains.

YB1

This was the other half of the paired duty with the previous day's *MC5*, leaving at 7.02am on the Goods to Melton Constable arriving there six and a half hours later at 1.28pm, after which it went on shed until the next day at 6.35am. The Goods had stops totalling 205 minutes at Caister (49), Hemsby (10), Martham (10), Potter Heigham (39), Stalham (33), Honing (13), North Walsham (13), Felmington (11), Aylsham North (12) and Corpusty (15), with the crew changing at Stalham and returning home with the 6.45am Melton-Yarmouth goods.

YB2

The day began at 6.25am for a trip working to White Swan yard returning to Yarmouth by 7.00am and then it was another four hours before taking the 11.15am to Lowestoft (arr. 11.47am) and returning with the12.33pm arriving Yarmouth at 1.06pm. Some four hours of inactivity was interrupted with the 4.55pm to Melton Constable arriving there at 6.34pm. The end of a long day was the 5.55pm ex-King's Lynn (taking over from a Melton D16) at 7.15pm back to Yarmouth (arr. 8.47pm) and on to Yarmouth Beach shed.

YB7

A late start on the 12.42pm to Peterborough as far as Melton Constable arriving 2.14pm and handing over to a Melton D16. Next came a short trip with the 3.55pm to Fakenham (arr. 4.13pm) returning on the 4.30pm to Yarmouth (arr. 7.04pm) and on to Yarmouth Beach shed less than seven hours after it left.

The impact of the 4MTs did not go unnoticed in the enthusiast press, the *Railway Observer* noting in its September 1951 issue: *A visit to the western end of the M&GN demonstrated the vast changes in locomotive power which have taken place in recent years. The most numerous class*

is now the Ivatt Class 4, nine of these being noted at Spalding in the space of one hour, excluding one or two more passing on the avoiding line. The 4-8pm from Spalding to Nottingham left behind 43065 and 43086, the pilot coming off at Bourne. This appears to be a regular working.

Similar comments appeared in April 1952: *There is now little 'G.N.' character left on this section, especially from the Peterborough end as Class 4 2-6-0s work nearly all trains. The exceptions to this are the daily Melton Constable working to Peterborough, which is worked by a G.E. Claud which seemingly works the train for a week. A B12/3 (normally 61540) pays an occasional visit to Peterborough from South Lynn and an evening fitted freight train is scheduled to be worked by a Class 5 engine (e.g. a K2). Other than these incidents Class 4s monopolise the work, there being 16 at South Lynn (43090-3/5, 43104-11/42-4) and 11 at Melton Constable (43145-55). The class is quite popular because of their capacity for the work they have to do, their easy ability to be worked tender first, and at the end of the day, they can be quickly put away in the shed.*

The position was the same at the eastern end of the line: *A few days observation along these lines reveals that on the M.&G.N. with the exception of 61520 (32F) all traffic on the Yarmouth end of the line is handled by Class 4MTs. On the Yarmouth-Lowestoft Section (N.&S. Jt.), however, F6 2-4-2Ts are used with only occasional use of 4MTs, only one appearing during a week's observation.*

End of the Line

Between the end of the war and the mid-1950s competition from the roads had increased considerably; the freight business was seriously damaged by the Transport Act of 1953 which deregulated road haulage. It went into a sharp decline and despite attempts to reverse the trend in 1958 by slashing prices, the fate of the line became inevitable. Passenger numbers had fallen away to almost nothing from many stations. On 11 June 1958 the formal closure procedures clanked into action and a decision was handed down by the Central Transport Consultative Committee at the end of November that, to all intents and purposes, the M&GN would close on 28 February 1959. Some peripheral passenger and freight services were to be retained but the essence of the system would be no more.

The Last Day

In its own inimitable style the *Railway Observer* produced a comprehensive report of the final day's operations.

The last day dawned fine and remained so which was fortunate for enthusiasts from all parts of the country travelling over the line.

The 6-51 a.m. ex-Kings Lynn to Nottingham was headed by 4MT 43085 (40F) tender first into Saxby. Here the train changed engines outside the station to a Fowler tank which had previously brought in stock to form the 9-55 a.m. Saxby to Kings Lynn. After waiting for the 9-8 a.m.

43088 arriving at Peterborough North with the 6.59am from Yarmouth on the last day of the M&GN, Saturday 28 February 1959. R.J. Buckley, Initial Photographics.

Leicester (London Road) to Peterborough (East) headed by Cl. 2 40452, departure of the 9-55 was a few minutes late.

Between Saxby and Castle Bytham the permanent way was recently re-laid with flat-bottom track as this section remains open for ironstone traffic. The station at Bourne would still have done credit to several main lines.

At Spalding the reversal produced a G.N. representative - J6 64172 (40F), where an elderly gentleman joined to travel to Holbeach and was overheard to say that although he had lived at Holbeach all his life he had never before travelled on the line.

After leaving Sutton Bridge and crossing Cross-Keys swing bridge, which owing to its cost of maintenance was given as one of the reasons for closing the line, the J6 got away in fine style reaching 60-65 m.p.h. before having to shut off, for crossing the Ouse at South Lynn.

South Lynn depot had a dejected air; although the building was only completed last November it was to be emptied of engines that night pending transfer of Kings Lynn's steam engines there in April.

The last through train from Birmingham (1-45 p.m.) to Yarmouth Beach arrived at Leicester (London Rd.) behind 4F 44542 (17B) which gave way to Mogul 43060 (40F Spalding) for its journey over the M.&G.N. line.

No.43060 had previously worked the last Yarmouth to Birmingham train in the morning as far as Leicester. A large placard, on which was painted a portrait of an M.&G.N. 4-4-2T and in large letters 'That's Yer Lot,' was attached to the smoke box door. Prior to departure several press photographs were taken and interviews with the driver, fireman and intending passengers were held but punctually at 3-15 p.m. this train left for the last time.

Engines noted on the Saxby-Bourne line in the afternoon included 43061 (40F) on yard pilot duty at Bourne and 43058 (40F)

on the 4-25 p.m. through train to Nottingham.

At Saxby 4F 43954 (16A) in spotless condition was noted on the 4-20 p.m. Nottingham-Kings Lynn which it worked through to Spalding.

At the end of the line at mid-day the dilapidated and roofless shed at Yarmouth Beach contained 43017 and 43157. D2571 stood silently in the yard, A fifty-nine year old driver although embittered at being sacked with one week's notice after thirty-four years' service, counted himself fortunate to have a pension of £2 16s.0d. per week to look forward to as a result of joining a G.N. superannuation scheme many years ago.

The last through train from Yarmouth Beach to Peterborough North left punctually behind 43145 adorned with many chalked inscriptions and bearing a bunch of balloons on the smokebox door. Enterprising enthusiasts aboard, not content with the limited variety of M.&G.N. tickets still available at Yarmouth, had telephoned down the line and were met at certain stations by staff whereupon a lightning transaction took place and further souvenirs were safe. The guard shook hands with many of his colleagues at stations en route to South Lynn. At Peterborough the withered remnant of one balloon remained.

43145 returned on the last train from Peterborough, the 8-37 p.m. to Melton Constable, but owing to funeral activities, was nearly 15 minutes late starting its run. Most of the passengers had come to Peterborough on the last up train which left Kings Lynn at 5-45 p.m. and made a last sentimental journey back to stations between Murrow and Sutton Bridge.

With the B.R. badge transformed into something looking like an out of work character from a Walt Disney cartoon down to the nude chalked on the chimney, 43145 gave what must have been the line's most striking display of informal locomotive decoration ever.

'Running out, please pass', 'We will never pass this way again', 'Bless 'em all!' The inscriptions left no doubt about the way in which the enthusiasts and railwaymen looked upon the closure. A laurel wreath with a board inscribed 'Farewell M.&G.N.' was officially presented and Driver Watts of Melton Constable gave a noisy farewell on the hooter.

When 43145 swung off the main line at Westwood box, fog detonators announced the arrival on M. & G.N. metals proper. After the train had passed over Rhubarb Bridge and down the incline to Paston crossing, practically every toilet roll aboard had found a new use, and many windows had lengths streaming from them.

A large reception committee was waiting at Murrow, one of the places hardest hit by the closure. Now the trains have gone, buses at Guyhirne, three miles away are the only connection with Peterborough and Wisbech.

Many passengers left the train at Murrow and joined people on the platform to sing 'Auld Lang Syne'. Then as everyone scrambled back into their places, and the train moved off again, the people left behind broke into cheers, augmented by car horns and more fog detonators. Rockets signalled the train's approach into Wisbech and here also the platforms were crowded. Most of the passengers, including certain top-hatted gentlemen, then left the train for the last time.

At Ferry and Tydd the country people said their farewells, and after the familiar handshakes with the driver and firemen, and, of course, more bangs, the train went on to Sutton Bridge. Here a crowd of over 200 waited on the curving platform and when the train pulled out some enthusiasts raced for their cars to drive along the nearby road into South Lynn alongside the train.

Through Walpole, Terrington and Clenchwarton, the train travelled and after crossing the Ouse, detonators every few yards announced arrival at South Lynn. Soon after 10-15 p.m. the train steamed slowly out of the station, and the red tail lamp soon disappeared into the night.

No time was wasted in starting the demolition and clearance work; the 4MTs were cleared out on 1 March to nearby Eastern Region sheds except for 43145 which was used for a short time on some of the dismantling work at the eastern end of the line.

43145 covered with 'end of line' chalked messages at Yarmouth Beach on the 12.56pm to Peterborough on the final day.

60

43108 at Melton Constable with the 1.16pm Peterborough-Yarmouth on the last day of the M&GN, 28 February 1959. R.J. Buckley, Initial Photographics.

43060 on 4 October 1953 at Spalding still has the early pattern guard irons attached to the frames; these would have been replaced by the pony truck mounted type when it went into Stratford Works for an Intermediate overhaul in January 1954. J.C. Hillyer.

4. THE DEVIL IN THE DETAIL

Unlike their Fowler and Stanier predecessors with their frequent changes of boiler and tender, the Ivatt 4MTs at a casual glance may appear to have had no significant differences. However, on closer study, the dedicated engine picker can identify a number of variants, both as built and with later modifications, together with numerous livery variations to catch out the unwary.

The engines were built at three different workshops and the worksplates attached to the front framing naturally reflected this. Horwich used standard LMS style cast iron oval worksplates with white letters and figures on a black background; Darlington and Doncaster applied LNER pattern oval brass plates with black lettering and works numbers. SC plates to signify the Self Cleaning apparatus in the smokebox were fixed below the shedplates on the smokebox doors from new, except probably for the Darlington engines up to around 43096, to which they were soon added. The plates seem to have disappeared from almost all the engines by the 1960s, although the equipment was not removed, officially at least.

When built, 3000-43049 had the massive and ineffectual double chimneys but following the tests with 43027 in 1949 all the others were built with a Black 5 pattern, 1ft 4in high, single chimney. As discussed at length in the first chapter the whole class was given new single chimneys, which were thinner and taller at 1ft 6in high, between 1953 and 1956. The top feed covers on the boilers of the first twenty were changed to the modified type cover fitted to 43020 onwards in the early 1950s. These had a small bonnet or 'top hat' fitted to cover the setscrews which projected above the centre portion. This arose from a re-design of the earlier type to reduce leakage problems and to allow minor steam leaks out instead of becoming trapped under the boiler

43158 in October 1961 has the guard irons on the pony truck as fitted to 43107 onwards; this kept them at a more constant height and position above the rail at all times. All the other engines were modified to this type by the mid-1950s. 43108 had just been fitted with AWS and the plate to protect the receiver is bent upwards; the conduit to the cab equipment and the battery box under the left hand cabside was clipped below the footplate. Note the slightly different mounting of the vacuum train pipe compared with 43060. R. Bruce, www.transporttreasury.co.uk

43079 on 25 September 1960 at Darlington. The prominent motion bracket and the bulk of those 17½in x 26in cylinders, inclined at 1 in 16, is emphasised by the high running plate. The large square box on top of the cylinder is the cover over the main steam feed to the cylinders from the header in the smokebox. It enters the steam chest between the piston valve heads. Presumably this was done at the top rather than the side (as was more usual) in view of height of the boiler. www.rail-online.co.uk

A close-up of 43088 taken on 20 June 1954 at Stratford illustrates numerous details including the curved footstep at the front of the tender with the vertical handrail following the shape. The lining on cab and tender is further out than on those from Horwich, and on the tender it stops to clear the cut-out for the tablet catcher. The 'RA4' is centrally positioned below the numbers, a Stratford trademark, unlike the engines painted at Doncaster where it was placed under the rear number. Note the tablet catcher, a term used on the Doncaster drawing of the apparatus, is stamped BR not M&GNJR, which would confound the suggestion that the 4MTs used second-hand equipment from withdrawn M&GN engines. Also in view are the hoses and the intermediate buffers between engine and tender. www.rail-online.co.uk

43148 on 29 June 1963 at New England with its damaged front end framing; it was repaired at Horwich during a Light Casual from 15/7/63-23/8/63. K.C.H. Fairey.

43006 at Kirkby Stephen in 1965, when allocated to Workington. It is an illustration of how the 'face' of an engine can be transformed by changing a few details. It had been at Eastleigh for a Heavy Intermediate from 12/11/64-29/1/65 and now has short door straps, no handrail, numberplate positioned above upper door strap, no SC plate and the top lamp bracket moved downwards. These are in addition to the AWS, which was fitted in October 1961, and the bar on the tender coal space. www.rail-online.co.uk

3001 at Bletchley on 17 May 1948 wearing the plain black LMS 1946 style livery carried by 3000-3002 which had pale straw coloured sans serif 14in letters and 12in numbers with inset maroon lining and maroon edging and corresponding serif smokebox numberplate. The 4F power classification on 3000 was below the cab number which was positioned immediately below the cab windows. It was above the number on the other two; the cab numbers were lower and in line with the LMS letters on the tender which were positioned slightly above the horizontal line of rivets. L.T. Russell Collection, Allan C. Baker.

cladding and appearing in the most unlikely of places. Apparently the purpose of the cover was to prevent enginemen from battering the setscrews in the hope of releasing the clack valves which occasionally stuck open. They were there to allow adjustment to the lift of the clack following machining and grinding of the valve and/or its seat,.

Pony Trucks and Guard Irons
3000-43106 had prominent guard irons attached to the front frames. On 43107 onwards smaller guard irons were fixed to the pony truck. This kept them at a more constant height and position above the rail at all times. The early engines were all modified to this pattern by the mid-1950s.

Tablet catchers
The 4MTs used on the M&GN and Scottish Region single lines had automatic tablet exchange apparatus which was attached on both sides of the tender at the front in a recess cut out of the tanks. Eastern Region 43058-43069, 43080-43095, 43104-43111, 43137, 43142-43161 and Scottish Region 43138-43141 were built with the catchers. 43132-43136 had the cut-out on the tenders to allow the equipment to be fitted, although there is no evidence that this was ever done. The catchers were eventually removed in the early 1960s, but it is possible some were left on until the engines were withdrawn.

43012 and 43017 which worked on the Somerset & Dorset Joint line in 1949 and the early-1950s also had tablet exchange apparatus fitted but did not have the recess in the tanks as on the later engines.

BR Days
As with most steam classes which survived into the 1960s the 4MTs received a number of minor modifications. The most important was the provision of AWS equipment and over a hundred were fitted between March 1960 and January 1963. External indications were a protection plate under the front buffer beam to prevent the screw coupling damaging the receiver, a conduit under the left-hand running plate and a battery box below the cab on the left-hand side.

With the onset of electrification from around 1960 'electric overhead' warning flashes, white enamel plates with the symbolic warning sign of forked lightning (in red) were fixed to those parts of the locomotive where footplate crews might come into contact with overhead wires. Also, from late-1963 the upper lamp bracket was, for safety reasons, moved down to the right of the central door fastening, and the central lamp iron above the bufferbeam was also moved to the right to remain directly under it. This was a common modification, although many of the class were withdrawn without undergoing it.

Three minor, but most noticeable, changes which affected the appearance of the engines were the removal of the horizontal handrail on the smokebox door, shorter door straps and repositioning of the smokebox numberplate. This only occurred in the case of a handful of engines which passed through Swindon or Eastleigh Works during late 1964 and 1965. The handrail was removed from 43012, 43112 and 43115 at Swindon in 1964 and from 43006 and 43019 at Eastleigh in 1965. The smokebox number plates were moved to the door strap in GWR-style at Swindon on 43001, 43012, 43015, 43044, 43047, 43070, 43112 and 43115 in 1964; Eastleigh also lowered the plate on 43106 in September 1965, but this time below the strap.

Fox and Kinder in *British Railways Illustrated* noted a few more minor and unseen modifications. 43154 was reportedly built with wheels of a slightly larger diameter, presumably involving little more than extra tyre thickness (otherwise major structural modifications would have been required). The boilers of the engines on the Eastern Region were modified when removed for heavy repairs by having the lowest row of four tubes removed and the position of one of the tubes on the front plate used as a wash-out plug hole. To partly compensate, an additional tube was added to either side of the second or third row from the

M3003 at Edge Hill on 14 March 1948. It was built at Horwich on 17 January 1948 and was renumbered as 43003 week ending 2/9/50. 3003-3010 were delivered before the newly nationalised BR had determined its standard liveries and appeared with a hybrid insignia style. BRITISH RAILWAYS in 10in lettering replaced the LMS on the tender although the LMS cab numbers remained for the time being, with a letter 'M' about 5-6in high to signify the owning Region squeezed between the numbers and the power classification. A square plate carrying an 'M' was fixed ahead of the smokebox numberplate. T.J. Edgington.

The 'M' designation had been replaced by the BR 40000 prefix when 43011-43019 were delivered and this resulted in LMS serif pattern BR smokebox number plates and rather strange cab numerals which were in thinner, probably hand-painted, characters than on M3003-10. Those on 43011-43015 appeared to be the LMS figures without the maroon lining whereas 43016-43019 had smaller 10in numbers which matched the tender lettering.

By the time 43020 appeared in December 1948, the new standard BR liveries had been chosen. The 4MTs got the mixed traffic livery of black lined with grey, red and cream in LNWR style as depicted on 43022 since they were now officially recognised as mixed traffic engines. The cab numerals were in 8in high cream serif and the BRITISH RAILWAYS was now only 6in high, positioned on the central horizontal line of rivets on the tender. Also appearing for the first time with this batch were the BR standard serif smokebox number plates, which had slightly thinner and more angular figures than the LMS pattern. In recognition of the revised designation the power class figure was changed from 4F to a plain '4', placed immediately below the cab windows. www.rail-online.co.uk

bottom. The position of the original front plate wash-out plug (adjacent to the second or third row) was blanked out.

Tenders

The original tenders built with the first fifty London Midland engines had several features which were changed on the later batches. They all had a long rear ladder which reached to the bottom of the frames; on 43050 onwards it finished at footplate level. The tender cab floor mounting was changed from a 'hole in the wall cut-out' above the top footstep on 3000-43019 to a waisted-in shape on all subsequent engines – probably for safety reasons (it was a long way down).

The rectangular shaped side air vents faced outward, to ensure that any overflow went down the tender side, on 3000-43036 (and possibly 43037 and 43038) but were turned inwards into the coal space on the last tender of lot 193 built with 43039, and on all subsequent engines. The change was presumably intended to help keep the coal dust damped down, but there was an unfortunate consequence; after picking up water the volume of the inflow, if the fireman didn't get the scoop up quickly enough, could inundate the coal space and even sweep a large proportion of the contents of the tender down onto the footplate.

The front handrails were straight and fixed to the tank on those tenders which did not have a cut-out for a tablet catcher; those with the cut-out had a curved handrail which followed the curve of the cab floor mounting. A vertical handrail was added to the rear end of the tank sides and footsteps were fitted below it on the frames from engines built from late-1951 onwards; from photographs 43116 appears to be last of the Horwich engines without the handrails: 43117-43136 definitely had them. Those from Doncaster are less certain: 43137-43144 did not have the handrails but 43158-43161 did; the pictures of 43145-43157 do not provide evidence either way. The handrails and steps were 'retro-fitted' in the early 1950s to all the tenders with short ladders; none of the long ladder examples were modified.

There were two more minor differences: firstly the rivet pattern on the tender tanks – Doncaster-built engines had flush rivets in the centre where the totem was positioned; all others from Horwich and Darlington had continuous lines of vertical and horizontal rivets. Secondly, tenders built at Doncaster had the prefix 'E' on the tender number plates and those from Darlington 'NE'.

A heavy steel bar attached to the rear of the tender coal space, matching the profile of cab roof, was applied to at

least twenty engines. These may have been connected with working under overhead electrified lines – they were fitted starting in early 1961 – but no definitive explanation seems to have survived. Allan Baker suggests that they were fitted to prevent coal being loaded above the loading gauge. Tenders attached to 43001, 43006, 43013, 43020, 43021, 43028, 43033, 43035, 43036, 43039, 43041, 43045, 43046, 43047, 43049, 43073, 43113, 43118, 43122 and 43137, most of which were allocated to the London Midland Region at the time, had the bars.

Liveries

Although always painted black, the 4MTs wore a variety of different insignia and linings, which varied both between batches and over time. The first three just sneaked into LMS livery but 3002-43049 carried a mix of styles as British Railways decided on its standard liveries; Doncaster and Darlington naturally added a few LNER touches to their engines.

3000-3002 emerged in plain black LMS 1946 style livery which had pale straw coloured sans serif 14in letters and 12in numbers with inset maroon lining and maroon edging and corresponding serif smokebox numberplate. Since they had been ordered as freight locomotives they each carried the 4F power classification, in the case of 3000 below

When deliveries began from the ex-LNER works the locomotives appeared in the plain black BR freight livery – as on 43075 brand new at Darlington on 27 September 1950, rather than the mixed traffic livery applied to 43020-43049. The two works also introduced some minor differences. Both used their own standard larger 10in cab numbers but on 43050-43069 Doncaster applied the LNER style RA4 lettering on the cabside, to the rear of and below the numbers. The corresponding 4MT was on the bufferbeam to the left of the coupling hook, whereas Darlington omitted these on 43070-43096. E. Haigh.

More livery variations emerged as the 4MTs went through works. 43050, originally plain black, was repainted with lining at Doncaster during a Heavy Intermediate overhaul in June/July 1953. It has large cab numbers, small BR emblem on tender. Unlike those from Horwich which had lining on the footplate angle and cylinder covers, the former LNER works left them plain black. The LM works used the '4' power classification and 8in cab numbers but Doncaster and Darlington continued with their 10in numbers; the former with the 'RA4' and '4MT'. The large size numerals meant that the lining was almost to the edges of the cab sheets whereas on the engines from Horwich it was inset; the tender has been fitted with a rear handrail but the lining goes beyond it. E. Blakey, www.transporttreasury.co.uk

43044 at Westbury on 11 June 1964, running in after a five month long General repair at Swindon, where it had been repainted with small cab numbers and tender emblem. The lining on the cab is inset as from Horwich; it stops short of the rear handrail on the tender but is longer than that applied by Horwich which finished several inches before the handrail. 43044 also has Overhead Line Warning flashes plus a 'Swindonised' smokebox front, albeit still with the horizontal handrail.
www.rail-online.co.uk

the cab number which was positioned immediately below the cab windows. It was placed above on the other two whose cab numbers were lower and in line with the LMS letters on the tender that were positioned slightly above the horizontal line of rivets.

3003-3010 were delivered while the nationalised railway was still considering its new liveries and therefore emerged with a hybrid insignia style. BRITISH RAILWAYS in 10in lettering replaced the LMS on the tender although the LMS cab numbers continued, with a letter 'M' about 5-6in high to signify the owning region squeezed between the numbers and the power classification. A square plate carrying an 'M' was fixed ahead of the smokebox numberplate.

The 'M' designation had been replaced by the BR 40000 prefix when the final nine engines in the lot were delivered and this resulted in LMS serif pattern smokebox number plates and rather strange cab numerals which were in thinner, probably hand-painted, characters than before on 43011-43015, which appeared to be the LMS figures without the maroon lining. 43016-43019 had smaller 10in numbers which matched the tender lettering.

The gap of six months before delivery of the next engine, 43020 in December 1948, saw a change to the new standard BR mixed traffic livery, lined grey, red

and cream in LNWR style as the 2-6-0s were now officially recognised as mixed traffic engines. The cylinders had a double red band but the footplate edge was too narrow for the red line. The cab numerals were the final BR pattern cream serif 8in high and the BRITISH RAILWAYS was now only 6in high, positioned on the central horizontal line of rivets on the tender. Also appearing for the first time on this batch were the standard BR serif smokebox number plates, which had slightly thinner and more angular figures than the LMS pattern. In recognition of the revised designation the power class figure was changed from 4F to a plain '4', placed immediately below the cab windows.

The next change came in July 1949 with the first engine of lot 200, 43040, when the smaller version of new BR 'lion on a wheel' emblem, positioned over the centre axle rather than centrally within the lining, replaced the lettering on the tender, all other details remaining the same.

The first ten engines received their BR numbers commencing with 3001 in August 1948, followed by 3002 in June 1950 and ending with M3010 in March 1951. The smokebox plate for 43001 was in the same LMS style numerals as used on 43011-43019; the others were fitted with BR pattern plates. 43000-43002 kept their LMS insignia tenders until their first

full repaint and thus ran with BR numbers while coupled to LMS tenders.

When deliveries began from the ex-LNER works in mid-1950 the locomotives appeared in the plain black BR freight livery, which may or may not have been an indication of their planned usage, and it was even reported by the Railway Observer that 43050 had '4F' painted on its bufferbeam. The two works inevitably managed to create some minor differences. Both used their own standard larger 10in cab numbers but on 43050-43069 Doncaster applied the LNER style RA4 lettering on the cabside, to the rear of and below the numbers and the corresponding 4MT on the bufferbeam to the left of the coupling hook, whereas Darlington omitted these on 43070-43096. Both placed the BR emblem centrally in line with the third vertical row of rivets, Doncaster using the area which had flush rivets for the purpose.

All the engines built after 1950 received the lined mixed traffic livery with the change starting mid-way through the Darlington lot on 43097, on the next lot from Horwich 43112-43136 and Doncaster's 43107-43111 and 43137-43161. Horwich continued to line the footplate angle and the cylinder covers but the former LNER works left them plain black. The London Midland works used the '4' power classification and 8in

70

The original tenders built with 43000-43049, as coupled to M3004 at Bletchley on 10 April 1948, had several features which were changed on the later batches. They had a long rear ladder which reached to the bottom of the frames; on 43050 onwards it finished at footplate level. The tender cab floor mounting was changed from a 'hole in the wall cut-out' above the top footstep on 3000-43019 to a waisted-in shape on all subsequent engines. The rectangular shaped side air vents faced outward on 3000-43036 (and possibly 43037 and 43038) to ensure that any overflow went down the tender side; on later tenders they were lengthened and turned inwards into the coal space. H.C. Casserley, courtesy R.M. Casserley.

71

cab numbers but Doncaster and Darlington did not follow suit, continuing with their 10in numbers; the former with the 'RA4' and '4MT'. Their use of the large size numerals meant that the lining was almost to the edges of the cab sheets whereas on the engines from Horwich it was inset; in all cases the tender lining was positioned to match. The lining on the tenders with tablet catcher cut-outs stopped at the edge of the cut-out. Horwich placed the small BR emblem centrally on the tank for those without the cut-out and rather strangely centred within the offset lining on those with the cut-out. Doncaster sensibly continued to use the flush riveted area, but Darlington positioned the crests centrally within the lined area.

What little uniformity in livery styles soon disappeared once the class started to undergo full repaints during works overhauls, with Stratford and Cowlairs throwing their own interpretations into the ring. Cowlairs painted shed allocations LNER style on the front buffer beams and Stratford positioned the 'RA4' characters centrally below the numbers. The bufferbeam power class also varied on the repaints – it was low down originally but moved higher on some of them and on others changed to 'Cl 4MT' or 'CLASS 4MT'. In the final years conformity crept in and the simple '4' cab above the numbers was used by all of the workshops.

The lining disappeared and re-appeared over the years. Both Stratford and Doncaster began lining out the 4MTs when they commenced Heavy/General repairs in 1953/54; Stratford dropped the lining in February 1955 and it is likely

that Doncaster did the same, leaving only Horwich applying the lining. Certainly engines built with lining were repainted in plain black in the late 1950s and early 1960s, and vice versa, but the size and positioning on the tenders also varied. It seems that Horwich decided to use a shorter length lining which cleared the tablet catcher cut-out on all tenders, irrespective of whether they had a cut-out. This meant that the lining stopped well short of the rear edge of the tanks because it was matched at the front end to the spacing on the cab. Doncaster and Darlington applied it uniformly on all edges to match their cab lining, only using the shorter length when they needed to avoid the cut-out.

In 1957 BR crests approved by the College of Arms replaced the emblem, at first with forward facing lions on each side, but after complaints from the College all lions faced left. Horwich, which always lined its 4MTs, used the smaller version of the crest and 8in cab numbers. Doncaster and Darlington chose the larger crest to go with the 10in numbers on lined engines but applied the small crests and 10in numbers on plain black repaints. As always there were exceptions; 43039, 43076 and 43077 carried 8in numbers and large crests when lined out. Most engines repaired at Swindon and Eastleigh in 1964/65 appear to have been given full repaints, lined out with 8in numbers, but 43015 emerged from Swindon with its original lining and 8in numbers and 43137 retained its 10in numbers, suggesting both were only partially repainted.

Right. **In April 1961 the** *Railway Observer* **reported a new development, the fitting of large racks or fenders at the rear of the coal space on 4MT tenders – these, it was said, resembled 'nothing so much as a rather austere brass bed-end'. This view of 43036 at Carlisle on 19 August 1964 illustrates the size of these structures. They were fitted to prevent coal being loaded above the loading gauge. Note that 43036 is not paired with its original tender because this one has inward facing vents and short rear ladder; it was no.4769 built with 43119. P. Chancellor.**

Below. **43157 on 27 May 1954 at North Walsham, demonstrating several changes from the earlier tenders, in addition to the provision of tablet exchange apparatus. It has inward facing rectangular shaped side air vents and a vertical handrail at the rear end of the tank sides with footsteps below it on the frames. The latter two features were (except for the first fifty) retrospectively fitted to the earlier tenders. The lining has been taken near to the edges of the tanks to match that on the cab and the BR emblem is placed centrally in the rivet-free area thoughtfully provided by Doncaster for that very purpose. www.rail-online.co.uk**

43097 was allocated to York when it was sent to Eastleigh for an Intermediate repair in 1965, from 1 February until 19 March. Much needs to be done when pictured on 6 March before it is ready for service, not just the wheels and motion but all that pipework around and below the cab.

43140 and unidentified fellow on 17 July 1960 at Manningham shed, Bradford. It was transferred from Dawsholm on the Scottish Region to West Auckland in November 1963, one of the nine Scottish based engines moved to the North Eastern Region in exchange for Crabs and BR Class 4 2-6-0s as part of a scheme to ease and speed-up repairs and to reduce the number of types of spares carried at depots. Paul Chancellor Collection.

5. ON THE RECORD

Health Warning

As pointed out in earlier volumes of this series, the Engine History Cards and Engine Record Cards, while containing much useful and even fascinating information, should be regarded as a *guide* to what happened to the engines, not an unimpeachable document to be afforded the status of gospel. It seems to be stating the obvious that the Cards only show what was written on them at the time but the temptation to read and interpret too much should be resisted.

Dates of leaving and entry to works were of course to some extent nominal and a day or two either side should always be assumed. Worse, the works were not above 'fiddling' dates slightly at the beginning or the end of a month to enhance the monthly figures, either of engines 'in' or engines 'out'. It was thus not entirely unknown for a locomotive to be out on the road with the figures showing it still in works and vice versa – for a few days at least. As with all BR steam locomotives, the record fades from about 1959-60 as the people involved realised their charges were on the way out. No-one responsible for the Cards bothered to record the last 'seeing out' mileages on the London Midland or other Regions

where the 4MTs ended up.

Although History Cards for those engines which were withdrawn from the London Midland Region went to the National Railway Museum, the only surviving information for those which worked on the Eastern, North Eastern and Scottish Regions are the Engine Record Cards. Although slightly less detailed then the History Cards, these have nonetheless allowed a reasonably complete picture to be produced for the remainder of the class, albeit a few of the cards are lacking details of the works visits. Some of the remaining gaps have been filled by reference to contemporary reports in the *Railway Observer* and *SLS Journal*.

Sheds...

Many shed moves at the end did not find their way onto the History Cards, although most seem to have been recorded on the Record Cards. However the Chief Accountant's Statistics Office at Derby kept going to the bitter end of BR steam and beyond, and so the London Midland Region shed allocations from around 1961 onwards were taken from the weekly Locomotive Stock Book Alteration Lists produced there. For the locomotives allocated to the Eastern, North Eastern

and Scottish Regions the Engine Record Cards were the primary source. The shed descriptions used are as written on the Cards and therefore translation is needed for some of the ex-LMS sheds: Bristol = Barrow Road; Leeds = Holbeck; Sheffield = Grimesthorpe. Transfer dates were for the week ending, although some moves recorded only on the Record Cards are the actual day of the transfer.

Repairs and Maintenance

Under the LMS motive power organisation which formed the basis of the BR system most sheds carried out minor running repairs and adjustments, including boiler wash-outs etc. Jobs which required the engine to return to Works were usually designated under one of the 'Classified Repair' codes. These were either 'Heavy, (**H**) or 'Light' (**L**), further sub-divided into 'Casual' (**C**), 'Intermediate' (**I**). 'Overhaul' (**O**), 'Service' (**S**) or 'General' (**G**). Occasionally engines were sent to Main Works for other reasons, such as modifications (e.g. fitting of AWS equipment if this did not coincide with a normally programmed visit) and in these cases the code **NC** (Non-Classified) was used. The other code which appears from time to time on the Engine Repair

43048 had been in the wars when photographed on 13 March 1960 at Horwich Works. It was recorded as out of traffic from 19/1/60-4/5/60, with 48 days awaiting works; the repairs, which were classified as Heavy General, were started on 15 March.
www.rail-online.co.uk

Colwick's allocation of 4MTs averaged around sixteen during 1963/64, but all had gone by the start of 1965. 43155 and another 4MT were there during that time. The angle of the shot shows off the high running plate and exposed motion to good effect. www.rail-online.co.uk

cards is **TRO**, which stands for 'Tender Repair Only'. Suffixes, usually after '**NC**' were **(EO)**, which signified 'Engine Only' and **Rect.**, or **Rect. (EO)** which was used when an engine had to be returned to Works soon after a works visit for 'rectification', i.e. tightening up bits that had come loose and loosening bits that were too tight. Eastern and North Eastern Region nomenclature differed slightly from the London Midland Region, using the abbreviations **IH, CL, NC** etc but these are self-explanatory.

According to the classification prescribed by the Board of Trade a heavy repair was any one during which an engine was reboilered or had its boiler removed from the frames. It was also when any two of the following were carried out:
Fitting new tyres to four or more wheels.
Fitting new cylinders.
Fitting new axles.
Re-tubing or otherwise repairing the boiler whilst still in the frames with not less than fifty firebox stays renewed.
Both turning wheels and refitting axleboxes.
Stripping and renewing both motion and brake gear.

Intriguingly, light repairs often involved major work such as fitting new axles, replacing cylinders, partially re-tubing or patching the boiler in situ, or refurbishing the motion, axleboxes, frames, etc. As long as only one of these items was involved, however, the repair was still regarded as light.

Most heavy repairs were 'generals' whilst most light repairs were 'intermediates'. General repairs were carried out either at set time intervals or at predetermined mileages beyond which it was deemed that an engine could not safely remain in service and were designed to return it virtually to 'as new' condition. Intermediate repairs were normally undertaken when some major component reached the stage where it had to be attended to before the engine was due for general repair, but the aim was to carry out as few intermediate repairs as possible. Thus HG repairs were usually done at approximately three yearly intervals, with either no, or one, Intermediate repair (either Light or Heavy) between.

Works...
Horwich Works was responsible for heavy repairs to the 4MTs based on the London Midland Region, and Doncaster, Darlington and Stratford at various times for those allocated to the Eastern, North Eastern and Scottish Regions.
On 10 August 1953 all the 4MTs in Eastern Region stock (those allocated to New England and the M&GN sheds) became the responsibility of Gorton Works for repair instead of Doncaster. 43094 was the first to go to Manchester for a Heavy Intermediate on 20 August, completed by 24 October, and 43127 had a General there between 2 October and January 1954. These were to be the only two to be dealt with at Gorton because the Eastern Region authorities changed their minds and decided to transfer the work to Stratford. By November, 43062 from New England and South Lynn's 43111 and 43142 were already there, and the London works carried out all the Heavy or Intermediate repairs on the Eastern Region engines during 1954 and the first half of 1955. Doncaster then took over, although for some unknown reason Stratford also did a few more from late 1957 until the end of 1959.

The engines allocated to the Scottish Region visited either Doncaster or Darlington for their main repairs, only going to Cowlairs for Light, or occasionally Intermediate, attention. The North Eastern Region 4MTs went to Doncaster for Heavy and General repairs throughout the 1950s, even after the Eastern Region transferred the work on its own engines from there to Stratford, until they were switched to Darlington from the start of 1959. Horwich took over both the Eastern Region and North Eastern Region work from mid-1962 until 1964; 43108 was the last from Doncaster on 11 May 1962 and

Stoke's 43115 on 27 September 1964, at the end of a Heavy Classified overhaul at Swindon which had begun on 20 May. The horizontal handrail has been removed, the top lamp iron lowered and the numberplate moved GWR style to the shorter length door strap, but it still has a pre-1957 crest on the tender. Only the smokebox has been repainted. The SC plate has vanished and two rivets have appeared at the bottom of the smoke box front. Had Swindon removed the self-cleaning plates and fitted a baffle plate at the bottom of the smokebox? www.rail-online.co.uk

43014 the final one from Darlington, in August 1962.

When steam repairs ceased at Horwich in May 1964, the engines then went to Cowlairs for Light or Intermediate overhauls. Heavy and General repairs had already been transferred to Swindon at the start of the year; in late-1964 and 1965, they were carried out at Eastleigh. It is interesting that most of the overhauls at Swindon took between four and five months; this was presumably due to little urgency being attached to the work, combined with the difficulty of obtaining spares. Somewhat ironically, given the events there in 1951, 43003 was the last BR steam locomotive to be repaired at Swindon, emerging in February 1965. 43019, 43073 and 43106 underwent the final repairs of all, off-works from Eastleigh in September 1965.

Two other shops did some minor work; Bow carried out LC or NC repairs on Devons Road engines 43000, 43001, 43020, 43021, 43022 and 43024 in early 1951 and each made return visits for the same purpose over the years up to 1957; Rugby did the same on 43022 in 1950, and between 1956 and 1958 attended to Nuneaton's 43001, 43002, 43022 and 43023.

Mileages
Total annual mileage was recorded on the History Cards up to around 1960 for the London Midland Region based engines and therefore only gives a partial indication for the class. It would have been fascinating to see what some of the M&GN engines managed to achieve during the 1950s! Having said that, a few snippets nevertheless can be extracted to show how the 4MTs compared with the engines they were designed to replace and the other LMS mixed traffic engines.

During their first full four years from 1949-52 43000-43019 averaged 29,000 miles per annum and 43020-43049 achieved 24,000 in 1950-52. For all those recorded the average dropped back to 24,000 p.a. over the period 1953-60. To put these into some sort of context this compared with around 37,500 p.a. for the LMS Black 5s between 1949 and 1960. Figures for their LMS predecessors when these engines were still relatively new were, in 1933-35, 27,590 p.a. for the 4F 0-6-0s and 37,560 p.a. for the Crab 2-6-0s. (The latter were generally employed at that time on long distance freight work). The corresponding mileages between general repairs were 111,372 for the 4Fs and 137,492 for the Crabs, compared with the 4MTs in 1952: 166,654; 1953 124,565; 1954 132,828.

'Improvements, Etc'
The History Cards had a section headed 'Improvements, Etc.' that recorded brief details of modifications or improvements applied to the engines. What was recorded here for the 4MTs was almost exclusively confined to the fitting of new chimney arrangements and AWS. This book uses the relevant 'off works' date for each particular modification rather than the 'period ending' date which was actually written on the Improvements section of the cards because clearly this makes more sense. Where a modification is known to have been applied but the date is not recorded a '?' is shown in the tables. The most common instance of this is the replacement chimney modification, most of which were not recorded; it is reasonable to assume most of these would have been done during the first works visit post-April 1953.

43038 and 43044 in the gloom of Stourton on 29 September 1961. 43038, which arrived there from Middlesbrough in September 1957 and stayed until withdrawn in May 1964, is in unlined black with large cab numbers, still fairly shiny after a repair at Doncaster completed in June. 43044 was shedded at Stourton for longer, from March 1952 until transferred to Manningham in October 1966. www.rail-online.co.uk

43019 at Lostock Hall on 2 February 1968, three months before withdrawal. It shows evidence of a Light Intermediate overhaul at Eastleigh from 25/6/65-1/9/65, with no horizontal hand rail and lowered upper lamp iron. Both number and shed plates have white painted borders as was common at this date. 43019 was one of the first 4MTs allocated to Lostock Hall in February 1966 when Lower Darwen shed closed. As 1968 dawned it was one of the last six remaining engines, all allocated to the Preston shed. N.E. Preedy.

Barrow Hill, the ex-Midland Railway shed at Staveley transferred to the Eastern Region in February 1958, had around half a dozen 4MTs on its books from 1960 and by January 1965 the allocation had reached nineteen. However almost all of them were withdrawn later that year with just a handful escaping, including 43082, pictured passing through the station on 11 July 1964 with a coal train.

43001 at Devons Road on 16 April 1955; it had arrived at the East London shed from Bletchley in January 1951. In the first three years of its life 43001 achieved a quite impressive mileage of 103,477, including 38,530 in 1949 while at Bletchley – an annual mileage that could stand comparison with any freight/mixed traffic type. 43001 kept its double chimney until a Heavy Intermediate at Horwich in mid-1956.

Derby's 43049 on 27 August 1955 at Litton between Monsal Dale and Millers Dale on the ex-MR line through the Peak District. It averaged some 25,000 miles a year between 1950 and 1954, only visiting Horwich once – for a Light Intermediate – over that whole period and then for less than a month.

6. THE COVERED WAGON CASEBOOK

(From an article compiled by Ray Fox and Mike Kinder published in British Railways
Illustrated Volume 12 No.10/11 July/Aug 2003)

The modern and highly beneficial features which the class enjoyed (many of which had already appeared on the Class 2) were numerous and included self cleaning smokeboxes and hopper ashpans. The latter enabled the disposal of ash through twin doors in seconds without any of the ritual manual toil hitherto required and regarded as part of the eternal order of things. Rocker grates were also fitted, though many firemen – and drivers – were wary of using these while on the road in case the sections jammed when still partially open, or a load of clinker fell through and burnt its way through the ashpan doors. One ex-fireman recalled that his drivers positively forbade their use while the train was moving. Long lap, long travel valves of generous dimensions (10 inch diameter) made the engines very fast runners when occasion demanded.

These same valve events also enabled them to slog up gradients more or less all day without suffering boiler pressure problems – at least when the initial steaming problems had been overcome and provided they had decent coal of course. There were outside water feed filter boxes on the tender framing, another feature later adopted on the BR Standards. These made filter cleaning a doddle – a wire brush under a running tap and no more forcing the youngest apprentice down into the tender tank! The boxes unfortunately could freeze and shatter in bad frost and 'fire devils' had to be brought into play at sheds. Such measures were a bit hit and miss however and Rugby for one (the idea caught on at other sheds too) made up copper pipes with flanges so that a fractured box could be by-passed and the engine kept running until a new box arrived. Remarkably, these sieve boxes were standard on all classes equipped with them – this included the BR Standards, Ivatt 2s and later Black 5s. The Ivatt 4s also had two excellent Monitor live steam injectors which could fill the boiler with remarkable efficiency and speed – embarrassing if the fireman's attention happened to be concentrated elsewhere!

As built, the steam pipes to the injectors and delivery pipes to the top feed, along with many others, were made of steel. This saved weight and cost but, owing to fractures caused by vibration and relative movement between boiler and frames, the steel pipes soon had to be replaced – usually at the first general repair – in traditional copper. In the long term, this was the best material for pipes on locos except where the position was completely stable. The engines had cast steel axleboxes with manganese steel liners on boxes and hornplates, and driving coupled wheel axleboxes with underfed oil to underkeeps. This method was much more effective than the more usual oil feed at the top while extensive grease lubrication saved many hours wielding the oil can. Moreover, to the great benefit of both crews and engines, it was done by the fitting staff. Another virtue these engines possessed was their positively electric powers of acceleration which were rated as superior even to those of the Fowler and Stanier 2-6-4Ts. Their working flexibility made them equally at home on passenger, freight and shunting duties; this, combined with a wide route availability, made them a god-send to the Operating Department,

43111 at Sutton Bridge on 28 February 1959, the last day of the M&GNR, with the 11.11am Peterborough-Yarmouth. The 4MTs were synonymous with the M&GN and much of their 'express' passenger work was done there, especially in the summer months on the numerous Saturday workings from the Midlands, though in many cases they only took over these workings at Spalding or South Lynn. These trains often comprised 12 or 13 coaches which could tax them to their limit.

43036 with a tablet catcher on the tender for use on the Somerset & Dorset, one of three 4MTs allocated to Bath at the beginning of the 1950s. They were very unpopular because of their poor steaming and their departure from the S&D was not mourned overmuch.

who could roster them far more intensively. Indeed, when the class arrived on the scene, many of the staff involved with them found a rapid decline in their overtime as a result of all these features.

Some compensation for this, though, was the comfort and convenience offered by these new engines, particularly the ability to remain warm and dry in winter and bad weather generally. This was an attribute sadly lacking on the 4Fs, and on many other classes. The day of the storm sheet flapping wildly in the wind had gone and crews found themselves snugly enclosed, though there were inevitably still some draughts – and the seats were still wooden tip-ups. Because of their anti-reflection qualities the angled spectacle glasses provided on both engine and tender were also welcomed, whilst the glass windshield, at the rear of the leading side window, was a highly desirable and effective feature, as were the damper controls, which could be set to fine adjustments without fear of subsequent movement. As Terry Essery observes in his book *Locomotives Compared*, the damper wheels, which projected from the floor, also afforded a very comfortable footrest for the fireman. There were twin pull-out regulator handles (originally, but only briefly, there were twin brake handles too) connected by a transverse rod. The right-hand one was not always appreciated by the fireman who could be on the receiving end if he didn't keep a weather eye open. They were useful during shunting operations when there was often only one man on the footplate, the other performing a more necessary duty elsewhere, such as brewing up or

participating in social activities. The fireman also had the benefit of a new home for the fire-irons, alongside the firebox on the fireman's side. The arrangement spared him the traditional movement of the fire-irons from the tender with all the attendant difficulties and dangers.

Despite all this the 4MTs got a rough reception at some depots. For example, in January 1951, Devons Road received 43000, 43001, 43020, 43021, 43022 and 43024 which proved highly unpopular. The crews complained about rough riding (the result of Horwich valve setting, which reportedly was resolved fairly rapidly, though complaints were still made), poor steaming and heavy coal consumption. 43001 and 43020 were reported to have lain dead on shed for at least two months while in May 1949 the driver of a badly ailing Jubilee, on a St Pancras-Manchester express, unequivocally declined the offer of help in the form of 43045!

Despite the indisputable weakness in the steaming capabilities of the early engines in their double chimney state, for which there is no lack of support whether from the official sources, ex-footplatemen or magazine columns, there are indications that things were not quite as grim as is implied. For example, in the first three years of its life 43001 achieved a quite impressive mileage of 103,477, including 38,530 in 1949 while at Bletchley – an annual mileage that could stand comparison with any freight/mixed traffic type. It was even superior to some of the Jubilee mileages for that year! Certainly it was hardly what one would expect of an engine that 'suffered from uncertain steaming except on the very lightest of

duties'. And, if it lay dead on shed for 'at least two months' in 1951 it must have been working every other day of the year. Apart from nineteen days undergoing a Light Casual at Bow, its engine history card records it as being out of service for only 71 days.

Similarly 43036, working from Bath Green Park over the Somerset & Dorset, a line finely calculated to test the steaming capacity of any engine to the limit, achieved an equally impressive mileage of 125,960 over the four years 1950-1953. The three examples allocated to Bath at the beginning of the 1950s (43013, 43017 and 43036) were very unpopular because of poor steaming. Their only redeeming feature in the eyes of their crews was the excellent coasting ability, which often saved the day. One of them was given two test runs on the 'Pines Express' between Bath and Bournemouth – rather a lot to expect of a class 4 engine, even in perfect condition, one feels, so it is hardly surprising that it proved unequal to the task. However, they were rostered to work heavy passenger trains on summer weekends and even the 'Pines' again on rare occasions. This proved very much an endurance test for the crews, who were only too thankful for the free-running qualities just mentioned. One summer Saturday a couple of them, 43017 and 43036, were put in charge of a 12 coach express on its way to Bournemouth, only to grind to a halt at Wellow, both in urgent need of a 'blow-up'. Their condition on arrival at Masbury summit was much the same. Needless to say, the departure of the 2-6-0s from the S&D was not mourned. It can only have been the dedication of the crews and their readiness to struggle on to their destinations that enabled at least 43036 to achieve the high mileages previously referred to.

In his *Four Thousand Miles on the Footplate*, O.S. Nock gives a graphic description of two journeys behind 43017 – the 8.40am Bournemouth-Bath with 320 tons and the 2.12pm back with 330 tons, both automatically piloted between Bath and Evercreech – showing how the crews maintained punctuality despite the constant fall in boiler pressure when the engine was working hard. A great pity they never had a modified single chimney example to try out.

Meanwhile Derby's 43049 averaged some 25,000 a year between 1950 and 1954, only visiting Horwich once – for a Light Intermediate – over that whole period and then for less than a month. On the evidence of those engine history cards that have survived, the single chimney version did not achieve any higher mileage than its predecessor. So, in respect of the steaming problems, the crews seem to have made the best of a bad job. Presumably, most of them soon found the merits of full regulator working – though it is quite clear that even that was very far from being a panacea. However, the locos certainly appear, on the whole, to have performed the work required of them. Dedication on the part of the crews surely made a major contribution to this, though the provision of so many modern features must have helped considerably.

The news columns of the various railway magazines certainly tell of some interesting movements by double chimney engines. For example in March 1950 Bristol's 43012 is recorded arriving at Normanton on the 1.30pm Aintree-Healey Mills and departing on the 12.22am Normanton-Birmingham express freight. In the same month Bath's 43013 (reputedly fitted with a chime whistle) worked the 4.00pm Bath-Brunswick and then visited Chesterfield, Royston and Tibshelf over the next three days.

Nottingham's 43033 deputised for a 2-6-4T on the 8.45am Northampton-Euston, the 5.05pm Euston-Watford and the 7.25pm Watford-Euston Parcels and was seen on local freights at Kings Langley and Willesden the following day. At the beginning of 1950, 43034 and 43035 were recorded working (individually) the Manchester-Heysham Boat Express, though the task proved too much for them. On May 31 1952, Saltley's 43046 passed through Hellifield with a Leeds excursion and was later seen on another excursion at Morecambe. On June 21 1952, Leicester's 43045 worked through to Southport with an excursion. But these examples are hardly the 'very lightest duties'.

There is, of course, insufficient evidence for precise total mileages, as the practice of recording annual mileages declined after about 1960. It is just possible that a few Ivatt Class 4s achieved over half a million miles but under, probably well under, half a million seems far more likely for the class as a whole. And, of course, very few achieved even half their declared 40 year life expectancy.

The 2-6-0s got off to an extremely inauspicious start, but the answer to the problem had been found and the remedy eventually applied. So, as a result of the chimney replacement (and blastpipe too in the case of double chimney engines) the class finally realised its full potential; the new levels of performance attained won wide appreciation. The caveat should be added, however, that despite general consensus around the capabilities and efficiency of the class once the chimney modifications had been effected, there were still some dissenting voices. One ex-fireman, for example, was critical of the steep inclination of the grate, the frequent difficulty of opening the pull-out regulator and the 'accessible' motion, which allowed generous deposits of dust and filth to penetrate every crack and crevice of both loco and crew. While conceding that the single chimney version was 'a somewhat better machine' than its double chimney predecessor, he took the view that there was 'hardly a notable advance in steam power'. On this point of course, it depends what you compare the Ivatt with. The strictly relevant comparison is with the 4F and obviously both in design and, eventually, in steaming capacity the Ivatt was light years ahead. Very interestingly, a 4F was actually fitted with new draughting arrangements for some tests in 1954 and its steaming rate was increased from 12,000 to 19,000lb/hr. Incredibly, nobody seemed to take any notice and no action was taken! Yet more support for the observations concerning the strange and obstinate reluctance of top management to make any attempt to improve chimney and draughting arrangements generally.

The work actually undertaken by the Ivatt Moguls indicates quite clearly that they fully achieved the degree of flexibility and versatility expected of

In the early 1950s the London-based 4MTs appeared quite regularly on Tilbury boat trains. Here Cricklewood's 43118 arrives at Tilbury Riverside on 20 March 1954 on a train connecting with P&O's liner Chusan.

43132 in May 1953 at Fort William, one of four from Eastfield despatched there for a few weeks in exchange for K2s to work on the Mallaig line while the ashpits there were being rebuilt. The 4MTs with their rocker grates and hopper ashpans were deemed ideal for the situation. Similarly, when the turntable was temporarily isolated as a result of this rebuilding, thus necessitating tender first working, the Ivatts, with their tender cabs, were again considered the best remedy.

them. Duties ranged from express (albeit of a secondary nature of course), stopping passenger and parcels, through every type of freight down to trip work, shunting and station pilot duties. They even encompassed banking, at Manchester Victoria and also at Tebay, where 43011, 43028, 43029 and 43035 spent three or four years in the late 1950s, though their primary function was to work mineral trains forward to the Barrow district.

A lot of their 'express' passenger work was done on the M&GN, particularly in the summer months on the numerous Saturday workings from such places as Birmingham, Leicester, Nottingham, Derby, Chesterfield, Mansfield and Kings Norton, though in many cases they only took over these workings at Spalding or South Lynn. Such trains often comprised 12 or 13 coaches which could tax their capabilities quite severely. By a wonderful piece of irony, the class they had been intended to replace often worked the western part of the journey – or even right through on the odd occasion, though the timekeeping of the 4F could be suspect. On the final day of the M&GN, February 28 1959, this uneasy and ironical partnership was still in place. The last through train from Birmingham to Yarmouth Beach, the 1.45pm, arrived at Leicester behind Burton's 44542 to be replaced by Spalding's 43060 which had worked the last Yarmouth-Birmingham into Leicester in the morning. Yet another 4F appeared on the 4.20pm Nottingham-Kings Lynn, 43954, which worked as far as Spalding. The last

through train from Yarmouth to Peterborough was hauled by 43145. The same engine returned on the last train from Peterborough, the 8.37pm to Melton Constable, adorned with balloons and bearing numerous chalked inscriptions, to say nothing of a nude on the chimney (again chalked, not real!). With toilet rolls streaming from the carriage windows, it was surely an early candidate for the Turner prize!

It only remains to be said that the Ivatt Class 4 seems to have served the M&GN efficiently and successfully during the last eight years of its life. By an even greater piece of irony, however, after the closure of the M&GN it was usually 4F 0-6-0s that were to be found on the holiday traffic from the Midlands to the East Anglia resorts, via the alternative Peterborough, Ely and Norwich route.

Other secondary expresses hauled at some stage by the Ivatt Class 4 Moguls included Bradford/ Leeds-Morecambe/ Heysham on which, according to The *Railway Observer* of March 1960, they were poor timekeepers, though no explanation is given. Other routes were Thornton-Glasgow, Leeds-York and Bridlington, Newcastle-Carlisle, the up Scarborough Flyer (as far as York), Middlesbrough-Scarborough and St. Pancras-Kettering – there is also a photo of 43042 piloting a Black 5 on the 10.05am Leicester-St. Pancras. In the early 1950s they appeared quite regularly on Tilbury boat trains. There is a photo, for instance, of Derby's double chimney 43031 at Barking with an Orient Line train from St. Pancras to

Tilbury and another, of Cricklewood's 43118, arriving at Tilbury Riverside with a train connecting with P&O's liner Chusan, whose destination was the Far East.

Perhaps the most remarkable instance was the appearance of Colwick's 43058 on the old Great Central on June 26 1964 with three coaches on the 8.15am Nottingham-Marylebone. This was not by choice, it should be added, but came about because of a derailment that had prevented the rostered stock and loco from reaching the station. This was just the sort of job an Ivatt 4 should have revelled in and things seem to have gone well, for it duly returned on the 2.38 from Marylebone in the afternoon.

The Ivatt 4s were also used occasionally to work a relief express – on August 1 1955, 43051 took a Newcastle-Leeds relief to the 4.15pm Newcastle-Liverpool and might even take over a top class express. For example, a Selby engine took over a Kings Cross-Newcastle train, though only as far as York, whilst 43127 worked the 8.25am Manchester-Marylebone from Aylesbury on June 9 1954. The train engine, V2 60820, had run hot; how successfully the Ivatt Mogul coped went unrecorded, unfortunately.

The Ivatts proved great favourites on excursions, particularly from the Midlands and the North East to Scarborough and Bridlington and again from the North East over Stainmore to Blackpool and Morecambe. Ivatt Class 4s worked stopping passenger trains from virtually every shed to which they were allocated and amongst the more interesting was the Langholm branch, a duty performed by Carlisle Canal's 43139 for more than ten years. And, as already stated, they worked every class of freight from C down. At the top end, for example, in 1952, before conversion, 43120 of Cricklewood is recorded making three trips weekly London-Leeds and back 'with little trouble', whilst either 43016 or 43030 was used on the 8.50pm Bradford-Nottingham Class C and returned on the 9.20pm Nottingham-Carlisle Class D at the beginning of 1958. Some of the Eastfield contingent worked seed potato trains from Scotland to Newcastle.

On the strength of all this material, then, together with the views of various enginemen, an attempt can be made at a final assessment. Indubitably, the modern features incorporated in the class were a massive advance on anything seen hitherto and were universally welcomed by engine crews and shed staff alike – despite the loss of overtime! On the mechanical side the engines proved wholly trouble-free throughout their lives, apart from the replacement of much of the steel pipework with copper. There was also a fairly general consensus of opinion (though certainly not unanimity) regarding their efficient and successful performance on the road, once Swindon had done its work on chimney dimensions. The views of one ex-fireman have already been mentioned and his complaint about dust and dirt in particular, funnelling down into the cab when the engine was running tender first unless the coal was kept well watered, was echoed elsewhere. And,

despite the enclosed cab, draughts were another cause of criticism, though all this of course is irrelevant to performance.

Complaints about rough riding (which have already been referred to, at Devons Road) were also quite common. The New England crews were apparently even more outspoken about this and at the end of 1951 their engines were banned from use on lodging turns. To be fair, incorrect driving methods could have been at least partly responsible. However, it was A.J. Powell (*Living with London Midland Locomotives*, Ian Allan, 1977) who inflicted, perhaps unintentionally, the ultimate vilification on the class. He strongly regretted the steep slope of the grate, which he regarded as a potential cause of constant trouble, and then went on to say: 'It would be fair to say the crews appreciated their convenience and comfort and regarded them as a better tool for passenger work than the 4F but inferior for real slogging freight work'! The compilers must express their strong disagreement with parts of this judgement and assume that it is based only on his experience with the double chimney variety. Certainly events post-chimney modifications do not support it. All the other views that the compilers have seen or heard expressed have been very favourable. In particular no mention has been made or found anywhere about problems with the steepness of the grate – those questioned denied the existence of any problem and emphasised the ease of firing and maintaining pressure. In general, the efficient performance of the class in East Anglia has already been referred to. In addition, the crews of

the North Eastern Region liked the class enormously – strong engines with no vices was the judgement. An old Darlington driver told one of the compilers that the Ivatt 4 was the best engine he had ever driven over Stainmore, whilst an ex-Buxton man was equally outspoken in his praise of them on the Manchester-Sheffield line, though he spoke of their hard riding. They are also recorded as being well received at Eastfield, whilst the Middlesbrough men had a high regard for them – though they too found them rather rough riding. Colwick men were delighted when they got them for the Nottingham-Grantham workings.

Lastly, the thoughts of Nuneaton crews on the subject. The sobriquet 'Covered Wagon', incidentally, seems to have been of Nuneaton origin, though the precise source/ explanation is unknown – either simply the presence of a tender cab or maybe some impresario on the footplate giving his rendering of a song, popular at the time of the first appearance of the engines, about a covered wagon rolling its way across the Wild West. So are legends born, though nicknames are often regional in nature; 'covered wagon' may well have been confined to London-Crewe.

Nuneaton had had examples on its books from the earliest days and had consequently suffered the double chimney experiences. There were still twelve of them there in October 1962, at which time they were all reallocated to Bescot and Crewe South. The verdict at Nuneaton was, in essence, that nothing ever went wrong and that the engines did everything that was asked

43139 at Carlisle Canal, where it was allocated from new for use on the Langholm branch, continuing right through until the line closed.

43002 moved to Nuneaton from Bletchley in September 1953. Nuneaton gave their 4MTs the sobriquet 'Covered Wagon', possibly because of the tender cab.

of them. At that time they were working freight trains to Northampton and Market Harborough, parcels to and from Leicester, morning and evening workmen's trains to Coventry and whatever else was required.

Over the years their regular duties from Nuneaton involved mainly local passenger trains to Leicester, Coventry, Leamington and Rugby and the many trip workings in the area, including coal trains to Washwood Heath. However, they did enjoy more exciting moments. One job that often cropped up, especially in winter when any of the overnight expresses from Scotland were running late, was the passenger train to Euston that had to be put on, for which they were great favourites. At holiday times they would be off with trips to North Wales, Buxton, Matlock, Dudley Zoo, Alton Towers and so on, whilst in the football season they would visit Hednesford, Banbury, Oxford, Burton and elsewhere. There was also the occasion when the Willesden crew, who worked the 3.42am Class C Nuneaton-Willesden, were given a Covered Wagon, which they hadn't experienced before, instead of the usual Crab. There was long and vociferous protest but authority finally prevailed. However, the following night, it was the same Willesden crew and they demanded a Covered Wagon instead of the Crab – a remarkable accolade.

Perhaps the compilers could be excused a brief digression at this point with an interesting little tale of the Nuneaton Ivatt 4 that inadvertently wandered onto forbidden territory.

Hawkesbury Lane Sidings lay approximately midway between Nuneaton and Coventry; from them ran a single track branch line, originally for the Wyken collieries but by this time serving Longford Power Station. Shortly before reaching the Power Station the branch crossed the Coventry Canal by means of a timber viaduct (not quite up to Brunel standard but certainly a famous local landmark) on which there was a severe weight restriction; only ex-Midland 2Fs and Ivatt Class 2s were allowed over it. However, on the occasion in question there happened to be a different Running Shift Foreman on the night turn at Nuneaton, Bill Powney, an ex-GW man who had just arrived from Chester, and he asked driver Bill Bennett, who was to take the 5.48am to Hawkesbury Lane and then wagons down to the Power Station, what sort of engine was normally rostered. The reply was an Ivatt 2-6-0 and Bill Powney made the pardonable error of putting 43003 on the job instead of the usual 46447. So Bill Bennett went off shed quite happily with the Ivatt 4, assuming that the Foreman knew all about the viaduct and the weight restrictions. It was only after they had actually crossed the viaduct and his fireman suddenly began to ask questions that serious doubts began to assail him. So, rather than risk the return journey over the viaduct, he rang Rugby Control but they had no answers.

Eventually he was put through to the District Superintendent and shortly afterwards one of the compilers was

despatched from Rugby in some haste, Light Engine, to sort the situation out. After a quick survey, the decision was taken to reduce the weight of 43003 by emptying the tender tank (leaving just enough water in the boiler to get it back to Hawkesbury Lane safely) and to get the driver of the Super D that was shunting Hawkesbury Lane to propel a raft of empty wagons down the branch to couple to the Ivatt and haul it back over the viaduct at snail speed. When the moment of truth arrived, Bill Bennett invited the compiler up onto the footplate to accompany them back over the viaduct, an offer diplomatically declined on the grounds of extra weight and the need to keep an eye on the viaduct from the side rather than above! Thankfully, though, the moment passed without mishap. However, the compiler advised the Nuneaton Shedmaster to contact the Civil Engineer at Derby and request a general inspection of the viaduct 'just in case'. This was duly done – without any mention of an Ivatt 4 of course – and the viaduct was declared to be in perfect condition.

Then there is the legend of Ernie Simmons, the fastest man in the West. There used to be a stopping passenger train, comprising three coaches, that left Nuneaton for Polesworth at 4.02pm. This was regularly worked by a Covered Wagon, running tender first, which ran round at Polesworth and then worked the stock as the 4.27pm stopping passenger all stations to Rugby. The driver in question had a reputation for being a 'ballast scorcher' and on this particular day, with 43023, ran the 14½ miles from Nuneaton to Rugby in 16 minutes flat, including stops at Shilton and Brinklow. From the Nuneaton start he tested the accelerative powers of the engine to the limit, taking four minutes up the 1 in 320 to the Bulkington Intermediate Block Signal (3½ miles) where the speed must have been well into the 70s. The wheels were rotating at over six times per second though a 9F, with wheels of smaller, 5ft diameter, once attained 90mph of course with no ill effects. There were rapid (and presumably almost infinitesimal) stops at Brinklow and Shilton and the same electric acceleration away and Rugby Midland was reached with a braking display that was worthy of its GC neighbour.

When it comes to a final verdict, both compilers must confess to a degree of sympathy for the Ivatt Class 4. A design that epitomised the functional necessities of the post-war era and the shape of things to come, its reception was a withering blast of opprobrium. Enthusiasts' aesthetic sensibilities were sorely offended, blissfully oblivious as they were to the exigencies of the time. Far more importantly, engine crews rapidly discovered that, amongst all the 'mod cons' incorporated, the ability to produce steam was conspicuously absent. And this most inauspicious and unfortunate start seems to have been followed by a fairly rapid decline into obscurity and anonymity where it remained for most of its existence, receiving little mention, let alone limelight.

It should perhaps be noted that they were at least called on to provide the motive power for railtours and some of the 'last' and 'commemorative' trips towards the end. For example, on October 2 1966, 43000 and 43063 were used on 'The Wansbeck Piper' railtour, organised by the Gosforth Round Table to mark the closure of the Woodburn branch, whilst on Easter Sunday 1967 43121 hauled the SLS 'Scottish Rambler' railtour which, amongst other delights, traversed the Haltwhistle-Alston branch.

What little reputation it had was frequently coloured by its looks and early performance in double chimney form. The numerous local derogatory sobriquets it was saddled with from the start - Doodlebugs, Beetlecrushers, Dirty Ducks, Clodhoppers, Flying Pigs - didn't help! However, despite the early adverse publicity and indisputable steaming problems, the verdict must be that, after modification, they were extremely capable, reliable, free steaming and free running engines, easy to work and easy to maintain, very economical on coal and water and trouble free when properly looked after. Indeed, one of the compilers would go so far as to say that, within their range, and taking into account their relatively small boilers, they were excellent machines. They never did replace the 4F and, in fact, regularly shared workings with them; on odd occasions indeed (the ultimate irony) the Ivatts worked in tandem with 4Fs and only outlived them by two years. Nonetheless, in terms of design, maintenance and performance they were far superior in every respect. An ex-Nuneaton fireman used to enquire most earnestly of any Midland men he met whether it was really true that their 4Fs had rising damp indicators instead of pressure gauges...

The compilers would also argue that their abilities were very much underused and underexploited, in part at least as a result of their versatility/flexibility and consequent availability for intensive usage which so endeared them to the Operating Department. There is no doubt that much of the work they did was of a very menial nature – witness the two coaches on the Carlisle-Langholm and the Selby-Goole trains or the single wagon and brake on the Tebay-Penrith shunt or station pilot work, to say nothing of the ultimate illustration, 43130 conveying two cans of water from Rose Grove to Settle Junction signalbox, the photo being appropriately captioned 'The most expensive water ever'.

On the other hand, such jobs had to be done and they were probably the most economical engines to do them. In the 1960s there is plentiful photographic evidence of them on the lowliest of jobs. But, unfortunately, when the steam locomotive is being used at low outputs of power, it is at its most inefficient. The report on 43027 in May 1952 emphasised: 'It is desirable to work with the highest permissible loads in order to operate the engine at the highest efficiency on a coal/ton mile basis' but quite clearly such a criterion was not, and obviously could not always be, satisfied. In the final years of steam, of course, it all became academic anyway.

Nuneaton had had examples on its books from the earliest days and had consequently suffered the double chimney experiences but the verdict there was, in essence, that nothing ever went wrong and that the engines did everything that was asked of them. 43034, pictured there on 29 May 1961, arrived from Lancaster in May 1949 and stayed until October 1962.

43000

Built as 3000 at Horwich 6/12/47
Renumbered 43000 w.e. 7/10/50

Boiler 12881
Tender 4650

Improvements and modifications
New chimney arrangement   16/12/53
Fitting A.W.S   30/3/61

Repairs
18/12/47-19/12/47	NC	Derby
8/3/48-15/3/48	NC	Derby
1/9/50-6/10/50	LI	Horwich
12/10/50-13/11/50	LC	Horwich
18/5/51-1/6/51	LC	Bow
17/11/51-30/11/51	LC	Horwich
22/6/52-8/9/52	LC	Bow
2/11/53-16/12/53	HG	Horwich
27/2/54-27/3/54	LC(EO)	Horwich
5/7/57-23/8/57	HI	Horwich
21/8/59-7/10/59	LC(EO)	Horwich
2/1/61-30/3/61	HG	Horwich
1/4/61-7/4/61	NC(EO)	Horwich

Mileage/(weekdays out of service)
1947	666 (6)
1948	29,436 (77)
1949	30,280 (81)
1950	25,788 (108)
1951	12,878 (113)
1952	12,735 (118)
1953	15,529 (92)
1954	16,899 (70)
1955	11,884 (87)
1956	12,404 (97)
1957	13,392 (113)
1958	19,799 (43)
1959	17,753
1960	19,009

Sheds
Crewe South	6/12/47
Bletchley	20/3/48
Devons Road	6/1/51
Nuneaton	12/10/57
Carlisle Upperby	15/4/61
Carlisle Canal	10/11/62
Carlisle Kingm'r	22/6/63
North Blyth	27/8/66 (loan)
North Blyth	10/12/66

Withdrawn w.e. 9/9/67

43000 stayed at Bletchley for almost three years before moving to Devons Road in January 1951, where it is pictured later that year. It still has the frame mounted guard irons and is in one of those hybrid livery combinations typical of the period. It has its new BR number, applied in October 1950 with 8in numerals on the cab side and a BR standard pattern numberplate, but LMS on the tender. 43000 remained at the London depot working local and trip freights until it was transferred to Nuneaton in October 1957.

43001

Built as 3001 at Horwich 20/12/47
Renumbered 43001 w.e. 7/8/48

Boiler 12882
Tender 4651

Improvements and modifications
New chimney arrangement	9/8/56
Fitting A.W.S	14/8/60

Repairs
10/3/48	NC	Horwich
14/6/48-4/8/48	NC	Horwich
24/7/50-7/9/50	LI	Horwich
7/6/51-29/6/51	LC	Bow
18/1/52-8/2/52	LC (EO)	Bow
14/2/53-14/4/53	HG	Horwich
20/4/53-9/5/53	LC	Horwich
12/6/56-9/8/56	HI	Horwich
6/7/57-9/8/57	LC (EO)	Horwich
21/7/58-7/8/58	LC (EO)	Rugby
20/10/58-4/11/58	LC (EO)	Horwich
8/4/60-12/8/60	HG	Horwich
4/64-11/64	?	Swindon

Mileage/(weekdays out of service)
1947	Nil (6)
1948	32,335 (79)
1949	38,530 (61)
1950	32,612 (76)
1951	15,411 (90)
1952	12,710 (111)
1953	13,422 (124)
1954	13,562 (72)
1955	13,570 (56)
1956	12,013 (126)
1957	14,260 (88)
1958	16,352 (84)
1959	22,025
1960	16,351

Sheds
Crewe South	20/12/47
Bletchley	6/3/48
Cambridge	16/10/50 (loan)
Bletchley	27/10/50
Cambridge	6/11/50 (loan)
Bletchley	13/11/50
Devons Road	6/1/51
Nuneaton	12/10/57
Bescot	20/10/62
Crewe South	22/6/63
Stoke	12/3/66
Crewe South	12/8/67

Stored serviceable
15/4/63-16/6/63
10/8/67-15/9/67

Withdrawn w.e. 16/9/67

43001 at Nuneaton on 2 September 1961; it was fitted with AWS in August 1960. It has retained its original tender with the square step, but has acquired one of those mysterious bars at the rear of the coal space. The Horwich style of short lining has been applied with the small version of the post-1956 BR crest. 43001 moved to the Midlands shed from Devons Road in October 1957 when that shed was taken over by diesels and stayed until October 1962 when it went to Bescot. www.rail-online.co.uk

43002

Built as 3002 at Horwich 31/12/47
Renumbered 43002 w.e. 10/6/50

Boiler 12878
Tender 4652

Improvements and modifications
New chimney arrangement 13/10/56
Fitting A.W.S 2/9/60

Repairs
9/3/48-10/3/48	**NC**	Horwich
14/4/50-10/6/50	**LI**	Horwich
4/9/51-7/9/51	**NC(EO)**	Crewe
16/12/52-13/2/53	**HG**	Horwich
19/2/53	**NC(Rect)**	Horwich
10/9/56-13/10/56	**HI**	Horwich
1/4/58-9/4/58	**LC(EO)**	Rugby
13/2/60-16/6/60	**HG**	Horwich
18/8/60-2/9/60	**NC(EO)**	Horwich
20/1/64-25/5/64		Swindon

Mileage/(weekdays out of service)
1947	Nil (12)
1948	36,430 (48)
1949	32,036 (82)
1950	29,882 (92)
1951	26,486 (81)
1952	17,987 (71)
1953	29,329 (66)
1954	21,616 (47)
1955	18,589 (78)
1956	21,184 (60)
1957	22,420 (42)
1958	19,290 (49)
1959	20,436
1960	15,431

Sheds
Crewe South	31/12/47
Bletchley	31/1/48
Cambridge	19/11/50 (loan)
Bletchley	26/11/50
Nuneaton	19/9/53
Bescot	20/10/62
Stoke	26/3/66
Workington	12/8/67 (loan)
Workington	19/8/67

Withdrawn w.e. 30/12/67

43002 at its home shed of Bescot on 27 August 1964 exhibits some of the subtle variations which delight the engine picker. It has a replacement tender, 4763 ex-43113, which has curved-in cab step and a coal space bar. 43002 has a lowered top lamp iron and smokebox number plate on the door strap, and full length lining on the tender, all souvenirs of a heavy repair at Swindon between January and May 1964. The AWS was fitted in September 1960 when it was at Nuneaton.

43003

Mileage/(weekdays out of service)
Year	Mileage
1948	34,230 (60)
1949	34,588 (49)
1950	22,859 (125)
1951	31,539 (104)
1952	22,670 (73)
1953	30,641 (33)
1954	18,591 (54)
1955	14,431 (97)
1956	18,774 (53)
1957	20,188 (62)
1958	21,649 (46)
1959	21,984
1960	21,146

Built as M3003 at Horwich 17/1/48
Renumbered 43003 w.e. 2/9/50

Boiler 12884
Tender 4653

Improvements and modifications
New chimney arrangement   25/11/55
Fitting A.W.S   23/9/60

Repairs
9/3/48-10/3/48	NC	Horwich
23/6/50-28/8/50	LI	Horwich
11/10/50-22/11/50	LC	Horwich
14/11/52-5/1/53	HG	Horwich
29/10/55-25/11/55	LI	Horwich
5/12/57-25/1/58	HG	Horwich
14/9/60-23/9/60	NC	Horwich
11/9/61-24/10/61	LI	Horwich
11/64-13/2/65	?	Swindon

Sheds
Crewe South	17/1/48
Bletchley	21/2/48
Cambridge	1/10/50 (loan)
Bletchley	9/10/50
Saltley	10/5/52 (loan)
Nuneaton	19/9/53
Bescot	20/10/62
Stoke	21/9/63
Crewe South	12/8/67

Stored serviceable
7/8/67-15/9/67

Withdrawn w.e. 16/9/67

43003 was the first BR-built 4MT, emerging from Horwich on 17/1/48 as M3003; it had been renumbered at the end of August 1950 after a Light Intermediate repair when it gained lining as well as its new smokebox plate. In this photograph it still has the original guard irons and double chimney which was not replaced with the new single chimney arrangement until November 1955. 43003 stayed at Bletchley for its first four years where the tender cab was appreciated by the crew when working tender first on the branch services operated from that shed.

43004

Built as M3004 at Horwich 24/1/48
Renumbered 43004 w.e. 9/12/50

Boiler 12885
Tender 4654

Improvements and modifications
New chimney arrangement 2/4/55
Fitting A.W.S 1/11/61

Repairs
31/1/48-12/2/48	NC	Horwich
6/3/48-9/3/48	NC	Horwich
1/11/50-5/12/50	LI	Horwich
16/9/52-25/10/52	HG	Horwich
4/3/55-2/4/55	HI	Horwich
5/4/55-7/4/55	NC	Nil
2/2/56-29/2/56	LC	Horwich
28/2/58-11/4/58	HG	Horwich
21/1/59-4/3/59	LC(EO)	Horwich
14/2/59-4/3/59	LI	Horwich
27/3/61-4/5/61	LI	Horwich
23/10/61-1/11/61	NC(EO)	Horwich
6/1/65-12/3/65	HI	Eastleigh
27/1/66-12/2/66	LI	Cowstairs

Mileage/(weekdays out of service)
1948	33,332	(58)
1949	35,760	(58)
1950	25,202	(102)
1951	39,625	(34)
1952	34,407	(57)
1953	40,039	(38)
1954	33,100	(54)
1955	32,856	(68)
1956	32,135	(70)
1957	32,058	(55)
1958	32,294	(68)
1959	30,376	
1960	27,556	

Sheds
Bletchley	24/1/48
Workington	9/12/50
Carlisle Upperby	22/6/63
Carlisle Kingmoor	2/5/64
Carnforth	30/4/66
Lostock Hall	24/6/67

Stored serviceable
16/5/66-5/12/66

Withdrawn w.e. 30/9/67

43004 at Carlisle in 1964; it had received AWS equipment in October 1961 and also has had the top lamp iron lowered. It was a Workington engine from late 1950, moving to Carlisle Upperby in June 1963 and then to Kingmoor week ending 2/5/1964. www.rail-online.co.uk

43005

Mileage/(weekdays out of service)

Year	Mileage	(weekdays out of service)
1948	36,295	(50)
1949	42,260	(57)
1950	32,584	(92)
1951	36,163	(48)
1952	21,731	(62)
1953	16,598	(101)
1954	21,158	(53)
1955	29,170	(55)
1956	33,282	(57)
1957	31,152	(63)
1958	28,363	(91)
1959	19,420	
1960	20,677	

Built as M3005 at Horwich 7/2/48
Renumbered 43005 w.e. 23/9/50

Boiler 12888
Tender 4655

Improvements and modifications

New chimney arrangement	13/1/54
Fitting A.W.S	18/11/60

Repairs

Date	Type	Works
9/3/48	NC	Horwich
16/8/50-19/9/50	LI	Horwich
23/11/53-13/1/54	HG	Horwich
13/8/56-13/9/56	HI	Horwich
21/8/57-26/9/57	LC(EO)	Horwich
25/8/58-13/11/58	HG	Horwich
10/11/60-18/11/60	NC(EO)	Horwich
8/8/62-14/9/62	LI	Horwich

Sheds

Crewe South	7/2/48
Bletchley	28/2/48
Cambridge	27/10/50 (loan)
Bletchley	6/11/50
Cambridge	13/11/50 (loan)
Bletchley	20/11/50
Nuneaton	19/9/53
Workington	16/4/55
Nuneaton	12/7/58
Bescot	20/10/62

Withdrawn w.e. 6/11/65

A typical Sunday at Bescot on 23 June 1963 with the shed yard full of engines, including 43005 which had been transferred from Nuneaton in July 1958. It remained there until withdrawn in November 1965. It was fitted with AWS in November 1960 and has Horwich style shortened tender lining.

43006

Built as M3006 at Horwich 14/2/48
Renumbered 43006 w.e. 11/11/50

Boiler 12886
Tender 4656

Improvements and modifications
New chimney arrangement   8/10/55
Fitting A.W.S   5/10/61

Repairs
22/3/48	NC	Horwich
10/10/50-9/11/50	LI	Horwich
21/8/52-30/9/52	HG	Horwich
29/4/53-19/5/53	NC(EO)	Horwich
2/9/55-8/10/55	HI	Horwich
29/10/56-20/11/56	LC(EO)	Horwich
31/8/57-11/10/57	HG	Horwich
1/1/61-17/2/61	HI	Horwich
4/9/61-5/10/61	LC	Horwich
30/1/63-21/2/63	LC	Horwich
12/11/64-29/1/65	HI	Eastleigh

Mileage/(weekdays out of service)
Year	Mileage (days)
1948	34,081 (34)
1949	38,749 (40)
1950	34,275 (62)
1951	39,266 (35)
1952	34,204 (65)
1953	35,715 (60)
1954	34,942 (52)
1955	28,737 (72)
1956	37,225 (73)
1957	26,390 (70)
1958	29,808 (60)
1959	33,617
1960	24,469

Sheds
Bletchley	14/2/48
Workington	20/3/48
Nuneaton	19/8/61 (loan)
Workington	9/9/61
Lostock Hall	6/1/68

Withdrawn w.e. 2/3/68

43006 at Eastleigh on 1 November 1964 waiting to be admitted to works for a Heavy Intermediate overhaul which lasted from until 29 January 1965, when it would emerge with a re-arranged smokebox door. 43006 had been sent to the south coast from its home shed at Workington, and was the first 4MT to be repaired at the Southern Region works following the imminent cessation of steam repairs at Swindon. It retains its original tender with the long ladder and no rear handrail and has shortened lining and a bar on the coal space. R.K. Blencowe.

43007

Built as M3007 at Horwich 21/2/48
Renumbered 43007 w.e. 21/10/50

Boiler 12893
Tender 4657

Improvements and modifications
New chimney arrangement   28/4/55
Fitting A.W.S   28/1/62 (P/E)

Repairs
9/3/48-10/3/48	NC	Horwich
12/9/50-17/10/50	LI	Horwich
16/6/52-8/8/52	HG	Horwich
10/3/55-28/4/55	HI	Horwich
13/6/55-11/7/55	NC	Horwich
12/9/56-11/10/56	LC(EO)	Horwich
5/11/57-6/12/57	HG	Horwich

Mileage/(weekdays out of service)
1948	30,897 (52)
1949	36,522 (60)
1950	34,817 (57)
1951	37,607 (37)
1952	34,224 (64)
1953	38,998 (42)
1954	32,652 (67)
1955	29,560 (84)
1956	32,999 (77)
1957	32,412 (68)
1958	29,442 (33)
1959	21,763
1960	33,939

Sheds
Workington	21/2/48
Nuneaton	12/7/58
Lancaster	7/11/59
Nuneaton	17/2/62
Watford	16/6/62
Willesden	3/4/65
Stoke	2/10/65
Crewe South	12/8/67

Withdrawn w.e. 16/9/67

43007 in 1963/64, one of the last to be fitted with AWS (in January 1962). Its first ten years were spent at Workington but it was in the South East from June 1962 until October 1965, at Watford and then Willesden before seeing out its days at Stoke and Crewe South. www.rail-online.co.uk

43008

Built as M3008 at Horwich 28/2/48
Renumbered 43008 w.e. 14/10/50

Boiler 12892
Tender 4658

Improvements and modifications
New chimney arrangement 5/5/55
Fitting A.W.S 9/10/61

Repairs
4/9/50-10/10/50	LI	Horwich
24/10/52-5/12/52	HG	Horwich
21/3/55-5/5/55	HI	Horwich
29/4/57-5/6/57	HG	Horwich
18/8/60-27/10/60	LI	Horwich
25/10/60-15/11/60	NC(EO)	Horwich
28/12/60-8/2/61	LC	Horwich
25/9/61-9/10/61	NC(EO)	Horwich
11/12/62-4/1/63	LC	Horwich
18/2/63-12/3/63	LC	Horwich
22/6/64-19/9/64	IH	Darlington

Mileage/(weekdays out of service)
1948	31,206 (32)
1949	38,908 (39)
1950	37,303 (53)
1951	37,926 (47)
1952	34,421 (62)
1953	41,374 (31)
1954	36,280 (42)
1955	31,832 (64)
1956	38,782 (27)
1957	32,207 (73)
1958	29,142 (86)
1959	28,267
1960	24,912

Sheds
Workington	28/2/48
Lostock Hall	6/1/68

Withdrawn w.e. 2/3/68

43008 ran as M3008 from February 1948 until October 1950. It was one of four 4MTs allocated to Workington at this time and it stayed there except for the last two months before withdrawal, moving to Lostock Hall in the first week of 1968. The engines initially took over from 4F 0-6-0s on the through goods workings from Workington to Carnforth, but they soon began to spend most of their time working passenger trains between Whitehaven and Carlisle, leaving 4Fs on the goods turns again.

43009

Built as M3009 at Horwich 6/3/48
Renumbered 43009 w.e. 30/9/50

Boiler 12894
Tender 4659

Improvements and modifications
New chimney arrangement   23/4/54
Fitting A.W.S   13/12/61

Repairs

22/8/50-26/9/50	LI	Horwich
16/5/52-19/6/52	HG	Horwich
11/3/54-23/4/54	LI	Horwich
17/8/55-23/9/55	HI	Horwich
16/12/55-20/1/56	LC	Horwich
10/10/56-14/11/56	LC(EO)	Horwich
2/8/58-8/10/58	HG	Horwich
5/5/59-28/5/59	LC(EO)	Horwich
16/10/59-20/11/59	LC(EO)	Horwich
2/1/60-28/1/60	NC(EO)	Horwich
30/11/61-13/12/61	NC	Horwich
1/5/63-12/6/63	LI	Horwich

Mileage/(weekdays out of service)

1948	34,228 (27)
1949	39,452 (41)
1950	35,204 (60)
1951	40,562 (33)
1952	35,101 (63)
1953	36,862 (50)
1954	34,920 (64)
1955	31,955 (78)
1956	32,295 (79)
1957	37,697 (31)
1958	28,871 (87)
1959	29,977
1960	21,000

Sheds

Workington	6/3/48
Nuneaton	25/6/60
Tebay	17/9/60

Withdrawn w.e. 26/11/66

Numbered M3009 from new in March 1948 it was allocated to Workington and stayed there until June 1960 when it moved to Nuneaton. It is in original condition and was not renumbered 43009 until September 1950. The location is not known and it is presumed to be somewhere near its home turf, so it is interesting to speculate about the working it was on with a GWR Collett coach as the first vehicle. www.rail-online.co.uk

43010

Built as M3010 at Horwich 20/3/48
Renumbered 43010 w.e. 10/3/51

Boiler 12887
Tender 4660

Improvements and modifications
New chimney arrangement 2/12/55
Fitting A.W.S 20/11/62

Repairs
12/2/51-3/3/51	**LI**	Horwich
31/1/53-11/3/53	**HG**	Horwich
13/4/53-28/4/53	**NC(EO)**	Derby
28/10/55-2/12/55	**HI**	Horwich
26/5/58-22/8/58	**HG**	Horwich
27/2/61-28/4/61	**LI**	Horwich
3/5/61-10/5/61	**NC(Rect)**	Horwich
12/11/62-20/11/62	**NC**	Horwich
13/4/64-26/6/64	**IH**	Darlington

Mileage/(weekdays out of service)
1948	18,600 (43)
1949	25,337 (59)
1950	22,699 (59)
1951	21,803 (66)
1952	27,049 (65)
1953	24,200 (83)
1954	26,689 (81)
1955	20,454 (118)
1956	27,243 (81)
1957	30,621 (49)
1958	19,620 (127)
1959	29,124
1960	24,507

Sheds
Derby	20/3/48
Saltley	18/12/48
Derby	14/5/49 (loan)
Saltley	28/7/56
Neasden	10/10/59
Wellingborough	2/4/60
Heaton Mersey	14/12/63 (loan)
Heaton Mersey	4/1/64
Workington	18/9/65

Withdrawn w.e. 30/12/67

M3010, at Derby on 29 June 1950, was the last 4MT delivered with the M-prefix which it kept until it became 43010 as late as March 1951. In its first few years it alternated between Derby and Saltley before going to Neasden in October 1959. R.J. Buckley, Initial Photographics.

43011

Built at Horwich 25/3/48

Boiler 12880
Tender 4661

Improvements and modifications
New chimney arrangement   16/6/53
Fitting A.W.S   6/11/61

Repairs
4/7/50-11/8/50	NC	Horwich
30/1/51-22/2/51	LI	Horwich
30/4/53-16/6/53	HG	Horwich
19/11/55-29/12/55	HI	Horwich
18/1/56-27/1/56	NC(Rect)	Horwich
19/6/59-7/8/59	HG	Horwich
25/10/61-6/11/61	NC(EO)	Horwich
10/9/62-5/10/62	LI	Horwich

Mileage/(weekdays out of service)
1948	19,439 (47)
1949	27,734 (47)
1950	23,312 (84)
1951	27,475 (82)
1952	26,310 (61)
1953	27,013 (62)
1954	22,904 (44)
1955	16,942 (93)
1956	19,270 (59)
1957	18,167 (72)
1958	21,675 (51)
1959	20,556
1960	25,042

Sheds
Derby	25/3/48
Eastern Region	19/6/48 (loan)
Derby	24/7/48
Saltley	14/5/49 (loan)
Saltley	10/12/49
Nuneaton	17/3/51 (loan)
Nuneaton	5/1/52
Tebay	18/5/57 (loan)
Tebay	5/10/57
Carlisle Upperby	9/7/60
Carlisle Canal	3/11/62
Carlisle Kingm'r	22/6/63
Carnforth	24/10/64
Workington	25/9/65

Withdrawn w.e. 11/2/67

43011, at Edinburgh St Margarets in the early 1960s, was the first 4MT to emerge new with the 40000 prefix though it had an LMS pattern smokebox numberplate. It received a single chimney in June 1953 and AWS in November 1961. It was allocated to all three Carlisle sheds beginning with Upperby in July 1960, then Canal in November 1962 as illustrated, and finally Kingmoor in June 1963. 43011 was one of the two loaned to the Eastern Region in mid-1948 prior to the decision to build the type for use on that Region. www.rail-online.co.uk

43012

Mileage/(weekdays out of service)
1948   23,838 (32)
1949   39,575 (47)
1950   24,025 (76)
1951   28,381 (33)
1952   29,635 (33)
1953   22,809 (68)
1954   26,089 (50)
1955   18,295 (72)
1956   27,399 (27)
1957   20,552 (87)
1958   17,460 (92)
1959   24,988
1960   22,417

Built at Horwich 10/4/48

Boiler 12879
Tender 4662

Improvements and modifications
New chimney arrangement   23/11/55

Repairs

9/8/50-11/9/50	**LI**	Horwich
7/2/53-27/3/53	**HG**	Horwich
22/10/55-23/11/55	**HI**	Horwich
17/7/58-11/9/58	**HG**	Horwich
10/7/61-29/8/61	**LI**	Horwich
? – 11/64	?	Swindon

Sheds

Bristol	16/4/48
Bath	29/1/49 (loan)
Bristol	1/4/50
Saltley	9/1/54
Sheffield	20/2/54
Kettering	21/9/57
Bournville	10/1/59
Saltley	20/2/60
Wellingborough	22/9/62
Heaton Mersey	14/1/64
North Blyth	27/8/66 (loan)
North Blyth	10/12/66

Stored serviceable
4/10/65-28/2/66
30/5/66-18/6/66

Withdrawn 26/4/67

Bournville's 43012 in 1959 at Nibley, north of Bristol on the ex-Midland main line to Birmingham. In its early days it spent several years at Bristol, including a spell on loan to Bath in 1949/50 where it worked on the SDJR, before moving to Saltley in January 1954. Never fitted with AWS, it ended its days at North Blyth in August 1966 until withdrawn the following April.
www.rail-online.co.uk

43013

Built at Horwich 17/4/48

Boiler 12890
Tender 4663

Improvements and modifications
New chimney arrangement 30/12/54
Fitting A.W.S 4/11/62 (P/E)

Repairs
21/11/48-7/12/48	LO	Derby
18/5/49-2/6/49	LC	Shed
15/8/51-12/9/51	LI	Horwich
15/11/54-30/12/54	HG	Horwich
16/1/58-19/2/58	LI	Horwich
12/12/60-3/2/61	HG	Horwich

Mileage/(weekdays out of service)
1948	13,831 (44)
1949	27,537 (63)
1950	31,754 (54)
1951	29,623 (76)
1952	32,886 (41)
1953	26,673 (62)
1954	21,186 (110)
1955	28,573 (59)
1956	28,467 (51)
1957	26,292 (73)
1958	27,644 (66)
1959	26,536
1960	25,182

Sheds
Bristol	17/4/48
Bath	13/8/49
Derby	2/2/52
Saltley	3/5/52
Wellingborough	22/9/62
Heaton Mersey	14/12/63 (loan)
Heaton Mersey	4/1/64

Withdrawn w.e. 16/10/65

Wellingborough's 43013 running tender first on a North London line freight at Cricklewood on 2 March 1963; it had only received its AWS equipment the previous October. The early pattern tender has a long ladder, no rear handrail and the elusive bar, plus Horwich's own brand of short lining.

43014

Built at Horwich 24/4/48

Boiler 12896
Tender 4664

Improvements and modifications
New chimney arrangement   14/8/54
Fitting A.W.S   3/6/61

Repairs

22/6/50-14/7/50	**NC**	Horwich
15/8/51-10/9/51	**LI**	Horwich
12/10/51-18/10/51	**NC(Rect)**	Horwich
17/6/54-13/8/54	**HG**	Horwich
6/5/58-13/6/58	**Gen**	Doncaster
25/5/61-3/6/61	**NC**	Darlington
28/5/62-11/7/62	**Gen**	Darlington
30/7/62-10/8/62	**Adj**	Darlington

Mileage/(weekdays out of service)

1948	20,062 (28)
1949	27,121 (48)
1950	23,408 (86)
1951	22,462 (80)
1952	24,562 (25)
1953	25,293 (26)
1954	19,470 (70)
1955	24,304 (26)
1956	21,779 (48)

Sheds

Sheffield	24/4/48
Saltley	25/12/48
Stourton	15/3/52
York	1/11/59
Manningham	8/9/63

Withdrawn w.e. 3/4/66

43014 went new to Saltley but moved north to Stourton, Leeds (then still part of the LMR) in March 1952 and then York in November 1959 where it is pictured on 15 September 1960. Its last shed was Manningham three years later; 43014 was withdrawn from there at the end of March 1966. www.rail-online.co.uk

43015

Built at Horwich 7/5/48

Boiler 12883
Tender 4665

Improvements and modifications
New chimney arrangement   ?
Fitting A.W.S   6/8/60

Repairs

20/5/49-10/6/49	LC	Horwich
3/5/51-28/5/51	LI	Horwich
6/6/51-8/6/51	Rect	Horwich
26/1/54-23/2/54	IH	Doncaster
26/7/56-12/10/56	IH	Doncaster
2/6/60-6/8/60	Gen	Darlington
22/8/62-19/9/62	CL	Horwich
21/1/63-6/2/63	NC	Darlington
3/64 -14/7/64	Inter	Swindon
13/10/64-3/12/64	U	Darlington
17/3/65-22/4/65	Cas	Darlington

Mileage/(weekdays out of service)

1948	16,935 (49)
1949	24,522 (58)
1950	21,781 (52)
1951	22,255 (48)
1952	27,382 (41)

Sheds

Sheffield	7/5/48
Dairycoates	16/2/52 (loan)
Dairycoates	11/4/52
West Hartlepool	26/6/55
Thornaby	17/6/62
West Hartlepool	23/10/62

Withdrawn w.e. 1/7/67

43015 at Thornaby in 1962 during its brief spell there, with an interesting livery combination – LMS pattern smokebox plate, large cab numbers and lining to the edges and a large BR crest. Originally allocated to Sheffield Grimesthorpe it went to Hull Dairycoates in February 1952, West Hartlepool in June 1955, then Thornaby in June 1962, before returning to West Hartlepool five months later. It received AWS in August 1960 and was withdrawn at the end of June 1967. www.rail-online.co.uk

43016

Built at Horwich 15/5/48

Boiler 12897
Tender 4666

Improvements and modifications
New chimney arrangement   ?
Fitting A.W.S   11/8/61

Repairs

Date	Type	Location
18/12/48-22/1/49	LC	Horwich
18/2/50-25/3/50	LC	Horwich
30/4/51-6/6/51	LI	Horwich
25/11/53-27/11/53	NC	Darlington
2/9/54-15/10/54	IH	Doncaster
13/1/59-20/2/59	Gen	Darlington
18/5/61-11/8/61	NC	Darlington
23/1/61-21/2/62	CL	Darlington
17/10/62-23/11/62	IH	Horwich

Mileage/(weekdays out of service)

Year	Mileage (days)
1948	23,264 (28)
1949	34,658 (56)
1950	25,803 (97)
1951	29,127 (58)
1952	17,840 (84)

Sheds

Shed	Date
Leeds	15/5/48
Heaton	11/2/52
Manningham	16/6/57

Withdrawn 30/1/66

43016 during 1962; it began its career at Leeds before moving to Tyneside (Heaton) in February 1952. It returned to the West Riding at Manningham in June 1957 and was withdrawn there in January 1966. 43016 received its AWS in August 1961. Paul Chancellor Collection.

43017

Built at Horwich 22/5/48

Boiler 12895
Tender 4667

Improvements and modifications
New chimney arrangement 17/2/54

Repairs

17/12/49-28/1/50	**LC**	Horwich
7/3/51-5/4/51	**LI**	Horwich
2/4/52-23/4/52	**LC(EO)**	Shed
4/9/53-16/9/53	**LC(EO)**	Shed
28/12/53-17/2/54	**HG**	Horwich
12/5/56-15/6/56	**HI**	Horwich
4/11/57-29/11/57	**HC**	Horwich
28/8/58-25/11/58	**HG**	Horwich
28/4/61-8/6/61	**HC(EO)**	Horwich
15/3/62-17/4/62	**LI**	Horwich
8/9/65-25/9/65	**NC**	Cowlairs

Mileage/(weekdays out of service)

1948	19,501 (44)
1949	29,246 (50)
1950	31,065 (63)
1951	31,147 (48)
1952	32,525 (61)
1953	22,652 (97)
1954	29,373 (72)
1955	30,249 (60)
1956	24,854 (72)
1957	27,641 (75)
1958	18,215 (138)
1959	26,446
1960	25,117

Sheds

Leeds	22/5/48
Saltley	25/12/48
Bath	10/12/49
Saltley	20/6/53 (loan)
Saltley	18/7/53
Bletchley	29/11/64
Workington	10/7/65 (loan)
Workington	24/7/65

Withdrawn w.e. 2/12/67

43017, waiting to emerge from the 1950s gloom of Birmingham New Street, had got the single chimney in February 1954. Although sent to Leeds from new it soon arrived at Saltley, at the end of 1948, but went to Bath twelve months later. Returning to Saltley in June 1953, it stayed until transferred to Bletchley in November 1964. www.rail-online.co.uk

43018

1948	23,783 (25)
1949	25,164 (77)
1950	22,660 (71)
1951	21,429 (86)
1952	27,235 (64)
1953	22,749 (84)
1954	29,327 (40)
1955	22,614 (98)
1956	32,207 (63)
1957	23,890 (59)
1958	26,790 (63)
1959	35,387
1960	32,958

Built at Horwich 29/5/48

Boiler 12889
Tender 4668

Improvements and modifications
New chimney arrangement	20/10/55
Fitting A.W.S	1/11/61

Repairs
28/7/51-1/9/51	LI	Horwich
30/4/52-20/5/52	LC(EO)	Horwich
4/4/53-19/5/53	HG	Horwich
15/9/55-20/10/55	LC	Horwich
3/11/55-1/12/55	LC(EO)	Horwich
24/2/56-27/3/56	LI	Horwich
1/11/57-21/11/57	LC(EO)	Derby
23/4/58-25/4/58	NC(EO)	Derby
2/5/59-4/6/59	HG	Horwich
16/10/61-1/11/61	NC(EO)	Horwich
17/4/62-16/5/62	LI	Horwich

Sheds
Nottingham	29/5/48
Colwick	19/6/48
Annesley	4/7/48
New England	11/7/48
Colwick	18/7/48
Nottingham	31/7/48
Leicester	5/7/52
Lancaster	11/10/58 (loan)
Lancaster	8/11/58
Kirkby Stephen	30/4/60
Carlisle Kingm'r	9/7/60
Watford	23/6/62
Willesden	3/4/65
Stoke	2/10/65

Withdrawn w.e. 22/10/66

43018 nearly consumed in its own steam; the date is not known though it would be late on, in its Willesden/Watford days on the Euston ECS jobs. Fitted with AWS in October 1961 it was shedded at Watford between June 1962 and April 1965 when it moved to Willesden. Its stay was brief and it went Stoke in October 1965 from where it was withdrawn twelve months later. transporttreasury.co.uk

43019

Built at Horwich 12/6/48

Boiler 12891
Tender 4669

Improvements and modifications
New chimney arrangement   6/1/54
Fitting A.W.S   31/10/62

Repairs
14/3/51-14/4/51	LI	Horwich
24/1/52-23/2/52	LC(EO)	Horwich
18/11/53-6/1/54	Gen	Horwich
21/5/54-19/6/54	LC(EO)	Horwich
27/5/55-8/7/55	HC	Horwich
3/9/56-10/10/56	LI	Horwich
27/6/58-15/7/58	LC(EO)	Horwich
7/1/61-29/3/61	HG	Horwich
23/10/62-31/10/62	LC	Horwich
25/6/65-1/9/65	LI	Eastleigh

Mileage/(weekdays out of service)
1948	16,512 (24)
1949	25,136 (58)
1950	22,014 (69)
1951	21,472 (72)
1952	22,718 (45)
1953	17,416 (79)
1954	22,360 (59)
1955	23,708 (69)
1956	21,217 (55)
1957	18,597 (69)
1958	24,181 (46)
1959	11,235
1960	11,782

Sheds
Derby	12/6/48
Saltley	25/12/48
Nottingham	10/12/49
Cricklewood	1/11/52
Wellingborough	22/9/62
Stoke	28/9/63 (loan)
Stoke	12/10/63
Lower Darwen	6/2/65
Lostock Hall	19/2/66

Stored serviceable
29/7/63-16/9/63
27/6/66-5/7/66
21/11/66-16/1/67

Withdrawn w.e. 4/5/68

43019 had travelled south from Lower Darwen for a Light Intermediate repair at Eastleigh which took place 25/6/65-1/9/65. Photographed on 5 September the smokebox front no longer has a top handrail and the upper lamp iron has been lowered. It was equipped with AWS in late 1962 and has retained its original tender. This was not been repainted because it still has the short lining from it last visit to Horwich Works.

43020

Built at Horwich 17/12/48

Boiler 12948
Tender 4670

Improvements and modifications
New chimney arrangement   13/7/54
Fitting A.W.S   23/9/60

Repairs

28/3/51-27/4/51	**LC**	Bow
6/12/51-5/1/52	**LI**	Horwich
7/3/52-23/4/52	**LC(EO)**	Bow
24/10/52-14/11/52	**LC(EO)**	Bow
16/1/54-17/2/54	**NC**	Bow
31/5/54-13/7/54	**HG**	Horwich
11/6/56-17/7/56	**LC(EO)**	Bow
23/3/57-7/5/57	**HI**	Horwich
18/12/58-27/1/59	**LC**	Horwich
27/6/59-30/7/59	**LC(EO)**	Horwich
2/5/60-23/9/60	**HG**	Horwich
28/3/61-25/4/61	**LC(EO)**	Horwich

Mileage/(weekdays out of service)

1948	181 (-)
1949	26,291 (24)
1950	21,351 (73)
1951	12,302 (119)
1952	14,814 (110)
1953	16,221 (54)
1954	13,426 (122)
1955	15,028 (54)
1956	14,685 (86)
1957	14,807 (77)
1958	17,010 (64)
1959	17,941
1960	12,731

Sheds

Crewe South	17/12/48
Nuneaton	8/1/49
Devons Road	6/1/51
Nuneaton	8/3/58
Crewe South	20/10/62

Withdrawn w.e. 8/10/66

43020 in original double chimney condition at Devons Road on 10 May 1952. Like the other 4MTs allocated to the shed at Bow, it had several Unclassified or Casual Repairs in the workshops there in the early 1950s. F.W. Goudie, transporttreasury.co.uk

43021

Built at Horwich 22/12/48

Boiler 12949
Tender 4671

Improvements and modifications
New chimney arrangement   28/4/54
Fitting A.W.S   25/10/61

Repairs
9/3/51-22/3/51	**LC**	Bow
4/8/51-28/9/51	**LI**	Horwich
25/3/52-9/4/52	**LC(EO)**	Bow
13/3/54-28/4/54	**HG**	Horwich
29/10/56-7/12/56	**HI**	Horwich
6/5/58-30/5/58	**LC(EO)**	Horwich
1/6/60-30/9/60	**HG**	Horwich
9/10/61-25/10/61	**LC(EO)**	Horwich

Sheds
Crewe South	22/12/48
Nuneaton	8/1/49
Devons Road	6/1/51
Sutton Oak	8/3/58
Lancaster	4/10/58 (loan)
Lancaster	6/12/58
Nuneaton	17/2/62
Watford	16/6/62
Stoke	3/4/65
Crewe South	3/6/67

Withdrawn w.e. 16/9/67

Mileage/(weekdays out of service)
1948	83 (-)
1949	23,620 (48)
1950	24,368 (45)
1951	13,016 (109)
1952	16,362 (69)
1953	15,415 (78)
1954	16,201 (80)
1955	15,047 (65)
1956	13,815 (104)
1957	15,375 (54)
1958	20,175 (64)
1959	42,233
1960	19,334

43021 around 1950, as built, still with its original guard irons. The double chimney was replaced in April 1954. 43021 spent its first two years at Nuneaton before moving to Devons Road in January 1951. It returned briefly to Nuneaton in 1962 after spells at Sutton Oak and Lancaster. www.rail-online.co.uk

43022

Built at Horwich 30/12/48

Boiler 12951
Tender 4672

Improvements and modifications
New chimney arrangement   25/6/54
Fitting A.W.S   1/12/60

Repairs

31/8/50-7/9/50	**LC**	Rugby
28/2/51-9/3/51	**LC**	Bow
16/6/51-6/7/51	**LC**	Bow
6/11/51-28/12/51	**LI**	Horwich
7/2/52-16/2/52	**LC(EO)**	Bow
14/6/52-11/7/52	**NC(EO)**	Bow
5/12/52-24/12/52	**LC**	Bow
2/5/54-25/6/54	**HG**	Horwich
12/9/56-23/10/56	**LC(EO)**	Rugby
29/10/56-23/11/56	**LC(EO)**	Bow
3/1/57-22/2/57	**HI**	Horwich
1/11/57-23/11/57	**LC(EO)**	Horwich
16/6/59-10/7/59	**LC(EO)**	Horwich
23/11/60-1/12/60	**NC(EO)**	Horwich
27/7/61-3/10/61	**HG**	Horwich
15/5/65-24/6/65	**LC**	Eastleigh

Mileage/(weekdays out of service)

1949	23,866	(45)
1950	23,136	(46)
1951	10,789	(119)
1952	14,829	(105)
1953	17,167	(68)
1954	16,355	(83)
1955	14,794	(59)
1956	11,770	(130)
1957	11,989	(122)
1958	15,806	(53)
1959	18,871	
1960	23,148	

Sheds

Nuneaton	30/12/48
Devons Road	6/1/51
Bescot	3/8/57 (loan)
Devons Road	17/8/57
Sutton Oak	8/3/58
Nuneaton	6/6/59
Crewe South	20/10/62
Bescot	19/1/63
Stoke	28/11/64

Withdrawn w.e. 19/11/66

43022 on 27 August 1964 at Bescot. It was allocated there from January 1963 until November 1964. AWS was fitted in November 1960 and 43022 was withdrawn from Stoke in November 1966.

43023

Built at Horwich 8/1/49

Boiler 12962
Tender 4673

Improvements and modifications
New chimney arrangement   13/11/53
Fitting A.W.S   16/9/60

Repairs

20/6/51-13/8/51	LI	Horwich
19/3/52-17/4/52	LC(EO)	Horwich
5/10/53-13/11/53	HG	Horwich
25/1/54-5/2/54	LC(EO)	Horwich
11/12/56-12/1/57	HI	Horwich
21/1/57-9/2/57	LC(TO)	Horwich
11/9/58-23/10/58	LC(EO)	Rugby
25/8/59-16/10/59	HG	Horwich
31/8/60-16/9/60	NC	Horwich
21/11/60-14/12/60	LC(EO)	Horwich
28/8/61-18/10/61	LC	Horwich
8/7/65-21/8/65	?	Cowlairs

Mileage/(weekdays out of service)

1949	25,178 (30)
1950	25,403 (44)
1951	21,567 (94)
1952	25,678 (74)
1953	22,201 (87)
1954	22,830 (48)
1955	18,614 (70)
1956	19,044 (68)
1957	20,281 (61)
1958	18,702 (76)
1959	16,677
1960	19,416

Sheds

Nuneaton	8/1/49
Devons Road	6/1/51
Nuneaton	20/1/51
Kirkby Stephen	30/4/60
Carlisle Kingm'r	9/7/60
Carnforth	30/4/66
Workington	1/4/67

Stored serviceable
16/5/66-5/12/66

Withdrawn w.e. 30/12/67

43023 on 4F duties with a coal train at Parton near Whitehaven in November 1967, only a month before it was withdrawn. It spent its first ten years at Nuneaton before moving north, first to Kirkby Stephen and then Kingmoor and Carnforth before its final posting to Workington in April 1967. S.V. Blencowe.

43024

Built at Horwich 21/1/49

Boiler 12955
Tender 4674

Improvements and modifications
New chimney arrangement   8/7/54
Fitting A.W.S   10/5/61

Repairs

13/4/51-4/5/51	**LC**	Bow
21/9/51-25/9/51	**NC(EO)**	Bow
1/10/51-8/11/51	**LI**	Horwich
15/10/52-24/10/52	**LC(EO)**	Bow
19/6/53-1/7/53	**LC(EO)**	Bow
11/5/54-8/7/54	**HG**	Horwich
10/10/57-9/11/57	**HI**	Horwich
31/10/58-21/11/58	**LC(EO)**	Horwich
25/9/59-6/11/59	**LC(EO)**	Horwich
3/5/61-10/5/61	**NC(EO)**	Horwich
10/7/61-20/10/61	**HG**	Horwich

Mileage/(weekdays out of service)

1949	22,583 (45)
1950	26,083 (31)
1951	14,660 (97)
1952	17,434 (61)
1953	16,411 (77)
1954	14,893 (98)
1955	15,306 (51)
1956	14,683 (88)
1957	12,534 (98)
1958	19,924 (54)
1959	19,845
1960	24,087

Sheds

Nuneaton	21/1/49
Devons Road	20/1/51
Nuneaton	12/10/57
Crewe South	20/10/62

Withdrawn w.e. 27/5/67

43024 on 2 September 1961 in for attention at Horwich; something unpleasant under that dome perhaps? It was in for a Heavy General after a visit earlier in the year for the fitting of AWS. D. Forsyth, colourrail.co.uk

43025

Built at Horwich 28/1/49

Boiler   12953
Tender   4675

Improvements and modifications
New chimney arrangement   2/4/54
Fitting A.W.S   30/12/61

Repairs
18/9/51-11/10/51	LI	Horwich
13/10/52-22/11/52	LI	Horwich
20/2/54-2/4/54	HG	Horwich
21/1/57-6/3/57	HI	Horwich
8/7/58-26/8/58	LC(EO)	Horwich
21/1/59-13/3/59	HG	Horwich

Mileage/(weekdays out of service)
1949	25,351 (22)
1950	23,133 (52)
1951	19,097 (113)
1952	24,350 (68)
1953	26,719 (33)
1954	21,573 (65)
1955	23,127 (36)
1956	22,958 (27)
1957	29,663 (81)
1958	28,376 (77)
1959	28,592
1960	29,159

Sheds
Nuneaton	28/1/49
Sutton Oak	25/11/50
Workington	19/1/57

Withdrawn w.e. 18/9/65

Brand new 43025 at Crewe North on 6 February 1949, doubtless running in after its release from Horwich the previous week and before going to its first shed at Nuneaton. It stayed there until November 1950 when it moved to Sutton Oak at St Helens. F.A. Wycherley.

43026

Built at Horwich 10/2/49

Boiler 12950
Tender 4676

Improvements and modifications
New chimney arrangement   6/2/54
Fitting A.W.S   24/1/62

Repairs
11/4/51-8/5/51	**LI**	Horwich
14/10/52-27/11/52	**LC**	Horwich
21/12/53-6/2/54	**HG**	Horwich
9/8/54-20/8/54	**LC(TO)**	Horwich
12/10/56-10/11/56	**HI**	Horwich
3/1/57-25/1/57	**LC**	Horwich
16/12/58-22/1/59	**HG**	Horwich
25/2/60-25/3/60	**LC**	Horwich
12/1/62-24/1/62	**NC**	Horwich
20/9/62-25/10/62	**LI**	Horwich

Sheds
Crewe South	10/2/49
Sutton Oak	26/2/49 (loan)
Sutton Oak	2/4/49
Workington	19/1/57
Nuneaton	3/1/59
Workington	30/1/60
Northampton	23/6/62
Crewe South	20/10/62

Withdrawn w.e. 24/9/66

Mileage/(weekdays out of service)
1949	20,833 (33)
1950	24,208 (59)
1951	30,654 (42)
1952	23,440 (81)
1953	25,079 (40)
1954	21,865 (58)
1955	20,214 (45)
1956	21,051 (45)
1957	31,450 (74)
1958	28,658 (71)
1959	20,258
1960	25,881

43026 at Sutton Oak where it spent its first eight years. Its new chimney was fitted in February 1954 and it moved to Workington in January 1957. www.transporttreasury.co.uk

43027

Built at Horwich 19/2/49

Boiler 12956
Tender 4677

Improvements and modifications
Blastpipe	12/5/49
Single chimney	23/5/49
New chimney arrangement	13/1/55
Fitting A.W.S	25/8/61

Repairs
6/5/49-12/5/49	**NC**	Horwich
23/5/49	**NC**	Crewe
24/8/49-1/10/49	**LC**	Horwich
25/10/50-6/11/50	**NC**	Horwich
23/10/51-20/11/51	**LI**	Horwich
29/11/54-13/1/55	**HG**	Horwich
5/9/56-13/10/56	**LI**	Horwich
19/2/58-31/3/58	**LC**	Horwich
24/8/59-15/10/59	**HI**	Horwich
10/8/61-25/8/61	**LC**	Horwich
23/1/62-5/3/62	**HG**	Horwich
1/8/63-23/8/63	**LC**	Horwich
13/10/65-6/11/65	**LI**	Cowlairs

Mileage/(weekdays out of service)
1949	16,039 (79)
1950	26,881 (42)
1951	26,905 (55)
1952	26,885 (86)
1953	23,547 (98)
1954	17,171 (130)
1955	27,380 (90)
1956	24,070 (104)
1957	29,078 (65)
1958	22,602 (97)
1959	22,144
1960	27,654

Sheds
Crewe South	19/2/49
Sutton Oak	2/4/49
Nuneaton	25/11/50
Saltley	17/3/51 (loan)
Saltley	11/1/52
Derby	3/5/52
Bournville	10/1/59
Saltley	20/6/59
Kirkby Stephen	23/4/60 (loan)
Kirkby Stephen	25/6/60
Carlisle Kingm'r	9/7/60
Carnforth	24/10/64
Workington	1/4/67
Lostock Hall	6/1/68

Withdrawn w.e. 4/5/68

43027 was the engine used in the first tests of the class between Crewe and Holyhead in 1949, following which it was the only member of the original fifty to run with a single blastpipe arrangement until the whole class was modified from 1953 onwards. It is pictured at Carlisle Kingmoor on 13 July 1963, having been fitted with AWS in August 1961. 43027 was shedded there from July 1960 until it moved to Carnforth in October 1964 before going to Workington in April 1967. It finally ended up at Lostock Hall in January 1968 and was one of the last survivors, withdrawn only in May 1968. D. Forsyth, Paul Chancellor Collection.

43028

Built at Horwich 3/3/49

Boiler 12954
Tender 4678

Improvements and modifications
New chimney arrangement   31/3/54
Fitting A.W.S   24/11/61

Repairs
28/3/51-7/4/51	**LC**	Horwich
7/3/53-10/4/53	**LI**	Horwich
27/2/54-31/3/54	**HG**	Horwich
8/10/56-2/11/56	**HI**	Horwich
14/4/58-23/5/58	**LC(EO)**	Horwich
1/4/61-5/6/61	**HG**	Horwich
7/11/61-24/11/61	**NC(EO)**	Horwich
13/4/65-17/4/65	**Cas**	Cowlairs
?-14/9/65	**HI**	Cowlairs

Mileage/(weekdays out of service)
1949	18,131 (31)
1950	25,063 (38)
1951	25,665 (46)
1952	24,467 (29)
1953	21,887 (68)
1954	23,180 (53)
1955	20,905 (65)
1956	20,978 (43)
1957	22,137 (59)
1958	21,098 (82)
1959	23,819
1960	18,231

Sheds
Crewe South	3/3/49
Sutton Oak	2/4/49
Tebay	12/1/57
Carlisle Upperby	9/7/60
Carlisle Canal	10/11/62
Carlisle Kingm'r	22/6/63
Heaton Mersey	25/1/64
Kingmoor	7/3/64
Workington	13/5/67
Carlisle Kingm'r	21/10/67

Withdrawn w.e. 2/12/67

43028 shunting at Carlisle on 27 June 1960, a week before it was transferred from Tebay to Upperby. The tender still has the early BR emblem and AWS has not yet been fitted – this was done in November 1961.

43029

Built at Horwich 15/3/49

Boiler 12960
Tender 4679

Improvements and modifications
New chimney arrangement   11/12/53
Fitting A.W.S   21/8/61

Repairs
13/3/51-29/3/51	LC	Horwich
7/2/52-14/3/52	LI	Horwich
10/11/53-11/12/53	HG	Horwich
22/2/56-5/4/56	HI	Horwich
14/11/59-8/1/60	HG	Horwich
13/1/60	NC(Rect)	Horwich
10/8/61-21/8/61	NC(EO)	Horwich
?-11/9/65	LI	Cowlairs

Mileage/(weekdays out of service)
1949	19,514 (23)
1950	22,832 (44)
1951	23,188 (47)
1952	26,837 (64)
1953	23,935 (69)
1954	27,914 (28)
1955	21,643 (66)
1956	25,715 (59)
1957	20,818 (76)
1958	15,793 (62)
1959	14,899
1960	23,703

Sheds
Crewe South	15/3/49
Sutton Oak	2/4/49
Tebay	12/1/57
Carlisle Upperby	9/7/60
Tebay	17/9/60
Lostock Hall	22/4/67

Withdrawn w.e. 30/9/67

43029 at Preston on station pilot duties. The LNER-style TEBAY depot name on the bufferbeam derived from a Light Intermediate repair at Cowlairs in late 1965. It also has AWS, fitted in August 1961, a lowered top lamp iron and white painted number and shed plate. 43027 was transferred from Tebay to Lostock Hall in April 1967 and was withdrawn from there in September. B. Taylor.

43030

Built at Horwich 25/3/49

Boiler 12959
Tender 4680

Improvements and modifications
New chimney arrangement   ?
Fitting A.W.S   21/1/61

Repairs
23/4/51-21/5/51	**LI**	Horwich
8/2/55-11/3/55	**IH**	Doncaster
23/4/58-15/5/58	**CL**	Doncaster
17/11/60-21/1/61	**Gen**	Darlington
17/3/64-16/4/64	**Unsch**	Darlington

Mileage/(weekdays out of service)
1949	31,726 (20)
1950	31,640 (36)
1951	29,039 (74)
1952	16,160 (78)

Sheds
Leeds	25/3/49
Heaton	11/2/52
Manningham	16/6/57

Withdrawn 19/10/66

43030 at Heaton on 6 June 1955; it had received its new tall chimney during a Heavy Intermediate overhaul at Doncaster completed the previous March. Originally shedded at Leeds, it moved to Heaton in February 1952, staying there until its final transfer to Manningham in June 1957, from where it was withdrawn in October 1966.

43031

Built at Horwich 5/4/49

Boiler 12958
Tender 4681

Improvements and modifications
New chimney arrangement   13/11/54

Repairs

31/12/51-29/1/52	LI	Horwich
11/10/54-13/11/54	HG	Horwich
25/1/57-28/2/57	LI	Horwich
20/12/58-23/1/59	LC	Horwich
25/7/61-13/9/61	HG	Horwich
18/9/61-9/10/61	NC(Rec)	Horwich

Mileage/(weekdays out of service)

1949	23,547 (28)
1950	25,830 (62)
1951	17,825 (96)
1952	25,681 (82)
1953	21,112 (25)
1954	15,323 (61)
1955	25,189 (37)
1956	20,985 (65)
1957	19,022 (55)
1958	17,154 (100)
1959	17,535
1960	12,567

Sheds

Derby	5/4/49
Cricklewood	7/2/53
Wellingborough	22/9/62
Heaton Mersey	14/12/63 (loan)
Heaton Mersey	4/1/64

Withdrawn w.e. 12/3/66

43031 at Leicester in the early 1960s showing the short lining and long rear ladder on the tender. 43031 was for long a Midland Division engine before going to its final shed of Heaton Mersey in December 1963.

43032

Built at Horwich 14/4/49

Boiler 12961
Tender 4682

Improvements and modifications
New chimney arrangement   ?
Fitting A.W.S   ?

Repairs
1/2/52-27/2/52	LI	Horwich
4/8/52-11/9/52	LC	Horwich
1/12/54-28/1/55	HG	Horwich
7/2/57-20/2/57	LC(EO)	Horwich
13/1/58-22/2/58	HI	Horwich
13/1/61-10/2/61	CL	Doncaster
20/12/61-20/1/62	Gen	Doncaster

Mileage/(weekdays out of service)
1949	17,866 (24)
1950	24,389 (32)
1951	22,436 (27)
1952	21,376 (68)
1953	27,821 (61)
1954	20,779 (119)
1955	25,517 (80)
1956	23,758 (81)
1957	20,966

Sheds
Sheffield	14/4/49
Millhouses	27/9/52
Colwick	16/9/61

Withdrawn w.e. 10/1/65

43032 at Hope on 14 April 1952 was a Sheffield engine from new, moving the short distance to Millhouses in September 1952. It lost its double chimney in January 1955 and moved to Colwick in September 1961. H.K. Boulter.

43033

Built at Horwich 5/5/49

Boiler 12957
Tender 4683

Improvements and modifications
New chimney arrangement   18/9/54

Repairs

17/9/51-27/10/51	LI	Horwich
25/3/52-23/4/52	LC(EO)	Horwich
29/7/54-18/9/54	HG	Horwich
22/9/56-1/11/56	LI	Horwich
13/9/57-11/10/57	LC	Horwich
28/1/60-6/7/60	HG	Horwich
20/4/64-3/7/64	IH	Darlington

Mileage/(weekdays out of service)

1949	20,550 (34)
1950	24,237 (59)
1951	20,227 (89)
1952	28,159 (63)
1953	27,473 (47)
1954	23,209 (85)
1955	26,721 (82)
1956	25,666 (107)
1957	33,089 (61)
1958	22,743 (94)
1959	18,155
1960	16,022

Sheds

Nottingham	5/5/49
Saltley	10/5/52
Nottingham	24/5/52
Derby	15/6/57
Bournville	10/1/59
Saltley	20/2/60
Trafford Park	22/9/62
Heaton Mersey	8/2/64
Tebay	27/11/65
Lostock Hall	22/4/67

Withdrawn w.e. 2/3/68

43033 with the 12E shed code for Tebay daubed on. It had arrived from Heaton Mersey in November 1965 and stayed until April 1967. The Tebay 4MTs were occasionally used as bankers up to Shap, although the shed's 2-6-4Ts were much more common and they also sometimes worked as pilots. 43033 escaped AWS fitting, in common with its Midland Division classmates in the early 1960s, but it has acquired a tender bar. D. Forsyth, colourrail.co.uk

43034

Built at Horwich 18/5/49

Boiler 13057
Tender 4684

Improvements and modifications
New chimney arrangement   28/8/54
Fitting A.W.S   27/10/60

Repairs
30/5/51-29/6/51	**LI**	Horwich
21/6/54-28/8/54	**HG**	Horwich
25/10/57-22/11/57	**LI**	Horwich
17/10/60-27/10/60	**NC**	Horwich
2/1/61-1/5/61	**HG**	Horwich

Mileage/(weekdays out of service)
1949	21,829 (31)
1950	34,352 (36)
1951	31,432 (64)
1952	35,119 (49)
1953	35,689 (48)
1954	27,192 (85)
1955	21,976 (44)
1956	19,425 (64)
1957	19,797 (69)
1958	22,329 (40)
1959	21,725
1960	21,077

Sheds
Lancaster	21/5/49
Nuneaton	27/11/54
Crewe South	20/10/62

Withdrawn w.e. 3/6/67

Nuneaton's 4MTs were regular visitors to Leicester where 43034 was photographed in the early 1960s collecting parcels from the Post Office sidings by the station. It received AWS in October 1960 and was transferred to Crewe South two years later. It has the usual London Midland Region short tender lining and small BR crest. www.rail-online.co.uk

43035

Built at Horwich 26/5/49

Boiler 12964
Tender 4685

Improvements and modifications
New chimney arrangement   18/6/54
Fitting A.W.S   19/10/61

Repairs
18/4/51-11/5/51	**LI**	Horwich
17/5/54-18/6/54	**HG**	Horwich
20/6/57-15/7/57	**HI**	Horwich
5/7/60-11/11/60	**HG**	Horwich
2/10/61-19/10/61	**NC(EO)**	Horwich

Mileage/(weekdays out of service)
1949	23,662 (18)
1950	35,084 (40)
1951	35,046 (51)
1952	33,813 (46)
1953	33,907 (46)
1954	31,256 (63)
1955	24,701 (38)
1956	18,557 (50)
1957	22,467 (75)
1958	19,767 (61)
1959	17,767
1960	10,720

Sheds
Lancaster	26/5/49
Nuneaton	27/11/54
Sutton Oak	5/3/55
Tebay	12/1/57

Withdrawn w.e. 20/11/65

43035 in the 1950s, between the fitting of a single chimney during a Heavy General overhaul completed at Horwich in June 1954 and repainting with the later BR crest in mid-1957.

43036

Built at Horwich 3/6/49

Boiler 12963
Tender 4686

Improvements and modifications
New chimney arrangement   3/12/54
Fitting A.W.S   9/11/62

Repairs

Date	Type	Location
27/2/51-3/3/51	LC	Horwich
1/4/52-3/5/52	LI	Horwich
19/5/53-8/6/53	LC(EO)	Shed
25/10/54-3/12/54	HG	Horwich
24/1/55-11/2/55	LC	Horwich
19/12/55-12/1/56	LC	Horwich
12/2/57-16/3/57	LI	Horwich
29/10/58-11/11/58	HG	Horwich
17/2/60-27/7/60	HG	Horwich
9/10/62-9/11/62	LI	Horwich

Mileage/(weekdays out of service)

Year	Mileage (days)
1949	18,122 (19)
1950	29,966 (52)
1951	31,335 (44)
1952	31,877 (59)
1953	32,282 (68)
1954	24,417 (87)
1955	23,933 (92)
1956	30,915 (47)
1957	29,599 (68)
1958	23,723 (85)
1959	20,096
1960	16,989

Sheds

Shed	Date
Bristol	3/6/49
Bath	13/8/49
Bristol	20/6/53 (loan)
Bristol	18/7/53
Saltley	3/10/53
Neasden	10/9/60 (loan)
Saltley	26/11/60
Trafford Park	22/9/62
Carlisle Kingmoor	7/3/64
Carnforth	24/10/64
Workington	18/9/65

Withdrawn w.e. 7/5/66

The size of that bar on the rear coal space is apparent in this picture of 43036 on 19 March 1961 at Saltley. The tender is ex-43119 with a short ladder and rear handrail and steps plus the usual short Horwich lining. Apart from a brief loan spell at Neasden in 1960, 43036 stayed at Saltley until transferred to Trafford Park in September 1962, after which it was fitted with AWS. www.rail-online.co.uk

43037

Built at Horwich 15/6/49

Boiler 12962
Tender 4687

Improvements and modifications
New chimney arrangement   29/7/54
Fitting A.W.S   1/9/61

Repairs

21/2/52-18/3/52	**LI**	Horwich
17/6/54-29/7/54	**HG**	Horwich
4/4/56-21/4/56	**LC**	Horwich
30/8/57-28/9/57	**LI**	Horwich
18/8/58-4/9/58	**CL**	Stratford
21/10/59-18/11/59	**NC**	Stratford
8/8/61-1/9/61	**Gen**	Doncaster

Mileage/(weekdays out of service)

1949	15,059 (17)
1950	23,736 (45)
1951	14,539 (69)
1952	16,459 (52)
1953	16,964 (49)
1954	14,741 (81)
1955	22,098 (44)
1956	18,981 (66)
1957	16,915

Sheds

Sheffield	12/6/49
Canklow	28/10/50
Millhouses	1/5/60
Canklow	31/12/61
Retford (GC)	23/9/62
Barrow Hill	4/5/63

Withdrawn w.e. 11/4/65

43037 on 6 October 1963 at Staveley Barrow Hill. It lost its lined black during a General overhaul at Doncaster in August 1961, emerging also with large cab numbers and small BR crest. 43037 did not stray far in terms of its sheds with two periods at Canklow and one at Millhouses before going to Retford GC in September 1962 and finally Barrow Hill in May 1963; it was withdrawn in April 1965.

43038

Built at Horwich 23/6/49

Boiler 13253
Tender 4688

Improvements and modifications
New chimney arrangement   ?
Fitting A.W.S   3/6/61

Repairs

14/11/51-12/12/51	LI	Horwich
8/10/52-14/10/52	NC	Doncaster
18/12/53-16/1/54	IH	Doncaster
11/3/54-22/3/54	NC	Doncaster
17/1/56-7/2/56	NC	Doncaster
23/8/56-29/9/56	CL	Darlington
17/9/58-22/10/58	Gen	Doncaster
26/1/60-5/2/60	NC	Darlington
23/5/61-3/6/61	NC	Darlington

Mileage/(weekdays out of service)

1949	13,339 (14)
1950	25,736 (32)
1951	19,878 (66)
1952	25,134 (38)

Sheds

Sheffield	23/6/49
Dairycoates	16/2/52
Kirkby Stephen	22/5/55
Middlesbrough	13/11/55
Stourton	15/9/57

Withdrawn 23/5/64

43038 at its final shed Stourton in 1961 having arrived there in September 1957 from Middlesbrough. It is unlined with large cab numbers and had AWS from June 1961. It was an early withdrawal, in May 1964. R.K. Blencowe.

43039

Built at Horwich 4/7/49

Boiler 12965
Tender 4689

Improvements and modifications
New chimney arrangement   11/9/54
Fitting A.W.S   1/6/61

Repairs

17/10/50-22/11/50	LC	Horwich
19/3/52-24/4/52	LI	Horwich
21/8/52-25/9/52	LC(EO)	Horwich
24/7/54-11/9/54	HG	Horwich
2/7/57-3/8/57	Gen	Doncaster
7/3/60-14/4/60	Gen	Darlington
16/5/61-1/6/61	NC	Darlington
2/8/62-24/8/62	CL	Horwich
18/9/63-29/10/63	IH	Horwich

Mileage/(weekdays out of service)

1949	18,101 (17)
1950	24,239 (104)
1951	32,708 (34)
1952	28,487 (88)
1953	32,452 (33)
1954	25,129 (91)
1955	30,804 (63)
1956	33,702 (73)

Sheds
Holbeck 9/7/49

Withdrawn 7/12/66

43039 at Carnforth on 21 May 1960. It was one of only three in the class to remain at one shed – it arrived at Leeds Holbeck in July 1949 and was withdrawn from there in December 1966. The double chimney was replaced in September 1954. K. Fairey, colourrail.co.uk

43040

Built at Horwich 30/7/49

Boiler 12966
Tender 4690

Improvements and modifications
New chimney arrangement   26/5/53

Repairs

20/6/52-1/7/52	**LC**	Shed
30/12/52-13/2/53	**LI**	Horwich
27/4/53-26/5/53	**LC(EO)**	Horwich
16/2/55-3/3/55	**LC**	Horwich
17/10/55-1/12/55	**HG**	Horwich
17/4/57-24/5/57	**HI**	Horwich
24/4/61-17/6/61	**HG**	Horwich

Mileage/(weekdays out of service)

1949	14,216 (17)
1950	25,501 (58)
1951	20,028 (76)
1952	23,773 (51)
1953	26,748 (89)
1954	28,376 (38)
1955	21,803 (107)
1956	39,008 (35)
1957	31,659 (50)
1958	26,259 (77)
1959	22,784
1960	27,435

Sheds

Nottingham	30/7/49
Derby	19/4/58
Bournville	10/1/59
Saltley	20/6/59
Trafford Park	22/9/62
Carlisle Kingm'r	27/6/64
North Blyth	27/8/66 (loan)

Withdrawn w.e. 26/11/66

Nottingham's 43040 at Castle Bromwich in the Birmingham suburbs on 14 July 1955. It got its new chimney arrangement in May 1953. After transfer to Derby in April 1958 it returned to Birmingham the following year with spells at Bournville and Saltley.

43041

Built at Horwich 18/8/49

Boiler 12967
Tender 4691

Improvements and modifications
New chimney arrangement 27/8/53

Repairs

17/1/52-8/2/52	LI	Horwich
31/7/53-27/8/53	LC(EO)	Horwich
17/8/54-7/10/54	HG	Horwich
11/7/56-25/8/56	LI	Horwich
27/6/60-20/10/60	HG	Horwich
18/4/62-2/5/62	LC	Horwich
26/8/63-4/10/63	LI	Horwich

Mileage/(weekdays out of service)

1949	9,419 (12)
1950	25,032 (27)
1951	23,149 (45)
1952	21,761 (36)
1953	21,782 (75)
1954	25,886 (80)
1955	29,880 (85)
1956	25,062 (108)
1957	30,153 (67)
1958	18,574 (109)
1959	23,482
1960	10,850

Sheds

Sheffield	18/8/49
Saltley	20/3/54
Derby	8/5/54
Saltley	10/1/59
Trafford Park	22/9/62
Lower Darwen	13/2/65
Lostock Hall	19/2/66

Stored serviceable
5/9/66-21/11/66

Withdrawn w.e. 12/8/67

With a rather unusually dressed 'driver' 43041 in 1963, in common with other Midland Division 4MTs had not been fitted with AWS although its tender had acquired one of the curious bars. It had moved from Saltley to Trafford Park in September 1962 and made the short trip to Lower Darwen in February 1965 before reaching Lostock Hall a year later. It was withdrawn from there in August 1967. www.rail-online.co.uk

43042

Built at Horwich 27/8/49

Boiler 13375
Tender 4692

Improvements and modifications
New chimney arrangement 26/2/54
Fitting A.W.S 1/12/62 PE

Repairs
25/1/52-22/2/52	**LI**	Horwich
12/8/52-3/9/52	**LC(EO)**	Horwich
15/1/54-26/2/54	**HG**	Horwich
23/1/57-25/2/57	**LI**	Horwich
26/2/59-9/4/59	**HG**	Horwich

Mileage/(weekdays out of service)
1949	9,616 (7)
1950	24,668 (33)
1951	22,154 (40)
1952	20,870 (66)
1953	24,242 (54)
1954	23,716 (78)
1955	21,583 (89)
1956	20,693 (72)
1957	21,891 (65)
1958	20,144 (56)
1959	23,055
1960	22,155

Sheds
Sheffield	27/8/49
Kettering	21/9/57
Heaton Mersey	22/9/62

Withdrawn w.e. 19/2/66

The driver demonstrates the advantage of having everything outside as he oils 43042 in 1955 at Sheffield Grimesthorpe (otherwise known as Brightside – the names seemed poles apart). Delivered new to Sheffield in August 1949, 43042 had been modified with the new chimney arrangement in September 1954 and left for Kettering in September 1957. www.rail-online.co.uk

43043

Built at Horwich 15/9/49

Boiler 13376
Tender 4693

Improvements and modifications
New chimney arrangement   ?
Fitting A.W.S   26/8/60

Repairs

15/10/51-14/11/51	**LI**	Horwich
31/1/55-3/3/55	**Gen**	Doncaster
13/12/56-3/1/57	**CL**	Doncaster
19/7/57-12/8/57	**CL**	Doncaster
2/2/59-13/3/59	**Gen**	Darlington
3/5/60-26/8/60	**CL**	Darlington
10/9/62-18/10/62	**IH**	Horwich

Mileage/(weekdays out of service)

1949	10,199 (6)
1950	33,310 (43)
1951	22,653 (98)
1952	20,808 (48)

Sheds

Saltley	15/9/49
Heaton	16/2/52
Holbeck	16/6/57
Neville Hill	1/3/64
Normanton	6/9/64

Withdrawn 30/9/67

43043 was transferred from the London Midland Region at Saltley to the North Eastern Region at Heaton, where it is pictured in February 1952. The double chimney was almost certainly replaced during a General overhaul at Doncaster in early 1955. 43043 moved to Holbeck in June 1957, then Neville Hill in February 1964 and finally Normanton the following September; it was withdrawn three years later. www.rail-online.co.uk

43044

Built at Horwich 29/9/49

Boiler 13378
Tender 4694

Improvements and modifications
New chimney arrangement   6/11/53
Fitting A.W.S   24/1/62

Repairs
18/4/51-26/4/51	**LC**	Shed
16/10/51-15/11/51	**LI**	Horwich
6/10/53-6/11/53	**LC(EO)**	Horwich
19/11/54-1/1/55	**HG**	Horwich
20/3/58-1/4/58	**NC**	Doncaster
8/10/58-13/11/58	**Gen**	Doncaster
17/12/57-22/1/60	**CL**	Darlington
9/1/62-24/1/62	**NC**	Darlington
16/1/64-9/6/64	**Gen**	Swindon

Mileage/(weekdays out of service)
1949	9,204 (4)
1950	32,463 (48)
1951	23,525 (68)
1952	26,294 (18)
1953	20,724 (60)
1954	19,454 (69)
1955	21,561 (27)
1956	20,909 (37)

Sheds
Saltley	29/9/49
Stourton	15/3/52
Manningham	2/10/66
Holbeck	30/4/67

Withdrawn 9/9/67

43044 at York around 1965-1966. The smokebox betrays its visit to Swindon for a General repair which lasted almost five months from January until June 1964. Interestingly only the numberplate was moved, the upper lamp iron and handrail remaining in their original position. 43044 received its AWS in January 1962 and as the painted 55B shedcode implies it was shedded at Stourton where it remained until its transfer to Manningham in October 1966. Its final shed was Holbeck in April 1967 before withdrawal in September. www.rail-online.co.uk

43045

Built at Horwich 10/10/49

Boiler 13377
Tender 4695

Improvements and modifications
New chimney arrangement   22/1/55
Fitting A.W.S   21/7/61

Repairs
12/5/52-7/6/52	LI	Horwich
15/10/52-13/11/52	LC(EO)	Horwich
8/12/54-22/1/55	HG	Horwich
3/6/57-9/7/57	HI	Horwich
24/12/58-28/1/59	LC(EO)	Horwich
28/10/59-24/12/59	HG	Horwich
21/6/61-21/7/61	NC(EO)	Horwich

Mileage/(weekdays out of service)
1949	6,235 (6)
1950	26,617 (44)
1951	23,322 (63)
1952	22,151 (77)
1953	28,684 (30)
1954	24,332 (67)
1955	26,420 (62)
1956	26,239 (82)
1957	18,792 (78)
1958	27,350 (67)
1959	34,231
1960	43,773

Sheds
Leicester	10/10/49
Lancaster	11/10/58 (loan)
Lancaster	8/11/58
Kirkby Stephen	30/4/60
Carlisle Canal	11/11/61
Carlisle Kingmoor	22/6/63
Carnforth	31/10/64
Workington	18/9/65

Withdrawn w.e. 3/9/66

43045 about 1962; this looks to be its home shed, Carlisle Canal, to which it was transferred the previous year from Kirkby Stephen. A. Robey, transporttreasury.co.uk

43046

Boiler 13379
Tender 4696

Improvements and modifications
New chimney arrangement   9/10/54

Repairs
12/9/51-10/10/51	LI	Horwich
11/8/54-24/9/54	HG	Horwich
11/9/57-22/10/57	HI	Horwich
31/7/61-15/11/61	HG	Horwich
20/9/65-13/11/65	LI	Cowlairs

Sheds
Bristol	19/10/49
Saltley	10/5/52 (loan)
Bristol	24/5/52
Saltley	1/11/52
Trafford Park	22/9/62
Lower Darwen	19/6/65
Lostock Hall	19/2/66

Stored serviceable
28/11/66-25/1/67

Withdrawn w.e. 25/11/67

Mileage/(weekdays out of service)
1949	4,401 (4)
1950	28,739 (31)
1951	25,346 (63)
1952	29,196 (38)
1953	28,552 (57)
1954	25,281 (85)
1955	28,844 (61)
1956	27,493 (49)
1957	24,662 (91)
1958	28,197 (66)
1959	17,204
1960	19,175

Saltley's 43046 hurries along at Halesowen Junction, 9 May 1953. It was originally a Bristol engine, moving to Saltley in late 1952 and then to Trafford Park. It was never fitted with AWS and lasted until November 1967, after spells at Lower Darwen from June 1965 and Lostock Hall from February 1966. transporttreasury.co.uk

43047

Built at Horwich 2/11/49

Boiler 13381
Tender 4697

Improvements and modifications
New chimney arrangement   11/12/54

Repairs
10/10/51-20/10/51	LC	Shed
5/3/52-31/3/52	LI	Horwich
1/11/54-11/12/54	HG	Horwich
30/7/55-11/8/55	LC	Horwich
14/9/57-16/10/57	HI	Horwich
25/10/60-22/12/60	HG	Horwich
2/1/61-5/1/61	NC	Horwich
14/2/64-15/7/64	HI	Swindon

Sheds
Bristol	2/11/49
Saltley	13/6/53
Wellingborough	22/9/62
Heaton Mersey	14/12/63 (loan)
Heaton Mersey	4/1/64
Workington	14/5/66

Stored serviceable
1/11/65-25/11/65

Withdrawn w.e. 30/12/67

Mileage/(weekdays out of service)
1949	4,823 (3)
1950	28,973 (44)
1951	26,194 (46)
1952	24,512 (63)
1953	28,715 (42)
1954	21,912 (92)
1955	29,983 (58)
1956	22,342 (101)
1957	27,016 (73)
1958	29,377 (54)
1959	28,224
1960	21,781

Double chimney 43047 at the Midland (Barnwood) shed at Gloucester on 10 May 1953 shortly before its transfer to Saltley the following month. It was fitted with a single chimney in December 1954 but as a Midland Division engine in the late 1950s/ early 1960s was never fitted with AWS. A.R. Carpenter, transporttreasury.co.uk

43048

Built at Horwich 12/11/49

Boiler 13383
Tender 4698

Improvements and modifications
New chimney arrangement   13/5/54
Fitting A.W.S   9/1/63

Repairs
11/12/50-25/1/51	LC	Horwich
15/3/52-9/4/52	LI	Horwich
3/4/54-13/5/54	HG	Horwich
18/6/54-9/7/54	NC(EO)	Horwich
21/7/54-7/8/54	LC(EO)	Horwich
23/4/55-21/5/55	LC	Horwich
27/8/56-5/10/56	HI	Horwich
19/1/60-4/5/60	HG	Horwich
23/11/62-9/1/63	LI	Horwich

Mileage/(weekdays out of service)
1949	3,662	(1)
1950	29,231	(53)
1951	24,404	(67)
1952	26,703	(62)
1953	24,208	(90)
1954	22,792	(105)
1955	26,992	(106)
1956	26,135	(95)
1957	29,312	(66)
1958	18,875	(63)
1959	17,645	
1960	18,907	

Sheds
Derby	12/11/49
Kettering	21/9/57
Heaton Mersey	22/9/62
Trafford Park	22/6/63
Heaton Mersey	21/9/63
North Blyth	27/8/66 (loan)
North Blyth	10/12/66

Stored serviceable
6/6/66-18/8/66

Withdrawn 10/5/67

Local 43048 heads a mixed freight with a Gresley full brake in the middle at Kettering on 29 March 1962. It was one of the last 4MTs to be fitted with AWS, during a Light Intermediate at Horwich completed in January 1963. 43048 had a short stay at Trafford Park in 1963, returning to Heaton Mersey after three months before its final destination, North Blyth. www.rail-online.co.uk

43049

Built at Horwich 25/11/49

Boiler 13380
Tender 4699

Improvements and modifications
New chimney arrangement   16/4/55
Fitting A.W.S   15/11/62

Repairs

21/1/52-23/2/52	**LI**	Horwich
3/3/55-16/4/55	**HG**	Horwich
15/5/56-2/6/56	**LC(EO)**	Horwich
8/7/57-22/8/57	**HI**	Horwich
11/7/60-4/11/60	**HG**	Horwich
5/11/62-15/11/62	**LC**	Horwich
7/5/64-30/5/64	**LI**	Horwich

Mileage/(weekdays out of service)

1949	1,988 (6)
1950	29,676 (46)
1951	22.952 (73)
1952	28,250 (77)
1953	26,311 (65)
1954	21,520 (103)
1955	26,439 (109)
1956	24,435 (107)
1957	27,196 (77)
1958	29,580 (46)
1959	30,897
1960	18,810

Sheds

Derby	25/11/49
Saltley	28/7/56
Heaton Mersey	22/9/62
Carlisle Kingmoor	14/11/64

Withdrawn w.e. 5/8/67

In somewhat murky conditions, Derby's 43049 has an up local at Lenton South Junction, Nottingham on 21 July 1956. It had been the last 4MT built with a double chimney, which it kept until April 1955. A. Lathey, transporttreasury.co.uk

43050

Built at Doncaster 20/7/50

Works number   2057
Tender   4700

Improvements and modifications
New chimney arrangement   ?
Fitting A.W.S   18/3/61

Repairs

Date	Type	Works
27/3/52-25/4/52	CL	Doncaster
17/6/53-22/7/53	IH	Doncaster
20/10/53-29/10/53	NC	Darlington
6/4/55-22/4/55	NC	Doncaster
21/6/56-29/6/56	NC	Darlington
5/2/57-12/3/57	Gen	Doncaster
15/6/57-12/7/57	CL	Doncaster
16/7/58-29/7/58	NC	Doncaster
19/1/61-18/3/61	Gen	Darlington
4/1/62-11/1/62	NC	Darlington
25/9/64-7/11/64	Unsch	Darlington
9/11/64-13/11/64	Adj	Darlington

Sheds

Darlington	20/7/50
Middlesbrough	24/9/50
Haverton Hill	29/4/56
Darlington	21/10/56
West Hartlepool	27/3/66
Manningham	10/4/66
Wakefield	30/4/67
North Blyth	14/5/67

Stored serviceable
27/3/66-10/4/66
30/4/67-14/5/67

Withdrawn w.e. 9/9/67

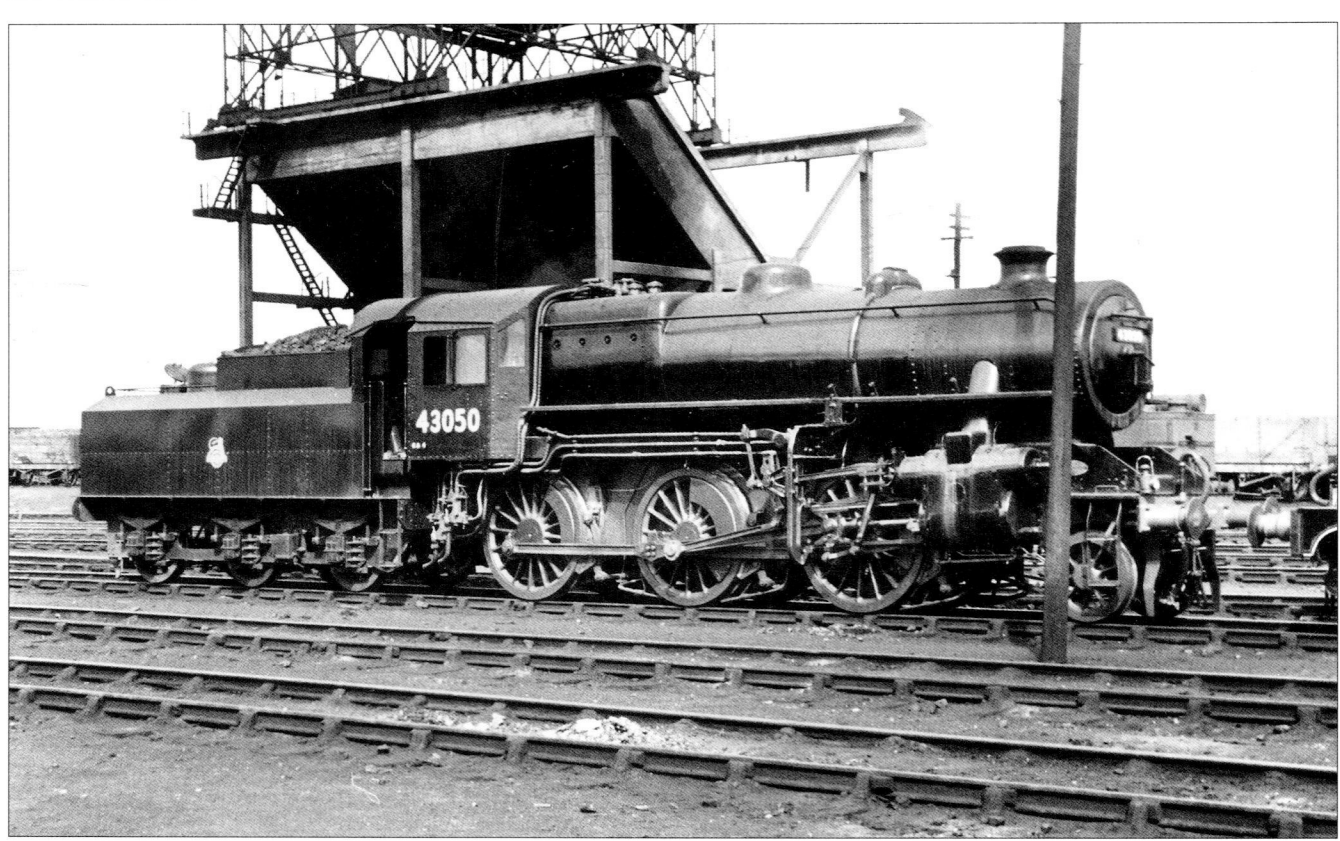

The first Doncaster-built 4MT, 43050 brand new on 29 July 1950 at Darlington in plain black with large numbers, RA4 on the cab and with 4F on the bufferbeam. It was allocated to Darlington for a couple of months, presumably for 'running-in' purposes, moving to Middlesbrough at the end of September, where it stayed for almost six years. Two original features would be changed fairly quickly: the guard irons on the frames were replaced by a pony truck mounted version and the tender was fitted with steps and a handrail at the rear end of the tank side. A.G. Forsyth, Initial Photographics.

43051

Built at Doncaster 2/8/50

Works number 2058
Tender 4701

Improvements and modifications
New chimney arrangement   ?
Fitting A.W.S   12/8/61

Repairs

13/8/51-22/8/51	CL	Doncaster
21/1/53-18/2/53	IH	Doncaster
11/5/53-15/5/53	NC	Darlington
7/2/55-2/3/55	CL	Doncaster
28/5/56-11/7/56	IH	Doncaster
28/8/56-6/9/56	NC	Doncaster
18/5/61-12/8/61	Gen	Darlington
12/4/62-30/4/62	CL	Darlington

Sheds

Darlington	2/8/50
Middlesbrough	24/9/50
Stourton	15/9/57
Selby	14/9/58
Neville Hill	8/3/59
Selby	5/4/59
Neville Hill	17/5/59
Stourton	22/2/63
Manningham	9/2/64

Withdrawn w.e. 23/1/67

One of the distinctive overhead electric masts is in the background at Lancaster on 24 August 1958 as 43051 from Stourton waits on shed. The guard irons on the pony truck frame and the rear tender steps and handrail are easy to spot but less obvious is the replacement chimney which was two inches taller than the original one. The final modification for 43051 was the fitting of AWS in August 1961.

43052

Built at Doncaster 10/8/50

Works number 2059
Tender 4702

Improvements and modifications
New chimney arrangement   ?
Fitting A.W.S   25/1/62

Repairs

21/11/52-19/12/52	**IL**	Doncaster
17/6/53-13/7/53	**CH**	Doncaster
1/11/55-3/12/55	**IH**	Doncaster
23/10/58-4/12/58	**Gen**	Doncaster
29/11/61-25/1/62	**Gen**	Horwich

Mileage/(weekdays out of service)

1956	24,915
1957	19,943
1958	17,355
1959	30,966
1960	28,424

Sheds

Scarborough	10/8/50
Selby	7/7/51
Saltley	16/5/59 (loan)
Saltley	23/5/59
Lancaster	11/7/59 (loan)
Nuneaton	17/10/59 (loan)
Lancaster	7/11/59
Nuneaton	7/11/59 (loan)
Nuneaton	30/4/60
Lancaster	17/9/60
Nuneaton	17/2/62
Northampton	16/6/62
Crewe South	20/10/62

Withdrawn w.e. 5/11/66

One of the 4MTs originally delivered to the North Eastern Region but transferred to the London Midland Region in May 1959, 43052 from Crewe South at Willesden on 28 July 1963. In the previous four years it had bounced back and forth between Nuneaton and Lancaster. It has received a Horwich repaint with short wide spaced lining and small cab numbers during a General repair from November 1961 to January 1962 when it was also fitted with AWS. 43052 was withdrawn from Crewe South at the end of October 1966.

43053

Built at Doncaster 21/8/50

Works number 2060
Tender 4703

Improvements and modifications
New chimney arrangement   ?
Fitting A.W.S   20/2/62

Repairs

30/7/52-12/8/52	NC	Doncaster
23/4/53-8/6/53	IH	Doncaster
2/10/53-9/10/53	NC	Darlington
5/3/56-4/4/56	Gen	Doncaster
28/9/59-4/11/59	CH	Darlington
31/10/61-20/2/62	CH	Darlington

Sheds

Dairycoates	21/8/50
Low Moor	14/6/59
West Hartlepool	1/11/59
Manningham	8/9/63

Stored serviceable
26/5/63-8/9/63

Withdrawn w.e. 20/4/64

43053 at its home shed West Hartlepool on 26 August 1962; it had spent four months in store the previous year and was an early withdrawal in April 1964 from its final shed, Manningham. It had been equipped with AWS in February 1962.

141

43054

Built at Doncaster 29/8/50

Works number   2061
Tender   4704

Improvements and modifications
New chimney arrangement   ?
Fitting A.W.S   11/60

Repairs
3/56- p/e 14/4/56   **Gen**   Doncaster
? – 11/60   ?   Darlington
Others not recorded

Sheds
Darlington   29/8/50
Middlesbrough   24/9/50
Saltburn   25/7/54
Middlesbrough   3/2/57
Saltburn   24/2/57
Middlesbrough   15/9/57
Thornaby   1/6/58
Selby   16/11/58
Neville Hill   8/3/59
Selby   5/4/59
Neville Hill   17/5/59
Manningham   30/1/66

Withdrawn w.e. 7/12/66

While allocated to Neville Hill 43054 double heads another 4MT with what appears to be an excursion train. It had two short spells away at Selby and finally left the Leeds shed in January 1966 for Manningham where it survived until the end of the year.

43055

Built at Doncaster 1/9/50

Works number 2062
Tender 4705

Improvements and modifications
New chimney arrangement   ?
Fitting A.W.S   24/3/62

Repairs

30/10/52-28/11/52	**IL**	Doncaster
23/11/54-17/12/54	**IH**	Doncaster
20/2/58-26/3/58	**Gen**	Doncaster
7/12/61-24/3/62	**Gen**	Darlington
29/7/63-30/8/63	**CasL**	Horwich

Sheds

Darlington	1/9/50
West Hartlepool	25/1/52
Kirkby Stephen	22/5/55
Gateshead	10/6/56
Heaton	25/11/56
Holbeck	16/6/57
York	1/11/59
West Hartlepool	21/11/65
Darlington	28/11/65
West Hartlepool	27/3/66
York	3/4/66
South Blyth	31/7/66
North Blyth	23/10/66

Stored serviceable
6/3/66-27/3/66

Withdrawn w.e. 1/7/67

43055 at York on 2 May 1964 shows the final Darlington lined livery with large cab numbers, wide spaced full length lining and large BR crest. AWS was fitted in March 1962 while it was shedded at York, having been transferred from Holbeck in June 1957.

43056

Built at Doncaster 16/9/50

Works number   2063
Tender   4706

Improvements and modifications
New chimney arrangement   ?
Fitting A.W.S   16/6/60

Repairs
4/6/52-13/6/52	**NC**	Doncaster
10/12/52-7/1/53	**CL**	Doncaster
8/2/54-8/3/54	**IH**	Doncaster
24/8/55-13/9/55	**NC**	Doncaster
15/1/57-16/2/57	**Gen**	Doncaster
25/4/60-16/6/60	**Gen**	Darlington
2/2/61-14/3/61	**CL**	Darlington
11/3/64-13/5/64	**Unsch**	Swindon

Sheds
Darlington	16/9/50
West Auckland	22/5/55
Blaydon	10/6/56
Heaton	23/9/56
Holbeck	P/E 13/6/57
York	1/11/59
Darlington	11/6/61
West Hartlepool	13/2/66

Withdrawn w.e. 31/12/66

The angled cab front of 43056 reflects the Darlington sunlight on 27 July 1964. It has the final Darlington lined livery with large numbers and crest inboard of wide spaced lining. It made the long trek to Swindon for an Unscheduled repair in March 1964 but unlike most of the others which went there its looks were not spoilt when it emerged two months later. 43056 was fitted with AWS in June 1960 before its transfer from York to Darlington in June 1961. Its final destination was West Hartlepool in February 1966 and it was withdrawn from there ten months later. R.K. Blencowe.

43057

Built at Doncaster 22/9/50

Works number   2064
Tender   4707

Improvements and modifications
New chimney arrangement   ?
Fitting A.W.S   26/1/62

Repairs
13/8/53-17/9/53	**IH**	Doncaster
31/12/54-24/1/55	**NC**	Doncaster
19/9/56-16/10/56	**Gen**	Doncaster
5/5/60-20/5/60	**NC**	Darlington
20/11/61-26/1/62	**Gen**	Darlington

Sheds
Darlington	22/9/50
West Auckland	22/5/55
Blaydon	10/6/56
Alnmouth	11/11/56
Middlesbrough	16/6/57
Thornaby	1/6/58
Selby	16/11/58
York	13/9/59
Neville Hill	20/9/59
York	18/10/59
Thornaby	12/2/61
Darlington	5/5/63
West Hartlepool	28/11/65

Withdrawn w.e. 31/12/66

43057 at home at Darlington on 19 May 1964. This was its first shed in 1950 and it stayed for five years, going to numerous North Eastern Region sheds before returning in May 1963. The AWS was fitted in January 1962 and it is in final Darlington lined livery – large numbers, wide spaced lining and large BR crest. 43057 was withdrawn from West Hartlepool at the end of 1966. P.H. Groom.

43058

Built at Doncaster 29/9/50

Works number 2065
Tender 4708

Improvements and modifications
New chimney arrangement   ?

Repairs
8/10/52-7/11/52	**IL**	Doncaster
18/5/54-29/7/54	**IH**	Stratford
15/6/57-26/7/57	**Gen**	Doncaster
20/12/60-20/1/61	**Gen**	Doncaster

Sheds
New England	29/9/50
Grantham	23/11/52
New England	14/3/54
Boston	8/6/58
Colwick	11/1/64

Withdrawn w.e. 26/12/64

43058 at Boston in 1961 in plain black with small BR crest, large numbers and Overhead Line Warning flashes. It still has its tablet catcher, and was the first to be so fitted for use on the M&GN when delivered to New England in September 1950. It moved to Boston the year before the M&GN closed and remained there until the shed closed at the end of 1963, when it went to Colwick until withdrawn at the end of 1964. www.rail-online.co.uk

43059

Built at Doncaster 11/10/50

Works number 2066
Tender 4708

Improvements and modifications
New chimney arrangement   ?

Repairs
8/7/53-4/8/53	**IH**	Doncaster
30/1/57-1/3/57	**Gen**	Doncaster
24/8/60-6/10/60	**Gen**	Doncaster
4/2/63-27/2/63	**NC**	Horwich

Sheds
New England	11/10/50
Boston	29/12/57
Colwick	30/12/62
Barrow Hill	20/6/64

Withdrawn w.e. 10/1/65

Colwick's 43059 on 21 August 1963 at Basford North with the 5.18pm Nottingham-Derby local. Originally a New England engine, it was one of eight 4MTs transferred to Boston In December 1957 when the sub-shed at Spalding was moved into the Lincoln District. It left for Colwick in December 1962 and spent its last six months at Barrow Hill before withdrawal in January 1965. It still has its tablet catcher but was never equipped with AWS. B.W.L. Brooksbank, Initial Photographics.

43060

Built at Doncaster 20/10/50

Works number   2067
Tender   4710

Improvements and modifications
New chimney arrangement   ?

Repairs

27/1/54-26/3/54	**IH**	Stratford
5/3/57-15/3/57	**NC**	Doncaster
2/1/58-31/1/58	**Gen**	Doncaster
5/12/61-6/1/62	**Gen**	Doncaster

Sheds

New England	20/10/50
Boston	8/6/58
Colwick	26/7/59
Lincoln	8/11/59
Colwick	29/9/62

Withdrawn w.e. 26/12/64

43060 on 18 July 1964 at a run-down Derby Friargate with the 1pm to Nottingham. The ex-Great Northern station was closed three weeks later and the 4MT did not last much longer, being withdrawn at the end of the year. It had followed several others from New England via Boston to Colwick, arriving there in September 1962.

148

43061

Built at Doncaster 27/10/50

Works number 2068
Tender 4711

Improvements and modifications
New chimney arrangement   ?

Repairs
19/5/53-19/6/53	HI	Doncaster
21/6/56-1/8/56	G	Doncaster
7/8/56-9/8/56	Adj	Doncaster
17/8/56-20/8/56	Adj	Doncaster
11/2/60-9/4/60	Gen	Doncaster
28/6/60-5/7/60	NC	Doncaster

Sheds
New England	27/10/50
Boston	29/12/57
Colwick	30/12/62

Withdrawn w.e. 5/1/64

43061 at Doncaster on 3 July 1960 after returning for a Non Classified 'rectification' visit following its General repair from 11 February to 9 April. Another Boston, ex-New England engine it was one of the earliest withdrawals, from Colwick at the end of 1963.

43062

Built at Doncaster 3/11/50

Works number 2069
Tender 4712

Improvements and modifications
New chimney arrangement   ?

Repairs
23/10/53-5/2/54	**IH**	Stratford
2/4/57-3/5/57	**Gen**	Doncaster
23/7/60-27/7/60	**NC**	Doncaster
21/9/61-25/10/61	**Gen**	Doncaster

Sheds
New England	3/11/50
Boston	29/12/57
Colwick	30/12/62
Barrow Hill	28/9/63

Withdrawn 20/6/65

The PW men stand aside for New England's 43062 at Peterborough in the 1950s. B. Richardson, www.transporttreasury.co.uk

43063

Built at Doncaster 10/11/50

Works number 2070
Tender 4713

Improvements and modifications
New chimney arrangement ?
Fitting A.W.S 11/10/62

Repairs
10/3/54-15/5/54	HI	Stratford
24/1/55-3/2/55	NC	Stratford
10/12/57-11/1/58	HG	Doncaster
14/1/60-30/3/60	LC	Horwich
17/7/61-2/10/61	HI	Horwich
4/10/62-11/10/62	NC	Horwich
22/5/63-25/6/63	LC	Horwich
7/8/63-26/8/63	LC	Horwich
22/11/63-20/12/63	NC	Horwich
30/1/64-21/2/64	NC	Horwich
12/3/65-30/4/65	HI	Eastleigh

Mileage/(weekdays out of service)
1958	27,646	(77)
1959	23,346	
1960	16,707	

Sheds
New England	10/11/50
Woodford	3/6/56
Saltley	24/3/62
Heaton Mersey	15/9/62
North Blyth	27/8/66 (loan)
North Blyth	10/12/66

Stored serviceable
4/10/65-14/3/66
30/5/66-18/8/66

Withdrawn w.e. 7/1/67

43063 in the late 1950s when allocated to Woodford Halse. It went there from New England in June 1956 and stayed until March 1962 when it moved to Saltley.

43064

Built as 3064 at Doncaster 17/11/50

Works number 2071
Tender 4714

Improvements and modifications
New chimney arrangement   ?

Repairs
? - w/e 6/9/52	?	Doncaster
1954	**HI**	Stratford
? - p/e 16/5/57	**Gen**	Doncaster
? – 7/61	**H**	Doncaster
Others not recorded		

Sheds
New England	17/11/50
Spital Bridge	26/11/50
New England	28/2/54
Boston	29/12/57
Colwick	30/12/62
Canklow	25/10/64
Langwith Junction	13/6/65

Withdrawn w.e. 20/6/65

43064, one of a large number of 4MTs at New England during the 1950s, passing Peterborough North box on 3 July 1956. It had originally been allocated to the ex-Midland shed at Peterborough Spital Bridge to cover a single M&GN diagram, swapping with 43084 in February 1954. Along with several others it went to Boston when the sub-shed at Spalding was transferred to the Lincoln District.

43065

Built at Doncaster 24/11/50

Works number   2072
Tender   4715

Improvements and modifications
New chimney arrangement   ?

Repairs
10/8/53-3/9/53	**IH**	Doncaster
26/4/55-9/5/55	**CL**	Stratford
8/11/56-12/12/56	**Gen**	Doncaster
4/2/57-12/2/57	**NC**	Doncaster
11/10/60-5/11/60	**Gen**	Doncaster

Sheds
New England	24/11/50
Neasden	1/3/53
New England	5/9/54
Boston	29/12/57
Colwick	30/12/62

Withdrawn w.e. 10/1/65

43065 was one of the group of ex-New England 4MTs which moved to Boston and then Colwick and is waiting in the middle road at Nottingham Victoria on 31 July 1964. It lasted only another six months, being withdrawn in the second week of January 1965. J.T. Clewley, www.transporttreasury.co.uk

43066

Built at Doncaster 1/12/50

Works number 2073
Tender 4716

Improvements and modifications
New chimney arrangement   ?

Repairs

18/7/51-27/7/51	**CL**	Doncaster
1/3/54-1/5/54	**IH**	Stratford
19/7/57-2/11/57	**Gen**	Stratford
8/8/60-12/8/60	**NC**	Doncaster
15/3/62-3/5/62	**Gen**	Doncaster

Sheds

New England	1/12/50
Neasden	1/3/53
New England	22/8/54
Boston	8/6/58
Colwick	30/12/62
Carnforth	10/10/64

Withdrawn w.e. 7/1/67

43066 at Carnforth on 20 July with a Class 7 freight. It has a lowered top lamp iron but no AWS. It was an Eastern Region engine until October 1964 when it moved to Carnforth, although it has retained its tablet catcher. B. Taylor.

43067

Built at Doncaster 14/12/50

Works number 2074
Tender 4717

Improvements and modifications
New chimney arrangement   ?
Fitting A.W.S   ?

Repairs
10/2/54-10/4/54	**IH**	Stratford
7/11/57-6/12/57	**Gen**	Doncaster
?-10/60	**H**	Doncaster
14/1/61-17/2/61	**Gen**	Doncaster
28/8/61-31/8/61	**NC**	Doncaster
28/2/63-19/3/63	**LC**	Horwich

Sheds
New England	14/12/50
Neasden	1/3/53
New England	22/8/54
Barrow Hill	24/11/63

Withdrawn w.e. 11/4/65

New England 's 43067 on a weed-killing weed train in the early 1960s; LNER brake leading and two former passenger coaches behind. 43067 stayed at the Peterborough shed until November 1963 when it moved to Barrow Hill. The record cards do not show when the AWS was fitted. B. Richardson, www.transporttreasury.co.uk

43068

Built at Doncaster 20/12/50

Works number 2075
Tender 4718

Improvements and modifications
New chimney arrangement ?

Repairs

5/1/54-27/2/54	**HI**	Stratford
7/7/57-16/8/57	**Gen**	Doncaster
3/3/60-30/4/60	**Gen**	Doncaster
9/8/60-12/8/60	**NC**	Doncaster

Sheds

New England	20/12/50
Neasden	1/3/53
South Lynn	25/7/54
Boston	1/3/59

Withdrawn w.e. 5/1/64

There are a few points to study on the tender of 43068 at Boston on 13 July 1963. It still has its tablet catcher, the short ladder, the additional handrail and oddly shaped rear steps are clearly visible. 43068 was unlined with small BR crest, and the flush rivets in the centre of the tank to accommodate the emblem also show up well. It left South Lynn for Boston on closure of the M&GN and was withdrawn from there at the end of 1963. R.K. Blencowe.

43069

Built Doncaster 29/12/50

Works number 2076
Tender 4719

Improvements and modifications
New chimney arrangement   ?
Fitting A.W.S   26/8/60

Repairs
27/5/53-3/7/53	**IH**	Doncaster
10/4/56-11/5/56	**Gen**	Doncaster
2/4/59-15/5/59	**Gen**	Darlington
15/8/60-26/8/60	**NC**	Darlington
20/10/60-26/11/60	**NC**	Darlington
3/4/63-24/5/63	**IH**	Horwich

Sheds
New England	29/12/50
Neasden	8/4/51
Dairycoates	30/3/52
Holbeck	6/6/65
Manningham	6/2/66

Stored unserviceable
26/6/66-4/9/66

Withdrawn w.e. 4/9/66

Although delivered to New England in 1950, 43069 was quickly moved to Neasden where it stayed for slightly over a year before joining the herd at Dairycoates in March 1952. It still had its original chimney when photographed on a short fitted freight near Selby. The 4MT power classification is just visible on the left-hand side of the bufferbeam. 43069 was fitted with AWS in August 1960 and moved to Holbeck in June 1965, finally ending up at Manningham in February 1966 where it was withdrawn six months later. R.K. Blencowe.

43070

Built at Darlington 10/8/50

Works number 2112
Tender 4720

Improvements and modifications
New chimney arrangement   ?
Fitting A.W.S   ?

Repairs

24/9/53-1/10/53	**NC**	Darlington
8/4/54-7/5/54	**IH**	Doncaster
6/8/58-20/9/58	**Gen**	Doncaster
2/5/61-12/5/61	**NC**	Darlington
7/9/61-16/9/61	**NC**	Darlington
5/2/64-2/7/64	**Gen**	Swindon

Sheds

Heaton	10/8/50
Holbeck	16/6/57
Manningham	18/1/59
York	1/11/59
Thornaby	12/2/61
Wakefield	29/7/62
Low Moor	5/1/64
Ardsley	3/1/65
Wakefield	10/10/65
West Hartlepool	5/2/67
North Blyth	2/7/67

Stored serviceable
25/3/62-29/7/62

Withdrawn w.e. 9/9/67

The first Darlington-built 4MT, ex-works and newly repainted with full lining after a Heavy Intermediate at Doncaster from 8 April to 7 May 1954. It has also gained the RA4 on the cab and a BR emblem slightly off centre to miss the vertical rivets – there was no flush riveted area on this batch. 43070 spent its first seven years allocated to Heaton before going to Holbeck in June 1957. www.rail-online.co.uk

43071

Built at Darlington 6/9/50

Works number   2113
Tender   4721

Improvements and modifications
New chimney arrangement   ?
Fitting A.W.S   8/3/62

Repairs

9/9/53-14/9/53	**NC**	Darlington
23/11/53-24/12/53	**IH**	Doncaster
4/10/56-7/11/56	**Gen**	Doncaster
8/1/62-8/3/62	**Gen**	Darlington

Sheds

Darlington	6/9/50
West Auckland	22/5/55
Blaydon	10/6/56
Alnmouth	11/11/56
Middlesbrough	16/6/57
Thornaby	1/6/58
Selby	16/11/58
York	13/9/59
Neville Hill	20/9/59
York	18/10/59
North Blyth	21/8/66

Withdrawn w.e. 6/3/67

43071 at York on 29 November 1964 in final Darlington condition, lined with large numbers and crest; the AWS was fitted in March 1962. It was shedded there from 1959 until its final year when it went to North Blyth in August 1966, prior to withdrawal in March 1967. D. Hawkins.

43072

Built at Darlington 8/9/50

Works number 2114
Tender 4722

Improvements and modifications
New chimney arrangement   ?
Fitting A.W.S   2/6/61

Repairs

9/3/53-16/4/53	IH	Doncaster
2/10/53-9/10/53	NC	Darlington
26/1/54-15/2/54	CL	Doncaster
13/5/54-21/5/54	NC	Doncaster
22/7/54-16/8/54	CL	Doncaster
27/8/56-6/10/56	Gen	Doncaster
2/10/59-23/10/59	NC	Darlington
29/4/60-17/5/60	NC	Darlington
23/5/61-2/6/61	NC	Darlington
12/10/61-19/10/61	NC	Darlington
16/10/62-21/11/62	Gen	Horwich

Sheds

Darlington	8/9/50
Middlesbrough	17/3/51
Thornaby	1/6/58
Darlington	11/9/60
Wakefield	29/7/62
Low Moor	19/8/62
Ardsley	24/3/63

Withdrawn w.e. 11/11/64

43072 at Wakefield on 19 August 1962 still with its 56A plate, although officially transferred to Low Moor on that date. One of several camera-shy 4MTs, it had received AWS equipment in June 1961 and went to Ardsley in March 1963. 43072 achieved its fifteen minutes of fame when it fell off a bridge onto a road at Laisterdyke, Bradford on 10 November 1964 and was cut up on site. A.G. Ellis.

43073

Built at Darlington 13/9/50

Works number 2115
Tender 4693

Improvements and modifications
New chimney arrangement   ?
Fitting A.W.S   21/9/61

Repairs

3/7/53-31/7/53	IH	Doncaster
12/10/53-17/10/53	NC	Darlington
1/2/55-16/2/55	CL	Doncaster
12/11/56-22/12/56	HG	Doncaster
18/2/60-14/4/60	HI	Horwich
21/4/60-22/4/60	NC(Rect)	Horwich
1/7/60-29/7/60	LC(TO)	Horwich
11/9/61-21/9/61	NC(EO)	Horwich
6/8/62-7/9/62	Gen	Horwich
6/8/62-12/9/62	Gen	Horwich
3/8/65-16/9/65	LC	Eastleigh

Mileage/(weekdays out of service)

1956	16,341
1957	25,487
1958	14,589
1959	19,851
1960	22,576

Sheds

Darlington	13/9/50
Middlesbrough	17/3/51
Thornaby	1/6/58
Stockton	1/3/59
Heaton Mersey	16/5/59 (loan)
Heaton Mersey	23/5/59
Lancaster	23/5/59 (loan)
Lancaster	20/6/59
Carlisle Upperby	4/10/59 (loan)
Carlisle Upperby	6/8/60
Crewe South	10/11/62
Stoke	21/9/63
Bletchley	23/1/65
Workington	10/7/65 (loan)
Workington	24/7/65

Withdrawn w.e. 19/8/67

43073 in the mid-1950s after its original chimney had been replaced and pony truck mounted guard irons fitted. Like many of the 4MTs built there it was shedded initially at Darlington, moving to Middlesbrough in March 1951 where it stayed until transferred to Thornaby in May 1958.

43074

Built at Darlington 22/9/50

Works number 2116
Tender 4724

Improvements and modifications
New chimney arrangement   ?
Fitting A.W.S   3/12/60

Repairs

9/6/53-14/7/53	**IH**	Doncaster
30/10/53-12/11/53	**NC**	Darlington
5/2/54-9/3/54	**CL**	Doncaster
8/3/56-24/3/56	**CL**	Doncaster
28/11/56-12/1/57	**Gen**	Doncaster
13/10/60-3/12/60	**Gen**	Doncaster
22/8/61-2/9/61	**CL**	Doncaster
17/4/64-31/7/64	**Unsch**	Swindon
16/10/64-6/11/64	**Unsch**	Darlington

Sheds

Darlington	22/9/50
Middlesbrough	17/3/51
Normanton	15/9/57
Manningham	21/1/62

Withdrawn w.e. 26/6/66

43074 with an ancient clerestory coach at York on 5 September 1961. It was originally plain black but received lining and a large BR crest during an overhaul at Doncaster. It was fitted with AWS in December 1960 and was withdrawn in June 1966.
www.rail-online.co.uk

43075

Built at Darlington 27/9/50

Works number 2117
Tender 4725

Improvements and modifications
New chimney arrangement   ?
Fitting A.W.S   10/6/61

Repairs

16/9/53-25/9/53	NC	Darlington
9/11/53-4/12/53	IH	Doncaster
24/1/57-26/2/57	Gen	Doncaster
1/5/61-10/6/61	Gen	Darlington
2/4/63-18/4/63	CL	Darlington

Sheds

Darlington	27/9/50
West Auckland	22/5/55
Gateshead	10/6/56
Heaton	25/11/56
Ardsley	16/6/57
Wakefield	15/9/57
Ardsley	8/6/58
Wakefield	7/6/59
Thornaby	5/3/61
West Hartlepool	20/1/63
Stourton	28/7/63
Neville Hill	1/3/64

Stored serviceable
25/3/62-17/6/62

Withdrawn w.e. 29/4/65

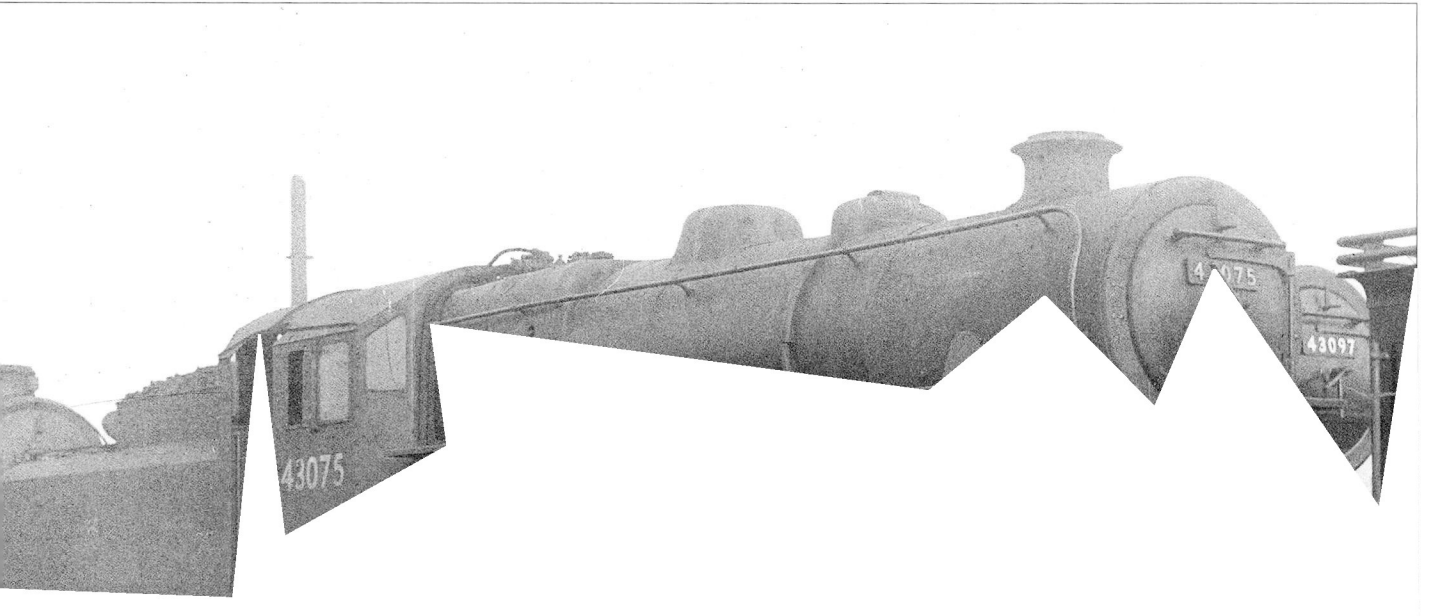

43075 at Darlington in September 1953 still with its original chimney which was probably replaced (along with the later pattern guard irons) during its next Heavy Intermediate at Doncaster a couple of months later. Although it stayed at Darlington for its first five years it then moved around to nine different North Eastern Region sheds before ending up at Neville Hill in early 1964.

43076

Built at Darlington 4/10/50

Works number 2118
Tender 4726

Improvements and modifications
New chimney arrangement   ?
Fitting A.W.S   25/8/60

Repairs

19/12/52-23/1/53	IH	Doncaster
9/9/53-18/9/53	NC	Darlington
18/7/55-10/8/55	CL	Doncaster
10/5/56-16/6/56	IH	Doncaster
16/9/57-26/9/57	NC	Doncaster
5/5/59-11/6/59	CL	Darlington
1/2/60-9/3/60	Gen	Darlington
18/8/60-25/8/60	NC	Darlington
23/3/61-7/4/61	NC	Darlington
7/8/64-29/8/64	Int	Cowlairs
24/2/65-17/4/65	U	Cowlairs

Sheds

Dairycoates	4/10/50
Royston	3/10/65
Holbeck	25/6/67
Low Moor	27/8/67

Stored serviceable
27/8/67-9/9/67

Withdrawn w.e. 9/9/67

43076 at Dairycoates on 4 August 1956 with a Trip working board above the front bufferbeam. The Hull shed, which had received eighteen of the class from new, lost its final four, including 43076, when they went to Royston in October 1965. It has later pattern guard irons, a new chimney and RA4 on the cab following overhaul at Doncaster. www.rail-online.co.uk

43077

Built at Darlington 6/10/50

Works number 2119
Tender 4727

Improvements and modifications
New chimney arrangement   ?
Fitting A.W.S   10/9/60

Repairs
1/5/51-15/5/51	CL	Doncaster
2/8/51-18/9/51	CH	Doncaster
6/5/53-10/6/53	IL	Doncaster
12/10/53-17/10/53	NC	Darlington
30/1/56-7/3/56	IH	Doncaster
17/8/59-23/9/59	Gen	Darlington
29/8/60-10/9/60	NC	Darlington
28/5/63-11/7/63	IH	Horwich

Sheds
Dairycoates	6/10/50
Goole	26/7/65
Royston	3/10/65
Manningham	5/2/67

Withdrawn w.e. 3/4/67

43077 ex-works at Darlington, probably after its General overhaul there from 17 August to 23 September 1959. It has wide spaced lining and large BR crest but, unusually for a non-Horwich repair, small cab numbers. 43077 was fitted with AWS in September 1960 and was transferred from its first shed, Dairycoates, to Goole in July 1965. It quickly moved on, to Royston three months later and then for its last two months before withdrawal at the end of March 1967, to Manningham. www.rail-online.co.uk

43078

Built at Darlington 13/10/50

Works number   2120
Tender   4728

Improvements and modifications
New chimney arrangement   ?
Fitting A.W.S   9/9/60

Repairs
13/2/52-5/3/52	**CL**	Doncaster
1/7/52-18/7/52	**CL**	Doncaster
10/6/53-17/7/53	**IH**	Doncaster
13/10/53-23/10/53	**NC**	Doncaster
24/4/56-28/5/56	**IH**	Doncaster
8/1/59-23/1/59	**NC**	Darlington
20/10/59-5/12/59	**Gen**	Darlington
29/8/60-9/9/60	**NC**	Darlington
3/4/63-21/5/63	**IL**	Horwich

Sheds
Dairycoates	13/10/50
Royston	3/10/65

Withdrawn w.e. 5/12/66

Another rare beast as far as the camera was concerned, 43078 on 15 July 1963 at Dairycoates which was its original shed in 1950. It left for Royston in October 1965 and was taken out of service there in December 1966. The AWS was fitted in September 1960 and the small cab numbers probably appeared after a 1963 Light Intermediate at Horwich. N.A. Machell.

43079

Built at Darlington 19/10/50

Works number 2121
Tender 4729

Improvements and modifications
New chimney arrangement   ?
Fitting A.W.S   23/9/60

Repairs

Date		Works
4/3/53-30/3/53	IL	Doncaster
23/11/53-5/12/53	NC	Darlington
11/10/54-26/10/54	NC	Doncaster
25/8/55-29/9/55	CL	Doncaster
1/8/56-5/9/56	IH	Doncaster
7/4/59-5/5/59	CL	Darlington
1/10/59-13/11/59	Gen	Darlington
13/9/60-23/9/60	NC	Darlington
4/63-17/5/63	IL	Horwich

Sheds
Dairycoates   19/10/50
Royston   3/10/65

Stored serviceable
5/9/65-3/10/65

Withdrawn w.e. 14/11/66

43079 in the early 1950s with its original guard irons and chimney. It was the fourth of the Dairycoates four to leave for Royston, in October 1965. www.rail-online.co.uk

43080

Built at Darlington 26/10/50

Works number   2122
Tender   4730

Improvements and modifications
New chimney arrangement   ?

Repairs

21/9/53-29/9/53	**NC**	Doncaster
21/12/53-6/2/54	**IH**	Stratford
15/1/57-26/1/57	**NC**	Doncaster
3/9/57-19/10/57	**Gen**	Doncaster
19/7/60-22/7/60	**NC**	Doncaster
31/1/62-8/3/62	**Gen**	Doncaster
24/7/64-1/10/64	**CL**	Darlington

Sheds

New England	26/10/50
Spital Bridge	28/2/54
New England	22/8/54
Boston	29/12/57
Colwick	30/12/62
Barrow Hill	1/65

Withdrawn 20/6/65

The first Darlington built one for the Eastern Region and M&GN operation, 43080 in 1961 at Boston; unlined with the small BR crest and still with tablet exchange apparatus. It was transferred to Boston in December 1957 when Spalding came under that shed's jurisdiction and remained there until the end of 1962 when it moved to Colwick, from where it was withdrawn in June 1965. www.rail-online.co.uk

43081

Built at Darlington 27/10/50

Works number   2123
Tender   4731

Improvements and modifications
New chimney arrangement   ?
Fitting A.W.S   ?

Repairs

Date	Type	Location
12/11/50-18/11/50	**Adj**	Darlington
21/5/52-10/6/52	**CL**	Doncaster
23/2/54-23/4/54	**IH**	Stratford
7/10/57-4/11/57	**Gen**	Doncaster
14/4/59-1/5/59	**CL**	Stratford
31/1/61-3/3/61	**Gen**	Doncaster

Sheds
New England   27/10/50

Withdrawn 3/1/65

43081 in the early 1950s with original guard irons and chimney; it was the only one of the large New England complement to remain there from delivery until withdrawal. www.rail-online.co.uk

43082

Built at Darlington 3/11/50

Works number 2124
Tender 4732

Improvements and modifications
New chimney arrangement ?
Fitting A.W.S ?

Repairs
5/4/54-29/5/54	**IH**	Stratford
23/5/58-8/8/58	**Gen**	Stratford
12/10/60-5/11/60	**NC**	Doncaster
15/3/63-25/4/63	**Gen**	Horwich

Sheds
New England	3/11/50
Barrow Hill	24/11/63
Langwith Junction	9/10/65

Withdrawn 14/11/65

43082 with two coaches in tow at Peterborough in June 1963. It had been repainted at Horwich with short lining and small cab numbers during a General repair from 15 March to 25 April 1963. Transferred away from New England in November to Barrow Hill, it was sent to Langwith Junction in late 1965, though this was probably one of those 'paper transfers' prior to withdrawal. www.rail-online.co.uk

43083

Built at Darlington 11/11/50

Works number 2125
Tender 4733

Improvements and modifications
New chimney arrangement ?

Repairs
5/5/53-10/6/53	**HI**	Doncaster
13/10/53-22/10/53	**NC**	Doncaster
3/6/56-14/7/56	**HI**	Doncaster
23/9/59-13/11/59	**Gen**	Stratford
28/6/60-5/7/60	**NC**	Doncaster
12/10/61-2/11/61	**CL**	Doncaster

Sheds
New England	11/11/50
Boston	29/12/57

Stored serviceable
1/12/63-22/12/63

Withdrawn w.e. 28/12/63

A stalwart of the M&GN at Bourne on 43083 20 May 1951, 43083 in original condition as delivered to New England the previous November. Its only other shed was Boston as part of the transfer of Spalding to the Lincoln District at the end of 1957. N. Fields.

43084

Built at Darlington 15/11/50

Works number   2126
Tender   4734

Improvements and modifications
New chimney arrangement   ?
Fitting A.W.S   ?

Repairs

? - p/e 15/10/55	**HI**	Doncaster
9/59	**H**	Stratford
Others not recorded		

Mileage/(weekdays out of service)

Sheds

New England	15/11/50
Grantham	25/5/52
New England	9/11/52
Barrow Hill	14/6/64
Stourton	18/7/65
Manningham	15/1/67
Wakefield	30/4/67
North Blyth	14/5/67
Normanton	25/6/67
Holbeck	9/7/67
Low Moor	27/8/67

Stored serviceable
30/4/67-14/5/67
27/8/67-9/9/67

Withdrawn w.e. 9/9/67

43084 engaged in some shunting in the early 1960s at Ramsey North, an ex-Great Northern and Great Eastern Joint station on the 13 mile long branch from Holme on the Huntingdon-Peterborough line. It had been closed to passengers in October 1947 although freight traffic survived until the 1970s. 43084 left New England in June 1964 for Barrow Hill but, unlike most of the others that were there at that date, it survived at various North Eastern Region sheds until September 1967. The AWS fitting date was not recorded.

43085

Built at Darlington 21/11/50

Works number   2127
Tender   4735

Improvements and modifications
New chimney arrangement   ?

Repairs
21/7/52-31/7/52	**NC**	Doncaster
13/4/54-5/6/54	**IH**	Stratford
4/6/57-13/7/57	**Gen**	Doncaster
21/5/60-22/7/60	**Gen**	Doncaster

Sheds
New England	21/11/50
Boston	29/12/57
Barrow Hill	30/11/63

Withdrawn w.e. 10/1/65

43085 moves off past one of the distinctive M&GN concrete post signals on 31 August 1958 at Gedney (between Spalding and Sutton Bridge) with the 10.53am Sunday Spalding-Hunstanton. It followed the common path from New England to Boston and then Barrow Hill in November 1963, from where it was withdrawn at the end of 1964. H. Ballantyne.

43086

Built at Darlington 24/11/50

Works number 2128
Tender 4736

Improvements and modifications
New chimney arrangement   ?

Repairs

17/2/54-15/4/54	**IH**	Stratford
10/3/58-9/5/58	**Gen**	Stratford
16/11/62-14/12/62	**HI**	Horwich

Sheds

New England	24/11/50
Melton Constable	24/6/57
New England	22/9/57
March	1/1/61
Cambridge	P/E 5/8/61
March	23/6/62
Lincoln	16/9/62
New England	11/1/64

Withdrawn 26/12/64

43086 approaches March level Crossing on 2 August 1960 with a very short fitted freight. After closure of the M&GN it stayed at New England until January 1961 when it moved to March for a few months. 43086 returned to Peterborough in January 1964 via Lincoln from September 1962 and was withdrawn by New England at the end of 1964. www.rail-online.co.uk

43087

Built at Darlington 29/11/50

Works number 2129
Tender 4737

Improvements and modifications
New chimney arrangement   11/5/54 est

Repairs
2/3/54-11/5/54	**IH**	Stratford
22/8/57-28/9/57	**Gen**	Doncaster
16/8/60-24/9/60	**Gen**	Doncaster
6/10/61-17/10/61	**CL**	Doncaster

Sheds
New England	29/11/50
Grantham	9/11/52
New England	23/11/52
Cambridge	23/6/57
Staveley	27/3/60
Grantham	4/11/62
Barrow Hill	12/5/63
New England	26/1/64

Withdrawn 26/12/64

43087 at Bletchley in March 1959. It was frequently found on the Cambridge-Oxford service while it was allocated to Cambridge between June 1957 and March 1960, when it left for Staveley. A. Swain, www.transporttreasury.co.uk

43088

Built at Darlington 1/12/50

Work number   2130
Tender   4738

Improvements and modifications
New chimney arrangement   ?
Fitting A.W.S   6/61

Repairs

1954	HI	Stratford
?-12/57	H	Doncaster
?-4/61	H	Doncaster
22/4/65-15/6/65	HI	Eastleigh

Sheds

New England	1/12/50
Barrow Hill	3/3/63
Crewe South	20/9/64 (loan)
Crewe South	10/10/64
Stoke	12/3/66
Croes Newydd	22/4/67 (loan)
Crewe South	3/6/67

Withdrawn w.e. 23/12/67

43088 at Stratford on 20 June 1954, was ex-works after a Heavy Intermediate repair there during which it received the new chimney arrangement. Its plain black was replaced in Stratford lined style, distinguishable by the central RA4 under the cab numbers. It was shedded at New England for over a decade, moving to Barrow Hill in March 1963. www.rail-online.co.uk

43089

Built at Darlington 7/12/50

Works number   2131
Tender   4739

Improvements and modifications
New chimney arrangement   ?
Fitting A.W.S   9/59

Repairs
11/12/51-12/12/51	**Adj**	Darlington
1954	**HI**	Stratford
2/56	**H**	Doncaster
9/59	**H**	Stratford
Others not recorded		

Sheds
New England	7/12/50
Neasden	8/4/51
Cambridge	22/8/54
Melton Constable	23/6/57
Cambridge	22/9/57
Kings Lynn	24/11/57
March	20/11/60
Staveley	27/11/60
Grimesthorpe	12/2/61
New England	9/7/61
Barrow Hill	14/6/64
Langwith	3/10/65

Withdrawn 14/11/65

Cambridge 4MT 43089 on 31 May 1956, waiting at Sandy probably with an Oxford to Cambridge train made up of ex-LMS stock. Sandy was effectively two stations side by side with separate buildings and stationmasters. This was the LNWR side building, demolished in the widening process of the 1970s. 43089 had been lined in Stratford style with the central RA4 under the cab numbers during a Heavy Intermediate there in 1954.

43090

Built at Darlington 9/12/50

Works number 2132
Tender 4740

Improvements and modifications
New chimney arrangement   ?
Fitting A.W.S   22/11/60

Repairs
19/12/50-20/12/50	**Adj**	Darlington
5/3/51-22/3/51	**NC**	Darlington
15/4/53-21/5/53	**IH**	Doncaster
21/9/55-1/11/55	**IH**	Doncaster
10/12/57-6/3/58	**Gen**	Stratford
21/10/60-22/11/60	**Gen**	Doncaster

Sheds
South Lynn	9/12/50
Kings Lynn	1/3/59
Staveley	27/11/60
Grantham	4/11/62
Barrow Hill	12/5/63

Withdrawn w.e. 11/4/65

Two schoolboys 'cabbing' 43090 on 16 July 1961 at Staveley GC shed. Unlined with a small BR crest, it had been fitted with AWS the previous November when it arrived at Staveley from Kings Lynn after spending its first years on the M&GN at South Lynn. It was withdrawn in April 1965. R.J. Buckley, Initial Photographics.

43091

Built at Darlington 13/12/50

Works number 2133
Tender 4741

Improvements and modifications
New chimney arrangement ?

Repairs
? - 2/58 **Gen** Stratford
? – 4/61 ? Doncaster
Others not recorded

Sheds
South Lynn 13/12/50
Boston 1/3/59
Colwick 5/1/64
Canklow 25/10/64

Withdrawn 6/6/65

43091 at Skegness in the early 1960s while allocated to Boston. It worked on the M&GN shedded at South Lynn from new until the line closed. www.colourrail.co.uk

43092

Built at Darlington 16/12/50

Works number 2134
Tender 4742

Improvements and modifications
New chimney arrangement ?

Repairs
? – 6/55   **Gen**   Stratford
1/58 – 2/58   ?   Stratford
? – 3/61   **H**   Doncaster
Others not recorded

Sheds
South Lynn   16/12/50
Boston   1/3/59
New England   5/1/64
Barrow Hill   9/1/65

Withdrawn 11/4/65

43092 newly repainted in unlined black, probably after a Heavy overhaul at Doncaster completed in March 1961. It was shedded at Boston at this time and moved to New England in January 1964 and then Barrow Hill in January 1965 for its last three months before withdrawal.

43093

Built at Darlington 20/12/50

Works number 2135
Tender 4743

Improvements and modifications
New chimney arrangement   ?

Repairs
29/12/50-2/1/51	**Adj**	Darlington
6/55-8/55	**Gen**	Stratford
? – 1/61	**H**	Doncaster
Others not recorded		

Sheds
South Lynn	20/12/50
Boston	1/3/59
Colwick	5/1/64
Canklow	25/10/64

Withdrawn 17/1/65

A work-stained 43093 from Boston, on shed at Doncaster around 1963. It moved to Colwick at the end of the year and then to Canklow in October before withdrawal three months later. www.rail-online.co.uk

43094

Built at Darlington 22/12/50

Works number   2136
Tender   4744

Improvements and modifications
New chimney arrangement   ?
Fitting A.W.S   5/11/60

Repairs

20/8/53-24/10/53	**HI**	Gorton
27/10/53-31/10/53	**Adj**	Gorton
16/5/57-6/7/57	**Gen**	Doncaster
13/10/59-22/1/60	**Gen**	Stratford
18/10/60-5/11/60	**NC**	Doncaster

Sheds

South Lynn	22/12/50
Swindon	27/2/51
South Lynn	15/10/51
Cambridge	28/10/51
South Lynn	10/10/52
Kings Lynn	1/3/59
Lincoln	18/9/60
New England	20/11/60

Withdrawn 5/1/64

43094 outside the old wooden shed at its South Lynn home on 25 April 1954. It was the 4MT subject to forensic examination at Swindon in 1951 which finally sorted out the steaming problems which characterised the early years of the class but still has its original chimney in this picture. It was also one of only two 4MTs which had a General overhaul at Gorton. When the M&GN closed in 1959 43094 moved the short distance to Kings Lynn and then to Lincoln briefly the following September before its final destination of New England two months later. 43094 was one of the first withdrawals, at the end of 1963. H.K. Boulter.

43095

Built at Darlington 23/12/50

Works number 2137
Tender 4745

Improvements and modifications
New chimney arrangement ?

Repairs

18/12/52-20/1/53	**Gen**	Doncaster
20/5/53-1/6/53	**CL**	Doncaster
7/2/55-1/4/55	**IH**	Stratford
15/11/57-18/1/58	**Gen**	Stratford
14/6/60-18/6/60	**NC**	Doncaster
7/3/62-13/4/62	**Gen**	Doncaster

Sheds

South Lynn	23/12/50
Boston	1/3/59
Lincoln	6/9/59
New England	11/1/64
Carnforth	10/10/64

Withdrawn w.e. 26/11/66

43095 at Stratford on 3 April 1955, newly repainted after a Heavy Intermediate overhaul. Characteristic central RA4 below the cab numbers, the works having ceased lining black engines a couple of months earlier. It was one of the last to be repaired there before Doncaster took over responsibility again for the Eastern Region 4MTs. It left the Region in October 1964 for Carnforth where it lasted until November 1966.

43096

Built at Darlington 29/12/50

Works number 2138
Tender 4746

Improvements and modifications
New chimney arrangement ?
Fitting A.W.S 11/11/60

Repairs

17/8/53-25/9/53	**IH**	Doncaster
8/10/54-4/11/54	**CH**	Doncaster
28/6/56-9/8/56	**Gen**	Doncaster
13/1/59-23/1/59	**NC**	Darlington
18/1/60-4/3/60	**Gen**	Darlington
26/4/60-3/5/60	**CL**	Darlington
27/10/60-11/11/60	**CL**	Darlington
1/3/63-29/3/63	**IL**	Horwich
18/3/65-3/4/65	**Unsch**	Cowlairs

Sheds

Selby	29/12/50
Neville Hill	6/6/57
Selby	15/9/57
York	13/9/59
Neville Hill	20/9/59
York	18/10/59
Dairycoates	11/6/61
Mirfield	22/7/62
Ardsley	9/12/62
Stourton	31/10/65
Manningham	11/12/66

Stored serviceable
17/6/62-23/7/62

Withdrawn 27/2/67

43096 fresh from the Paint Shop on 9 August 1956 at Doncaster after a General repair which began on 28 June. The BR emblem on the tender has been placed off centre to avoid the vertical rivets and the RA4 designation has been added at the lower rear edge of the cab side sheet. 43096 was always a North Eastern Region engine, starting at Selby and ending up at Manningham.

43097

Built at Darlington 24/1/51

Works number 2139
Tender 4747

Improvements and modifications
New chimney arrangement   ?
Fitting A.W.S   ?

Repairs
25/9/53-2/10/53	**NC**	Darlington
28/12/53-23/1/54	**Gen**	Doncaster
8/3/57-10/4/57	**Gen**	Doncaster
16/8/60-1/10/60	**Gen**	Darlington
1/2/65-19/3/65	**Inter**	Eastleigh

Sheds
Selby	24/1/51
Goole	13/9/59
York	29/7/62
North Blyth	21/8/66

Withdrawn 3/1/67

43097 early on, still with its original guard irons; it was the first Darlington built 4MT to be lined out. Allocated initially to Selby it was transferred to Goole in September 1959.

43098

Built at Darlington 1/2/51

Works number 2140
Tender 4748

Improvements and modifications
New chimney arrangement   ?
Fitting A.W.S   ?

Repairs
9/6/53-18/6/53	**NC**	Doncaster
15/9/53-24/9/53	**NC**	Darlington
5/3/54-1/4/54	**Gen**	Doncaster
30/3/57-2/5/57	**Gen**	Doncaster
26/11/57-7/12/57	**NC**	Doncaster
6/9/62-12/10/62	**Gen**	Horwich

Sheds
Selby	1/2/51
Goole	13/9/59
Normanton	3/10/65

Withdrawn 24/5/67

43099 at Darlington at an unrecorded date. It received its AWS equipment in late 1960 and was transferred to Normanton in October 1965, before moving to its last shed at Manningham where it was withdrawn in December 1966. S.B. Lee, colourrail.co.uk

43098 at its home shed of Selby on 14 August 1952. It still has the original guard irons and chimney and underneath the grime it was lined out. It went to Goole in September 1959 and stayed until October 1965 when it went to Normanton, from where it was withdrawn in May 1967. J. Robertson, www.transporttreasury.co.uk

43099

Built at Darlington 15/2/51

Works number 2141
Tender 4749

Improvements and modifications
New chimney arrangement   ?
Fitting A.W.S   ?

Repairs

3/8/53-2/10/53	IH	Doncaster
24/4/56-4/5/56	NC	Doncaster
25/10/56-5/12/56	IH	Doncaster
4/7/57-20/7/57	NC	Doncaster
12/8/60-8/10/60	Gen	Darlington
7/6/62-20/6/62	Tdr	Darlington
25/8/64-16/10/64	Unsch	Darlington

Sheds

Dairycoates	15/2/51
Copley Hill	14/6/59
Ardsley	4/10/59
Darlington	1/11/59
Normanton	3/10/65
Manningham	29/10/66

Stored serviceable
23/5/65-3/10/65

Withdrawn 7/12/66

43099 at Darlington at an unrecorded date. It received its AWS equipment in late 1960 and was transferred to Normanton in October 1965, before moving to its last shed at Manningham where it was withdrawn in December 1966. S.B. Lee, colourrail.co.uk

43100

Built at Darlington 19/2/51

Works number 2142
Tender 4750

Improvements and modifications
New chimney arrangement   ?
Fitting A.W.S   6/7/60

Repairs

8/7/53-6/8/53	IH	Doncaster
20/10/53-29/10/53	NC	Darlington
25/7/55-4/8/55	NC	Doncaster
12/7/56-25/8/56	IH	Doncaster
23/5/60-6/7/60	Gen	Doncaster
27/9/60	Weigh	Darlington
25/5/62-15/6/62	CL	Darlington
27/11/62-12/62	NC	Darlington
19/6/64-11/7/64	IL	Cowlairs
15/7/64-18/7/64	CL	Cowlairs

Sheds

Dairycoates	19/2/51
Copley Hill	14/6/59
Ardsley	4/10/59
West Hartlepool	1/11/59

Stored serviceable
16/6/63-28/7/63

Withdrawn 5/2/67

43100 in August 1962 at Hart near Billingham, possibly on PW work since there is no brake van behind the bogie bolster wagons. It was fitted with AWS in July 1960 while shedded at West Hartlepool, having reached there from Dairycoates via short spells in 1959 at Copley Hill and Ardsley; it was withdrawn in February 1967. N.E. Preedy.

43101

Built at Darlington 23/2/51

Works number   2143
Tender   4751

Improvements and modifications
New chimney arrangement   ?
Fitting A.W.S   2/11/62

Repairs

15/9/53-15/10/53	**Gen**	Doncaster
29/7/55-10/8/55	**NC**	Doncaster
29/7/57-27/8/57	**Gen**	Doncaster
6/4/61-19/4/61	**NC**	Darlington
26/9/62-2/11/62	**Gen**	Horwich
7/2/63-27/2/63	**NC**	Horwich
24/9/64-25/9/64	**Weigh**	Darlington

Sheds

Dairycoates	23/2/51
Middlesbrough	1/6/52
Kirkby Stephen	13/11/55
Gateshead	10/6/56
Heaton	25/11/56
Ardsley	16/6/57
Low Moor	15/9/57
Ardsley	8/6/58
Wakefield	7/6/59
Thornaby	5/3/61
Wakefield	29/7/62
Copley Hill	5/1/64
Ardsley	6/9/64
North Blyth	31/10/65

Stored serviceable
25/3/62-29/7/62

Withdrawn 27/3/67

43101 at Hull Botanic Gardens shed on 29 July 1951. It had been delivered new to Dairycoates in February but was not to stay on Humberside for long, departing to Middlesbrough in June 1952. This was the first of around a dozen moves before its final shed at North Blyth in late 1965 from where it was withdrawn in March 1967. B.G. Tweed.

43102

Built at Darlington 8/3/51

Works number 2144
Tender 4752

Improvements and modifications
New chimney arrangement   ?
Fitting A.W.S   4/5/61

Repairs
19/8/53	**NC**	Doncaster
26/8/53-30/9/53	**IH**	Doncaster
17/12/57-28/12/57	**NC**	Doncaster
20/3/59-30/4/59	**Gen**	Darlington
19/1/60-27/1/60	**NC**	Darlington
25/4/61-4/5/61	**NC**	Darlington
5/3/64-6/3/64	**Unsch**	Darlington
10/4/64	**Unsch**	Cowlairs

Sheds
Dairycoates	8/3/51
Middlesbrough	1/6/52
Thornaby	1/6/58
Darlington	11/9/60
Stourton	3/10/65

Stored serviceable
23/5/65-3/10/65

Withdrawn w.e. 7/12/66

The only known photograph of an Ivatt 2-0-0. The whole rear weight of Darlington's 43102 is carried on a couple of sleepers but all is quite safe with the pony wheels chocked. The half open top tender cab completes an odd scene. 43102 had been fitted with AWS in May 1961 and left Darlington for Stourton in October 1965, being withdrawn there in December 1966. www.rail-online.co.uk

43103

Built at Darlington 9/3/51

Works number 2145
Tender 4753

Improvements and modifications
New chimney arrangement   ?
Fitting A.W.S   2/10/61

Repairs

16/12/52-30/12/52	**CL**	Doncaster
28/9/53-24/10/53	**IH**	Doncaster
29/4/54-7/5/54	**NC**	Doncaster
15/1/57-23/2/57	**HG**	Doncaster
25/9/59-12/11/59	**HI**	Horwich
18/9/61-2/10/61	**NC(EO)**	Horwich
13/3/63-11/4/63	**Gen**	Horwich

Mileage/(weekdays out of service)

1956	19,472
1957	17,151
1958	21,272
1959	17,850
1960	32,148

Sheds

Dairycoates	9/3/51
Saltley	16/5/59 (loan)
Saltley	23/5/59
Kirkby Stephen	23/4/60 (loan)
Kirkby Stephen	25/6/60
Carlisle Kingmoor	9/7/60
Carnforth	24/10/64

Withdrawn w.e. 19/11/66

43103 on 13 July 1963 at Carlisle Kingmoor had been repainted in Horwich style with small numbers and short lining during a General repair there a few months earlier. The AWS had been fitted in October 1961, after its arrival at Kingmoor in July 1960 where it stayed until October 1964 when it was transferred to Carnforth, remaining there until withdrawn in November 1966. colourrail.co.uk

43104

Built at Darlington 16/3/51

Works number   2146
Tender   4754

Improvements and modifications
New chimney arrangement   ?

Repairs

26/4/53-29/5/53	**HI**	Doncaster
29/10/53-7/1/54	**NC**	Doncaster
24/8/55-1/10/55	**HI**	Doncaster
10/4/58-15/4/58	**NC**	Stratford
6/1/59-13/2/59	**Gen**	Stratford
15/6/60-18/6/60	**NC**	Doncaster

Sheds

South Lynn	16/3/51
Boston	1/3/59
Lincoln	6/9/59

Withdrawn 5/1/64

43104 from South Lynn at Stratford on 20 April 1958 after a short Unclassified repair completed a few days earlier. It left the M&GN on closure for Boston and quickly moved on to Lincoln in September 1959 and was an early withdrawal from there at the end of 1963.

43105

Built at Darlington 30/3/51

Works number   2147
Tender   4755

Improvements and modifications
New chimney arrangement   ?

Repairs

20/8/51-23/8/51	**CL**	Darlington
16/6/53-27/7/53	**HI**	Doncaster
14/1/54-22/1/54	**NC**	Doncaster
26/8/55-8/10/55	**HI**	Doncaster
24/4/56-3/5/56	**CL**	Doncaster
23/3/57-30/3/57	**HC**	Doncaster
1/4/59-15/5/59	**Gen**	Stratford
28/11/60-20/12/60	**LC**	Doncaster
19/12/62-25/1/63	**HI**	Horwich

Sheds

South Lynn	30/3/51
Stratford	1/3/59
Cambridge	P/E 5/8/61
March	23/6/62
Lincoln	16/9/62
New England	11/1/64
Carnforth	10/10/64

Withdrawn w.e. 27/5/67

43105 cutting a modern dash among the LNER types at South Lynn in April 1953. When the M&GN closed in 1959 it moved to Stratford and within a month went to the works there for a General repair. It was one of a handful of 4MTs to be repaired at Stratford around this time, Doncaster having taking over responsibility for them some years earlier. J.T. Clewley, transporttreasury.co.uk

43106

Built at Darlington 10/4/51

Works number 2148
Tender 4756

Improvements and modifications
New chimney arrangement   ?
Fitting A.W.S   26/1/63 PE

Repairs
2/6/53-10/7/53	HI	Doncaster
16/7/55 PE	LC	Shed
29/8/55-7/10/55	HI	Doncaster
20/4/57 PE	L	Shed
24/6/58-29/8/58	HI	Horwich
14/11/58-12/12/58	NC(EO)	Horwich
6/11/59-4/2/60	HC	Horwich
28/8/61-3/11/61	HI	Horwich
6/8/65-24/9/65	HI	Eastleigh

Mileage/(weekdays out of service)
1958	17,729 (123)
1959	25,647
1960	24,863

Sheds
South Lynn	10/4/51
Woodford Halse	8/7/56
Saltley	31/3/62
Wellingborough	23/6/62
Kettering	23/3/63
Trafford Park	17/8/63
Heaton Mersey	21/9/63
Carlisle Kingmoor	27/8/66
Lostock Hall	23/9/67

Stored serviceable
13/5/63-5/8/63
29/11/65-18/8/66

Withdrawn w.e. 22/6/68

43106, the only 4MT to be preserved, moved around the country during its time in BR service and was shedded at Woodford Halse when this picture was taken at Neasden on 3 June 1961. Intriguingly the smokebox plate has been moved from the usual position, something which was only done on other 4MTs in 1964/65 after repairs at Swindon and Eastleigh. It has Horwich style short lining to avoid the tablet catcher cut-out and small numbers and BR crest; it was not fitted with AWS until January 1963.

43107

Built at Doncaster 18/5/51

Works number   2077
Tender   4757

Improvements and modifications
New chimney arrangement   ?

Repairs
16/3/54-21/5/54	**HI**	Stratford
19/12/56-30/1/57	**HI**	Doncaster
29/12/58-2/1/59	**CL**	Stratford
28/9/59-27/11/59	**Gen**	Stratford
5/7/60-8/7/60	**NC**	Doncaster

Sheds
New England	18/5/51
South Lynn	17/6/51
Neasden	1/3/53
South Lynn	11/7/54
Boston	1/3/59

Withdrawn 28/12/63

43107, the first 4MT built with guard irons fixed to the pony truck, at Boston on 13 July 1963. Along with 43108-43111 it was originally to be built at Darlington but the order was transferred to Doncaster. This resulted in the motion of 43107 being stamped 43137, which was the next planned Doncaster engine after 43096. It was based on the M&GN at South Lynn until 1959 apart from a spell at Neasden in 1953/54 along with several others where they were dedicated to a particular group of freight workings. After the M&GN 43107 went to Boston and was withdrawn in December 1963. www.rail-online.co.uk

43108

Built at Doncaster 25/5/51

Works number 2078
Tender 4758

Improvements and modifications
New chimney arrangement ?

Repairs
15/7/53-19/8/53	**IH**	Doncaster
28/7/55-30/9/55	**Gen**	Stratford
21/4/58-20/6/58	**Gen**	Stratford
21/1/60-20/2/60	**CL**	Doncaster
26/3/62-11/5/62	**Gen**	Doncaster
9/3/64-9/4/64	**Cas**	Darlington

Sheds
New England	25/5/51
South Lynn	17/6/51
Boston	1/3/59
Colwick	26/7/59
Boston	22/1/61
Colwick	30/12/62
New England	5/1/64
Barrow Hill	3/1/65
Canklow	13/3/65
Langwith Junction	9/10/65

Withdrawn 14/11/65

43108 was one of sixteen 4MTs transferred to Boston after closure of the M&GN, but was quickly moved to Colwick although it returned to Boston in January 1961 until the end of 1962. Thus it was allocated to Boston when photographed at Colwick on 24 June 1962. 43108 lost its lining during a late General overhaul at Stratford completed in June 1958.

196

43109

Built at Doncaster 4/6/51

Works number   2079
Tender   4759

Improvements and modifications
New chimney arrangement   ?

Repairs
31/3/53-8/5/53	**IH**	Doncaster
25/5/55-5/7/55	**IH**	Doncaster
16/9/57-19/10/57	**Gen**	Doncaster
2/1/61-4/2/61	**Gen**	Doncaster
11/2/64-4/7/64	**Cas**	Swindon

Sheds
South Lynn	4/6/51
Boston	1/3/59
Barrow Hill	24/11/63
Canklow	13/3/65
Langwith Junction	9/10/65

Withdrawn 14/11/65

43109 in the early 1960s at Boston in the typical unkempt condition of the time. It was unlined and had been fitted with Overhead Warning plates. 43109 had arrived from South Lynn on 1 March 1959 with its fellow 4MTs and stayed at Boston until November 1963 when it moved to Barrow Hill. www.rail-online.co.uk

43110

Built at Doncaster 14/6/51

Works number 2080
Tender 4760

Improvements and modifications
New chimney arrangement ?

Repairs
22/7/53-26/8/53	**HI**	Doncaster
11/10/55-12/11/55	**HI**	Doncaster
11/4/57-18/4/57	**NC**	Doncaster
3/4/59-23/5/59	**Gen**	Stratford
9/7/60-15/7/60	**NC**	Doncaster
11/8/60-26/8/60	**NC**	Doncaster

Sheds
South Lynn	14/6/51
Kings Lynn	16/6/57
South Lynn	25/8/57
Boston	1/3/59

Stored serviceable
1/3/59-24/3/59

Withdrawn w.e. 28/12/63

43110 in front of the old shed at South Lynn in April 1953. It still has its original chimney and shows the Doncaster style of lining, widely spaced and with a gap to avoid the tablet catcher cut-out. 43110 went to Boston when the M&GN closed and was withdrawn there in December 1963. J.F. Clewley, www.transporttreasury.co.uk

43111

Built at Doncaster 4/7/51

Works number 2081
Tender 4761

Improvements and modifications
New chimney arrangement   ?
Fitting A.W.S   8/61

Repairs
11/53-?	?	Stratford
1/56-2/56	H	Doncaster
? - 5/58	H	Stratford
? – 8/61	H	Doncaster
Others not recorded		

Sheds
South Lynn	4/7/51
Boston	1/3/59
Colwick	26/7/59
Grimesthorpe	8/11/59
Barrow Hill	23/4/61
Grantham	4/11/62
Barrow Hill	18/5/63

Withdrawn w.e. 20/6/65

43111 had already lost its lined livery by 29 October 1956 when this photograph was taken at South Lynn. It had been given the new taller chimney by this date. Like most of the South Lynn 4MTs it went to Boston in March 1959. L.G. Marshall.

43112

Built at Horwich 29/3/51

Boiler 13733
Tender 4762

Improvements and modifications
New chimney arrangement   24/12/53
Fitting A.W.S   16/11/61

Repairs
16/11/53-24/12/53	LI	Horwich
8/8/57-5/9/57	HG	Horwich
19/2/59-17/4/59	LC(EO)	Horwich
6/3/61-9/5/61	LI	Horwich
25/10/61-16/11/61	NC(EO)	Horwich
?- 12/64	?	Swindon

Mileage/(weekdays out of service)
1951	22,077 (21)
1952	30,460 (32)
1953	25,181 (80)
1954	30,456 (39)
1955	25,773 (72)
1956	25,606 (69)
1957	21,692 (102)
1958	27,274 (70)
1959	33,402
1960	33,928

Sheds
Skipton	29/3/51
Lancaster	25/10/58 (loan)
Nuneaton	17/2/62
Northampton	16/6/62
Bescot	20/10/62
Stoke	21/9/63
Crewe South	12/8/67

Stored serviceable
7/8/67-15/9/67

Withdrawn w.e. 16/9/67

43112 at Swindon in late 1964 with the usual smokebox changes applied. It was the first engine from the final Horwich batch and went new to Skipton in March 1951. Its LMR peregrinations took it to Lancaster in 1958, Nuneaton, Northampton and Bescot in 1962 and then to Stoke in September 1963 before finally landing up at Crewe South in August 1967, to be withdrawn the following month. It was fitted with AWS in November 1961. J.N. Smith, transporttreasury.co.uk

43113

Built at Horwich 13/4/51

Boiler 13734
Tender 4763

Improvements and modifications
New chimney arrangement   28/10/55
Fitting A.W.S   28/9/61

Repairs
28/5/51-7/6/51	LC	Horwich
24/3/53-7/5/53	LI	Horwich
23/7/53-19/8/53	LC(EO)	Horwich
27/9/55-28/10/55	HG	Horwich
2/5/56-17/5/56	NC	Horwich
6/5/57-18/5/57	LC(EO)	Horwich
16/6/58-31/7/58	HI	Horwich
6/9/60-25/11/60	HG	Horwich
11/9/61-28/9/61	NC(EO)	Horwich
5/1/62-23/1/62	LC	Horwich
29/3/62-11/4/62	LC	Horwich
1/8/62-17/8/62	LC	Horwich

Mileage/(weekdays out of service)
1951	20,168 (26)
1952	30,028 (53)
1953	19,946 (133)
1954	24,468 (90)
1955	21,360 (104)
1956	28,087 (62)
1957	25,882 (71)
1958	27,180 (94)
1959	43,311
1960	29,502

Sheds
Skipton	13/4/51
Lancaster	25/10/58 (loan)
Nuneaton	17/2/62
Crewe South	20/10/62

Withdrawn w.e. 3/9/66

43113 at Horwich on 7 April 1962 during a Light Casual repair. It had received its AWS in the previous September. D. Forsyth, colourrail.co.uk

43114

Built at Horwich 9/5/51

Boiler 13735
Tender 4764

Improvements and modifications
New chimney arrangement   11/8/53
Fitting A.W.S   11/5/61

Repairs
25/6/53-11/8/53	**LC(EO)**	Horwich
6/5/54-11/6/54	**LI**	Horwich
7/7/55-10/8/55	**LC**	Horwich
16/8/56-28/9/56	**HG**	Horwich
1/6/59-8/7/59	**Gen**	Darlington
4/5/61-11/5/61	**NC**	Darlington

Mileage/(weekdays out of service)
1951	16,917(17)
1952	26,288(31)
1953	21,185(67)
1954	20,182(84)
1955	21,947(82)
1956	26,306(70)

Sheds
Sheffield	9/5/51
Leeds	24/3/56
Normanton	30/6/56

Withdrawn w.e. 30/11/63

43114 on a proper 4F duty at Dore with a coal train in the early 1950s. It had the dubious distinction of being the first of the class to be withdrawn, in week ending 30 November 1963. www.rail-online.co.uk

43115

Built at Horwich 19/5/51

Boiler 13736
Tender 4765

Improvements and modifications
New chimney arrangement   5/5/54
Fitting A.W.S   15/9/61

Repairs
21/2/53-18/3/53	LO	Horwich
29/3/54-5/5/54	LI	Horwich
4/5/55-23/6/55	LC	Horwich
16/3/57-17/4/57	HG	Horwich
2/5/60-16/6/60	HI	Horwich
28/8/61-15/9/61	NC(EO)	Horwich
20/5/64-1/10/64	HC	Swindon

Mileage/(weekdays out of service)
1951	15,193 (16)
1952	24,191 (35)
1953	25,556 (56)
1954	23,314 (65)
1955	23,014 (74)
1956	24,139 (56)
1957	23,753 (63)
1958	30,353 (54)
1959	38,822
1960	36,744

Sheds
Sheffield 19/5/51	
Derby	23/11/57
Lancaster	4/10/58 (loan)
Lancaster	8/11/58
Nuneaton	17/2/62
Northampton	16/6/62
Bescot	20/10/62
Stoke	21/9/63

Withdrawn w.e. 27/5/67

43115 at Bescot in June 1963, still with the pre-1957 BR crest. It was transferred there from Northampton in October 1962 and moved to its final shed, Stoke, the following September and was withdrawn there in May 1967. 43115 received its AWS in September 1961.

43116

Built at Horwich 1/6/51

Boiler 13737
Tender 4766

Improvements and modifications
New chimney arrangement   11/6/53
Fitting A.W.S   8/6/61

Repairs

4/5/53-11/6/53	**LI**	Horwich
21/5/54-24/6/54	**HI**	Horwich
15/11/56-18/12/56	**HG**	Horwich
21/3/60-3/5/60	**Gen**	Darlington
31/5/61-8/6/61	**NC**	Darlington

Mileage/(weekdays out of service)

1951	22,555 (13)
1952	34,067 (46)
1953	34,566 (48)
1954	33,331 (68)
1955	34,628 (51)
1956	29,192 (87)

Sheds

Leeds	1/6/51
Normanton	30/6/56

Withdrawn w.e. 22/5/66

43116 on local passenger duty at Hellifield on 23 July 1953. It had acquired the new chimney arrangement the month before during a Light Intermediate overhaul at Horwich. It was allocated at the time to Leeds Holbeck and remained there until June 1956 when it was transferred to Normanton. M.N. Bland, www.transporttreasury.co.uk

43117

Built at Horwich 9/6/51

Boiler 13738
Tender 4767

Improvements and modifications
New chimney arrangement ?
Fitting A.W.S 20/5/61

Repairs

5/3/53-8/4/53	LI	Horwich
15/6/56-10/8/56	HG	Horwich
?-27/2/67	CL	Doncaster
3/9/57-3/10/57	CL	Doncaster
10/2/59-20/3/59	Gen	Darlington
11/5/61-20/5/61	NC	Darlington
1/3/62-25/5/62	Gen	Darlington
27/9/65-12/11/65	CL	Darlington

Mileage/(weekdays out of service)

1951	20,635 (13)
1952	37,774 (30)
1953	32,865 (48)
1954	35,328 (42)
1955	28,398 (75)
1956	25,283 (101)

Sheds

Leeds	9/6/51
Stourton	3/10/65
Wakefield	30/4/67
North Blyth	14/5/67

Stored serviceable
30/4/67-14/5/67

Withdrawn 1/7/67

43117 at Kingmoor on 21 August 1952. Always a North Eastern engine, it finished up at North Blyth in May 1967, from where it was withdrawn at the end of the next month. transporttreasury.co.uk

43118

Built at Horwich 21/6/51

Boiler	13739
Tender	4768

Improvements and modifications
New chimney arrangement   15/1/54

Repairs
4/3/53-18/3/53		Horwich
11/12/53-15/1/54	**LI**	Horwich
13/10/56-16/11/56	**HG**	Horwich
19/9/60-18/11/60	**HI**	Horwich
21/11/63-3/1/64	**Gen**	Horwich

Mileage/(weekdays out of service)
1951	15,101 (14)
1952	29,995 (19)
1953	18,694 (63)
1954	25,959 (33)
1955	20,218 (83)
1956	20,181 (49)
1957	19,964 (37)
1958	19,941 (56)
1959	11,163
1960	12,178

Sheds
Nottingham	21/6/51
Cricklewood	1/11/52
Wellingborough	22/9/62
Stoke	22/9/63 (loan)
Stoke	12/10/63
Lower Darwen	6/2/65
Lostock Hall	19/2/66
Workington	11/3/67

Stored serviceable
29/7/63-16/9/63

Withdrawn w.e. 18/11/67

The usual shabbiness brightened up with white painted and polished number and shed plates on 43118 at Lostock Hall on 3 July 1966. The absence of AWS indicates a previous life on the Midland Division. D. Hawkins.

43119

Built at Horwich 30/6/51

Boiler 13740
Tender 4769

Improvements and modifications
New chimney arrangement   19/12/53

Repairs

9/1/53-5/2/53	**LC(EO)**	Horwich
17/4/53-12/5/53	**LC(EO)**	Horwich
12/11/53-19/12/53	**LI**	Horwich
12/4/56-26/5/56	**HG**	Horwich
11/10/58-28/11/58	**HI**	Horwich
21/3/59-13/4/59	**LC(EO)**	Horwich
22/8/63-11/10/63	**Gen**	Horwich
2/1/64-21/1/64	**Gen**	Darlington
11/3/65-16/3/65	**LC**	Eastleigh

Mileage/(weekdays out of service)

1951	15,922 (10)
1952	31,686 (29)
1953	22,000 (97)
1954	34,227 (34)
1955	27,608 (66)
1956	14,692 (101)
1957	17,311 (45)
1958	12,326 (122)
1959	10,672
1960	17,421

Sheds

Nottingham	30/6/51
St Albans	1/10/55
Cricklewood	16/1/60
Wellingborough	22/9/62
Kettering	30/3/63
Trafford Park	17/8/63
Lower Darwen	13/2/65
Lostock Hall	19/2/66
Tebay	26/11/66
Carnforth	31/12/66
Lostock Hall	24/6/67

Stored serviceable
13/5/63-5/8/63

Withdrawn w.e. 12/8/67

43119 entering Preston, 26 October 1963. 43119 went new to Nottingham but moved to St Albans in October 1955 and took over the Johnson 3F 0-6-0 duty on the freight-only Harpenden to Hemel Hempstead branch. It stayed there until January 1960 when it was transferred to Cricklewood before moving a further eight times, eventually arriving at Lostock Hall in June 1967, only to be withdrawn two months later. transporttreasury.co.uk

43120

Built at Horwich 11/7/51

Boiler 13742
Tender 4770

Improvements and modifications
New chimney arrangement   29/5/54

Repairs

18/12/52-14/1/53	LC(EO)	Horwich
27/4/54-29/5/54	LI	Horwich
13/4/55-13/5/55	LC	Horwich
28/11/55-6/1/56	LC	Horwich
10/9/56-17/10/56	HG	Horwich
17/2/59-2/4/59	HI	Horwich
20/2/63-22/3/63	Gen	Horwich
25/6/64-6/11/64	LC	Swindon

Mileage/(weekdays out of service)

1951	14,358	(16)
1952	30,434	(27)
1953	23,752	(27)
1954	24,105	(41)
1955	17,154	(94)
1956	19,253	(68)
1957	21,911	(52)
1958	18,933	(53)
1959	15,575	
1960	18,988	

Sheds

Cricklewood	11/7/51
Wellingborough	22/9/62
Heaton Mersey	14/12/63 (loan)
Heaton Mersey	4/1/64
Carlisle Kingmoor	19/6/65

Withdrawn w.e. 26/8/67

43120 at Swindon Works on the engine reception/exit roads, parallel to the main line in front of the main building. By chance another LMR mogul, Stanier 5MT 42954, having completed its overhaul by the look of it, is on the adjacent road. 43120 was in Wiltshire for a desultory five months, from June until November 1964. www.rail-online.co.uk

43121

Built at Horwich 10/8/51

Boiler 13741
Tender 4771

Improvements and modifications
New chimney arrangement   28/8/54
Fitting A.W.S   16/11/62

Repairs
20/7/54-28/8/54	**LI**	Horwich
28/11/56-9/1/57	**HG**	Horwich
18/12/58-6/2/59	**LC(EO)**	Horwich
2/7/59-1/9/59	**HI**	Horwich
2/2/60-22/3/60	**LC**	Horwich
10/11/62-16/11/62	**Gen**	Horwich

Mileage/(weekdays out of service)
1951	13,995	(11)
1952	30,613	(20)
1953	20,420	(46)
1954	21,432	(65)
1955	25,445	(58)
1956	21,713	(69)
1957	22,804	(36)
1958	18,277	(48)
1959	14,693	
1960	15,042	

Sheds
Cricklewood	10/8/51
Wellingborough	22/9/62
Heaton Mersey	14/12/63 (loan)
Heaton Mersey	4/1/64
Carlisle Kingmoor	19/6/65

Withdrawn w.e. 18/11/67

43121 at one of the ex-L&Y sheds (to judge from the water column) which formed its usual habitat in the last years after it had left the Midland Division. It had been one of four Ivatt 4s at Cricklewood in the 1950s, used on transfer freight work but also on passenger duties when required; in fact they often hauled boat trains from St Pancras to Tilbury (Riverside). 43121 even turned up at Liverpool Street on 16 May 1961 with a Tilbury boat train when it was diverted because the usual route was blocked. colourrail.co.uk

43122

Built at Horwich 21/8/51

Boiler 13775
Tender 4772

Improvements and modifications
New chimney arrangement   ?
Fitting A.W.S   7/10/62 PE

Repairs

26/9/57-26/10/57	**HG**	Doncaster
15/11/60-13/1/61	**HI**	Horwich
19/1/61-31/1/61	**NC(Rec)**	Horwich
23/11/64-21/1/65	**LC**	Eastleigh

Mileage/(weekdays out of service)

1956	15,832
1957	19,347
1958	24,488
1959	22,495
1960	24,212

Sheds

Dairycoates	21/8/51
Kirkby Stephen	22/5/55
Dairycoates	10/6/56
Saltley	16/5/59 (loan)
Saltley	23/5/59
Bletchley	28/11/64
Workington	10/7/65 (loan)
Workington	24/7/65

Withdrawn w.e. 18/3/67

43122 at Haresfield on 29 July 1961 with the 1.18pm Gloucester to Bristol stopping train. Originally a Dairycoates engine it was one of six transferred to Kirkby Stephen in 1955/6 for freight work over the Stainmore summit. 43122 returned to Hull until 1959 when it moved to Saltley for five years before a short stay at Bletchley from late 1964 until July 1965 and its final shed, Workington, until withdrawal in March 1967. B.W.L. Brooksbank, Initial Photographics.

43123

Built at Horwich 30/8/51

Tender 4773

Improvements and modifications
New chimney arrangement   ?
Fitting A.W.S   1/10/60

Repairs

30/11/53-11/12/53	**NC**	Doncaster
21/7/54-20/8/54	**IH**	Doncaster
4/7/55-21/7/55	**CL**	Doncaster
9/3/56-4/4/56	**CH**	Doncaster
14/7/58-13/8/58	**Gen**	Doncaster
13/9/60-1/10/60	**NC**	Doncaster
5/1/61-10/3/61	**Gen**	Darlington
13/12/62-22/12/62	**NC**	Darlington
18/9/64-14/10/64	**Unsch**	Darlington

Sheds

Selby	30/8/51
Dairycoates	13/9/59
West Hartlepool	11/6/61
York	24/4/66
North Blyth	23/10/66

Stored serviceable
13/3/66-24/4/66

Withdrawn w.e. 1/7/67

The white paint has been out to highlight the smokebox plates on 43123 at its home depot of Selby. It was there until September 1959 when it moved the short distance to Hull Dairycoates and was equipped with AWS in October 1960.
www.rail-online.co.uk

43124

Built at Horwich 13/9/51

Tender 4774

Improvements and modifications
New chimney arrangement   ?
Fitting A.W.S   16/3/61

Repairs
26/3/54-28/4/54	**IH**	Doncaster
15/12/54-11/1/55	**CL**	Doncaster
7/6/56-27/7/56	**Gen**	Doncaster
19/10/56-25/10/56	**NC**	Doncaster
4/4/60-13/5/60	**Gen**	Darlington
2/2/61-16/3/61	**CL**	Darlington
15/3/63-19/4/63	**IH**	Horwich
19/6/64-26/6/64	**NC**	Cowlairs

Sheds
Dairycoates	13/9/51
Kirkby Stephen	22/5/55
Darlington	1/7/56
Holbeck	15/9/57

Withdrawn 7/12/66

Holbeck's 43124 passes through Bingley on 7 July 1958 with an excursion made up of BR, LMS and pre-grouping stock. G.W. Sharpe.

43125

Built at Horwich 21/9/51

Tender 4775

Improvements and modifications
New chimney arrangement   ?
Fitting A.W.S   19/5/61

Repairs
7/4/55-12/5/55	**Gen**	Doncaster
24/10/57-27/11/57	**Gen**	Doncaster
11/5/61-19/5/61	**NC**	Darlington
10/5/62-6/7/62	**Gen**	Darlington

Sheds
Dairycoates	21/9/51
Heaton	3/11/51
Selby	16/5/54
West Auckland	22/5/55
Selby	10/6/56
Goole	13/9/59
Normanton	3/10/65
Manningham	27/2/67
Wakefield	30/4/67
Normanton	25/6/67

Stored serviceable
30/6/67-25/6/67

Withdrawn 9/9/67

43125 in the early 1960s at Goole alongside an Austerity 2-8-0, one of the engines which may have influenced the design of the 4MTs. It has had a Darlington repaint with wide spaced lining, large cab numbers and BR crest, and had AWS from May 1961. 43125 stayed on the North Eastern Region from new until withdrawn from Normanton in September 1967. www.rail-online.co.uk

43126

Built at Horwich 29/9/51

Tender 4776

Improvements and modifications
New chimney arrangement ?
Fitting A.W.S 5/5/61

Repairs
22/9/54-22/10/54	**IH**	Doncaster
24/3/59-6/5/59	**Gen**	Darlington
25/4/61-5/5/61	**NC**	Darlington
22/6/61-1/8/61	**CL**	Darlington

Sheds
Dairycoates	29/9/51
Heaton	3/11/51
Alston	7/6/53
Blaydon	28/3/54
Heaton	26/6/55
Ardsley	16/6/57
Sowerby Bridge	15/9/57
Heaton	19/7/59
Gateshead	12/6/60
Sunderland	11/9/60
Heaton	5/2/61
Gateshead	28/5/61
South Blyth	20/8/61
York	10/9/61

Withdrawn 5/4/66

43126 inside York shed; it was well travelled around the NER until it reached York from South Blyth in September 1961, staying until withdrawal in April 1966. Its tender was exchanged with that of 43133, which had a tablet catcher cut-out, while under repair at Darlington in July 1961; the AWS had been fitted there earlier in the year at a Non Classified visit for the purpose. transporttreasury.co.uk

43127

Built at Horwich 12/10/51

Tender 4777

Improvements and modifications
New chimney arrangement   ?
Fitting A.W.S   ?

Repairs
2/10/53-9/1/54	**Gen**	Gorton
26/9/56-27/10/56	**Gen**	Doncaster
27/11/59-14/1/60	**IH**	Doncaster
23/1/61-26/1/61	**NC**	Doncaster

Sheds
Dairycoates	12/10/51
Neasden	30/3/52
New England	18/7/54
Spital Bridge	22/8/54
New England	31/1/60
Retford	7/5/61
Barrow Hill	1/6/63 PE

Withdrawn w.e. 10/1/65

A grimy 43127 basks in the sunshine at Stamford Town on 22 June 1960. It had been fitted with AWS earlier in the year. It was one of only two 4MTs to be repaired at Gorton in late 1953 when the Eastern Region briefly made the Manchester works responsible for 4MT repairs, before deciding to send them to Stratford instead. Originally lined, it was painted plain black during a Heavy Intermediate overhaul at Doncaster completed in January 1960.

43128

Built at Horwich 20/10/51

Tender 4778

Improvements and modifications
New chimney arrangement   3/3/55
Fitting A.W.S   ?

Repairs

29/12/52-9/1/53	**CL**	Darlington
3/2/55-3/3/55	**IH**	Doncaster
21/8/56-5/9/56	**NC**	Doncaster
23/10/57-23/11/57	**Gen**	Doncaster
2/2/60-8/4/60	**CL**	Darlington
29/8/62-5/10/62	**Gen**	Horwich
24/2/64	**Weigh**	Darlington
6/4/64	**Weigh**	Darlington

Sheds

Dairycoates	20/10/51
Heaton	3/11/51
Alston	7/6/53
Kirkby Stephen	22/5/55
West Hartlepool	1/7/56

Withdrawn 12/7/65

43128 at Northallerton (shed in the background) in the late 1950s. It was working from West Hartlepool from July 1956 until its withdrawal in 1965. It received AWS at an unrecorded date, probably in October 1962. It was allocated to Alston to work the branch from Haltwhistle in June 1953 before joining several other 4MTs at Kirkby Stephen in May 1955, staying there until July 1956. B.K.B. Green Collection.

43129

Built at Horwich 1/11/51

Tender 4779

Improvements and modifications
New chimney arrangement   ?
Fitting A.W.S   13/5/61

Repairs

27/5/53-15/6/53	**CL**	Doncaster
14/9/55-22/10/55	**IH**	Doncaster
11/9/56-24/10/56	**CL**	Doncaster
1/8/58-15/8/58	**NC**	Doncaster
22/2/60-1/4/60	**Gen**	Darlington
9/5/61-13/5/61	**NC**	Darlington
13/10/61-10/11/61	**CL**	Darlington
13/3/62-26/3/62	**CL**	Darlington
4/63-17/5/63	**Gen**	Horwich

Sheds

Heaton	1/11/51
Darlington	16/6/57
Normanton	13/3/66

Withdrawn 24/6/67

43129 at Darlington on 19 June 1965. It only had three sheds; it started at Heaton, then went to Darlington in June 1957 and ended up at Normanton from March 1966 until withdrawn in June 1967. The AWS was fitted in May 1961. J.T. Clewley, www.transporttreasury.co.uk

43130

Built at Horwich 10/11/51

Tender 4780

Improvements and modifications
New chimney arrangement ?
Fitting A.W.S 30/6/60

Repairs
22/12/53-26/1/54	**IH**	Doncaster
7/2/55-18/2/55	**NC**	Doncaster
7/7/55-9/8/55	**CL**	Darlington
8/10/56-10/11/56	**Gen**	Doncaster
23/5/57-31/5/57	**NC**	Doncaster
3/5/60-30/6/60	**Gen**	Darlington
30/9/62-1/11/63	**IL**	Horwich

Sheds
Dairycoates	10/11/51
Kirkby Stephen	22/5/55
Darlington	23/9/56
Holbeck	15/9/57

Withdrawn 29/6/67

43130 followed a familiar trail from Hull Dairycoates to Kirkby Stephen in May 1955 and then to Darlington in September 1956. It moved to its final shed, Holbeck in September 1957 and was pictured there on 4 September 1960. It shows evidence of a recent overhaul at Darlington completed in June, when it was fitted with AWS and given a repaint with wide spaced lining with large numbers and crest; it was withdrawn in June 1967. R.K. Blencowe.

43131

Built at Horwich 21/11/51

Tender 4781

Improvements and modifications
New chimney arrangement   ?
Fitting A.W.S   7/10/60

Repairs
14/10/53-9/11/53	**IH**	Doncaster
14/12/56-15/1/57	**IH**	Doncaster
17/11/59-6/1/60	**Gen**	Darlington
26/9/60-7/10/60	**NC**	Darlington
26/4/62-9/5/62	**CL**	Darlington

Sheds
Dairycoates   21/11/51

Withdrawn 9/12/63

43131, always shedded at Dairycoates, was an early withdrawal in December 1963, shortly after this picture was taken at its home shed. It was fitted with AWS at Darlington in October 1960. The chalked figures on the buffer are a system employed by the shed to indicate when the locomotive was required. www.rail-online.co.uk

43132

Built at Horwich 1/12/51

Tender 4782

Improvements and modifications
New chimney arrangement   ?
Fitting A.W.S   ?

Repairs
5/5/54-2/6/54	**IH**	Doncaster
23/1/57-23/2/57	**Gen**	Doncaster
5/8/60-10/9/60	**Gen**	Darlington
12/4/62-13/6/62	**CH**	Darlington
11/7/62	**NC**	Cowlairs
9/3/64-1/5/64	**CL**	Swindon

Sheds
Eastfield	1/12/51
Fort William	2/5/53
Eastfield	4/7/53
Kipps	3/5/56
Greenock	5/3/62
Hurlford	20/12/62
Wakefield	3/11/63
Low Moor	5/1/64
Ardsley	3/1/65
North Blyth	31/10/65

Withdrawn 1/12/66

43132 with a cut-out on the tender for a tablet catcher, although it was never fitted with the device, at Eastfield on 9 July 1955. It was loaned to Fort William in May/June 1953, moving to Kipps in May 1956 and to Greenock and then Hurlford in 1962. It moved south to the North Eastern Region at Wakefield in November 1963. J. Robertson, transporttreasury.co.uk

43133

Built at Horwich 8/12/51

Tender 4783

Improvements and modifications
New chimney arrangement   ?
Fitting A.W.S   ?

Repairs

5/8/53-6/8/53	NC	Cowlairs
11/3/54-15/4/54	HI	Doncaster
31/12/54	NC(EO)	Cowlairs
7/10/55-8/10/55	NC(EO)	Cowlairs
29/3/57-30/5/57	Gen	Doncaster
9/2/60-16/3/60	Gen	Darlington
1/6/60-11/6/60	NC(TO)	Cowlairs
18/5/61-16/9/61	LC	Darlington
20/3/62-30/3/62	NC(EO)	Cowlairs
11/1/63-26/1/63	NC	Cowlairs
25/2/63-1/4/63	LI	Horwich
11/5/63-27/6/63	LC	Horwich

Sheds

Eastfield	8/12/51
Fort William	2/5/53
Eastfield	6/7/53
Kipps	3/11/56 PE
Motherwell	5/3/62
Greenock	17/3/62
Hurlford	20/12/62
West Auckland	3/11/63
Goole	2/2/64
York	19/7/64
South Blyth	31/7/66
North Blyth	23/10/66

Withdrawn w.e. 1/12/66

43133 at Bolton Trinity Street in 1963; 67B Hurlford plate indicating that it had been borrowed locally after visiting Horwich twice in that year for Light repairs. The date it was fitted with AWS is not recorded but was probably done during one of those visits.

43134

Built at Horwich 20/12/51

Tender 4784

Improvements and modifications
New chimney arrangement ?

Repairs

24/5/54-17/6/54	**IH**	Doncaster
7/10/55-8/10/55	**NC**	Cowlairs
22/5/57-21/6/57	**Gen**	Doncaster
16/4/59-20/4/59	**NC**	Cowlairs
7/6/61-21/9/61	**Gen**	Darlington
3/8/62-21/8/62	**CL**	Horwich

Sheds

Eastfield	20/12/51
Kipps	3/3/56
Greenock	5/3/62
Hurlford	29/12/62
Ardsley	3/11/63

Withdrawn 24/2/65

43134 at Eastfield on 27 September 1952, as delivered from Horwich the previous December in lined black. Two features distinguished the five ScR engines built at Horwich. The most obvious is the cut-out for a tablet catcher on the tender, but there was also a rectangular plate riveted to the lower edge of cab on the right-hand side. Starting life at Eastfield it went to Kipps in March 1956 and to Greenock and then Hurlford in 1962. It moved south to the North Eastern Region at Ardsley in November 1963 and was withdrawn in February 1965. www.rail-online.co.uk

43135

Built at Horwich 27/12/51

Tender 4785

Improvements and modifications
New chimney arrangement   ?

Repairs
5/4/54-5/5/54	**HI**	Doncaster
5/2/57-2/3/57	**Gen**	Doncaster
18/11/59-18/12/59	**Gen**	Darlington
9/8/62-1/11/62	**HI**	Horwich
5/11/62-8/11/62	**NC**	Horwich
11/4/63-12/4/63	**NC**	Cowlairs

Sheds
Eastfield	27/12/51
Fort William	2/5/53
Eastfield	6/7/53
Parkhead	8/7/60
Dawsholm	5/10/61
Thornaby	3/11/63
Stourton	24/5/64
Manningham	19/6/66

Stored serviceable
19/4/64-24/5/64

Withdrawn 30/10/66

43135 looking immaculate at Eastfield on 3 May 1952 shows off the Horwich version of lined black. It was one of the engines loaned to Fort William in May/June 1953 while the ashpits at Mallaig were being rebuilt. 43135 went to Parkhead in July 1960 and Dawsholm in October 1961 before going to Thornaby in November 1963. R.K. Blencowe.

43136

Built at Horwich 3/1/52

Tender 4786

Improvements and modifications
New chimney arrangement   ?

Repairs

13/5/54-14/6/54	**HI**	Doncaster
13/10/54-23/10/54	**CL**	Cowlairs
12/2/57-14/3/57	**Gen**	Doncaster
15/12/59-28/1/60	**Gen**	Darlington
23/1/64-12/2/64	**Unsch**	Darlington

Sheds

Eastfield	3/1/52
Perth	1/4/55
Eastfield	11/5/55
Parkhead	8/7/60
Dawsholm	5/10/63
Ardsley	3/11/63

Withdrawn w.e. 20/6/64

The last Horwich-built 4MT, 43136 in the late 1950s while allocated to Eastfield. It has the new chimney arrangement fitted during a Heavy Intermediate overhaul at Doncaster completed in June 1954. It moved to Parkhead in July 1960, Dawsholm in October 1963 and then to the North Eastern Region at Ardsley the following month. 43136 was withdrawn in June 1964.

43137

Built at Doncaster 13/7/51

Works number   2082
Tender   4787

Improvements and modifications
New chimney arrangement   ?

Repairs
6/2/53-19/3/53	IL	Doncaster
27/10/55-25/11/55	IH	Doncaster
16/5/57-17/5/57	NC	Cowlairs
21/4/59-28/5/59	Gen	Darlington
6/3/63-2/4/63	IH	Horwich
6/64-30/11/64	Unsch	Swindon

Sheds
South Lynn	13/7/51
Eastfield	13/8/51
Fort William	2/5/53
Eastfield	6/7/53
Grangemouth	27/2/61
Wakefield	3/11/63
Copley Hill	5/1/64
Wakefield	6/9/64
Ardsley	3/1/65
Wakefield	10/10/65
North Blyth	21/8/66

Stored serviceable
13/8/62-24/10/62

Withdrawn 9/9/67

43137 at Eastfield on 31 March 1956 with a tablet catcher fitted tender. Built at Doncaster in 1951, it was the first Scottish Ivatt in August 1951, although it was borrowed by South Lynn for a month before it went north to Eastfield. transporttreasury.co.uk

43138

Built at Doncaster 23/7/51

Works number 2083
Tender 4788

Improvements and modifications
New chimney arrangement   ?

Repairs

5/11/53-4/12/53	**HI**	Doncaster
26/8/57-29/8/57	**LC(EO)**	Cowlairs
21/1/58-14/2/58	**Gen**	Doncaster
10/3/58-13/3/58	**NC(Adj)**	Doncaster
3/5/58-9/5/58	**NC**	Doncaster
24/4/62-29/6/62	**Gen**	Darlington
10/9/63	**NC(EO)**	Cowlairs

Sheds

Eastern Region	23/7/51
Eastfield	13/8/51
Bathgate	15/4/54
Parkhead	9/7/60
Hawick	6/10/61
West Auckland	11/10/63 (loan)
West Auckland	3/11/63
Dairycoates	2/2/64
York	6/9/64
South Blyth	31/7/66
North Blyth	23/10/66

Withdrawn 27/3/67

43138 in 1951 at its home shed, Eastfield, has the final lined Doncaster livery with wide spaced lining and large cab numbers. It has a tablet catcher for working the single lines and went to Bathgate in April 1954 and Parkhead in July 1960 before arriving on the Waverley line at Hawick in October 1961.

43139

Built at Doncaster 27/7/51

Works number 2084
Tender 4789

Improvements and modifications
New chimney arrangement	19/1/54
Fitting A.W.S	7/8/61

Repairs
22/8/52-3/9/52	**NC**	Doncaster
14/12/53-19/1/54	**HI**	Doncaster
3/4/56-9/5/56	**HI**	Doncaster
5/6/57-19/6/57	**NC(EO)**	Doncaster
3/3/58-18/4/58	**HI**	Horwich
22/4/58-23/4/58	**NC(EO)**	Horwich
25/3/60-20/4/60	**LC**	Horwich
19/6/61-7/8/61	**HG**	Horwich
12/8/63-5/9/63	**LC**	Horwich
17/10/63-8/11/63	**LC**	Horwich
30/11/65-8/1/66	**LI**	Cowlairs

Mileage/(weekdays out of service)
1953	35,322 (42)
1954	31,916 (59)
1955	33,603 (57)
1956	34,644 (57)
1957	29,986 (83)
1958	32,104 (53)
1959	34,586
1960	27,080

Sheds
Eastern Region	27/7/51
Carlisle Canal	13/8/51
Carlisle Kingmoor	22/6/63

Withdrawn w.e. 30/9/67

43139, the Langholm branch engine for more than ten years, at Carlisle on 1 August 1957. It lost its lined livery during a Heavy Intermediate overhaul at Doncaster the previous year. 43139 was a Carlisle engine throughout, originally at the ex-LNER Canal shed until that closed in 1963 and then Kingmoor to withdrawal in September 1967.

43140

Built at Doncaster 3/8/51

Works number 2085
Tender 4790

Improvements and modifications
New chimney arrangement   ?

Repairs

7/11/51-26/11/51	**CL**	Doncaster
28/5/53-7/7/53	**Gen**	Doncaster
16/9/53-23/9/53	**NC(EO)**	Darlington
14/3/56-21/4/56	**IH**	Doncaster
10/6/59-1/8/59	?	Darlington
26/4/62-28/4/62	**CL(EO)**	Cowlairs
18/1/63-26/2/63	**IH**	Horwich

Sheds

Polmont	3/8/51
Grangemouth	31/1/59
St Rollox	3/4/59
Parkhead	13/7/60
Dawsholm	3/11/61
West Auckland	3/11/63
Thornaby	1/12/63
Darlington	7/6/64
North Blyth	15/11/64
Stourton	23/5/65
Normanton	15/1/67

Withdrawn 15/5/67

43140 at Dawsholm on 13 April 1963. It had returned to its home shed from a Heavy Intermediate at Horwich a few weeks earlier with only the smokebox repainted, the original Doncaster lining just visible under the grime. David Idle, www.transporttreasury.co.uk

43141

Built at Doncaster 13/8/51

Works number 2086
Tender 4791

Improvements and modifications
New chimney arrangement   ?
Fitting A.W.S   ?

Repairs
23/4/53-11/5/53   **NC**   Doncaster
29/6/53-24/7/53   **Gen**   Doncaster
19/1/56-23/2/56   **Gen**   Doncaster
12/2/57-28/2/57   **CL**   Doncaster
16/7/58-24/7/58   **NC**   Doncaster
22/9/59-28/10/59   **Gen**   Darlington
25/11/60-3/12/60   **CH(EO)**   Cowlairs
8/6/61-8/12/61   **CH**   Darlington
11/11/63-4/12/63   **HI**   Horwich

Sheds
Polmont   13/8/51
Hawick   2/6/58
Parkhead   8/7/60
Hawick   18/12/61
West Auckland   16/10/63 (loan)
West Auckland   3/11/63
Dairycoates   2/2/64
Low Moor   7/6/64
Ardsley   22/11/64
Normanton   31/10/65

Withdrawn 28/10/66

43141 at Hawick on 14 August 1962; it was twice shedded there, from June 1958 to July 1960 and again from December 1961 until transferred to the North Eastern Region in late 1963. It is in plain black, and has AWS equipment, probably fitted during a Heavy Classified repair at Darlington which took six months from June to December 1961.

43142

Built at Doncaster w.e 25/8/51

Works number 2087
Tender 4792

Improvements and modifications
New chimney arrangement   ?

Repairs

18/10/53-8/1/54	HI	Stratford
11/3/57-18/4/57	G	Doncaster
4/6/57-15/6/57	Adj	Doncaster
24/12/59-19/2/60	Gen	Doncaster
4/7/60-7/7/60	NC	Doncaster

Sheds

South Lynn	20/8/51
Boston	1/3/59
Retford	30/4/61
Boston	21/5/61

Withdrawn w.e. 28/12/63

43142 at Boston on 15 May 1960 with the breakdown train; it was at South Lynn until the M&GN closed whereupon it moved to Boston. It remained there except for three weeks at Retford in May 1961 and was withdrawn in December 1963. www.rail-online.co.uk

43143

Built at Doncaster 30/8/51

Works number 2088
Tender 4743

Improvements and modifications
New chimney arrangement   ?

Repairs

6/8/53-1/9/53	IH	Doncaster
5/10/55-5/11/55	IH	Doncaster
11/1/57-30/1/57	CL	Doncaster
27/8/57-6/9/57	CL	Stratford
10/3/59-24/4/59	Gen	Stratford
11/7/60-16/7/60	NC	Doncaster
PE 5/11/60	CL	Boston
14/6/63-16/8/63	HI	Horwich

Sheds

South Lynn	30/8/51
Boston	1/3/59
Barrow Hill	30/11/63

Withdrawn 20/6/65

A very unkempt 43143 at Willesden on 29 August 1964. It was a Barrow Hill engine and what it was doing at the London shed is an interesting question.

43144

Built at Doncaster 5/9/51

Works number 2089
Tender 4794

Improvements and modifications
New chimney arrangement   ?
Fitting A.W.S   5/61

Repairs
1954	**HI**	Stratford
?-p/e 19/1/57	**H**	Doncaster
12/59-1/60	?	Stratford
?- 5/61	?	Doncaster
Others not recorded		

Sheds
South Lynn	5/9/51
Neasden	1/3/53
South Lynn	25/7/54
Stratford	1/3/59
Boston	27/11/60
New England	5/1/64
Barrow Hill	3/1/65

Withdrawn 11/4/65

43144 at Doncaster, ex-works in newly applied plain black with small BR crest, probably when it was fitted with AWS in May 1961. It was one of the M&GN 4MTs sent to Neasden in 1953/54, returning to South Lynn and going to Stratford on its closure. It joined many of its classmates at Boston in November 1960, staying until the end of 1963 when it moved to New England and then Barrow Hill a year later. www.rail-online.co.uk

43145

Built at Doncaster 20/9/51

Works number   2090
Tender   4795

Improvements and modifications
New chimney arrangement   ?

Repairs
1954	HI	Stratford
?-p/e 19/1/57	H	Doncaster
?-3/60	H	Doncaster
Others not recorded

Sheds
South Lynn	20/9/51
Yarmouth Beach	30/9/51
Melton Constable	27/1/52
Norwich	1/3/59
Staveley	13/3/60
Colwick	23/9/62

Withdrawn 10/1/65

43145 on 16 July 1961 at Staveley GC shed appears to be out of use with its chimney covered. It had spent time at all three M&GN sheds, leaving for Norwich on closure. It moved to Staveley in March 1960 and finally Colwick in September 1962, being withdrawn from there in January 1965. R.J. Buckley, Initial Photographics.

43146

Built at Doncaster 9/51

Works number 2091
Tender 4796

Improvements and modifications
New chimney arrangement   ?

Repairs
3/5/54-19/6/54	**IH**	Stratford
31/10/55-13/12/55	**CL**	Doncaster
19/10/56-29/11/56	**Gen**	Doncaster
16/3/60-21/5/60	**Gen**	Doncaster
30/4/63-30/5/63	**LI**	Horwich

Sheds
Melton Constable	28/9/51
Norwich	1/3/59
Grimesthorpe	24/1/60
New England	9/7/61

Withdrawn 3/1/65

43146 looks immaculate on 20 June 1954 at Stratford after completion of a Heavy Intermediate overhaul there. Stratford dropped the lining from February 1955. www.rail-online.co.uk

43147

Built at Doncaster 8/10/51

Works number 2092
Tender   4797

Improvements and modifications
New chimney arrangement   ?

Repairs
1954	**HI**	Stratford
? - p/e 16/5/57	**Gen**	Doncaster
? – 12/60	**H**	Doncaster
Others not recorded		

Sheds
Melton Constable	8/10/51
Boston	1/3/59
New England	5/1/64

Withdrawn w.e. 26/12/64

43147 with the normal weekday two coach train drifting in off the Cromer line at Melton West junction in the late 1950s. It was always at Melton Constable, up to March 1959, moving then to Boston and later to New England at the end of 1963. Dr Ian C. Allen, www.transporttreasury.co.uk

43148

Built at Doncaster 17/10/51

Works number   2093
Tender   4798

Improvements and modifications
New chimney arrangement   ?

Repairs

6/5/54-3/7/54	**IH**	Stratford
16/5/55-4/6/55	**NC**	Stratford
21/12/55-4/1/56	**NC**	Doncaster
3/6/57-13/9/57	**Gen**	Stratford
29/11/60-4/1/61	**Gen**	Doncaster
15/7/63-23/8/63	**LC**	Horwich

Sheds

Melton Constable	17/10/51
Stratford	1/3/59
Colwick	14/2/60
Boston	22/1/61
Barrow Hill	30/11/63

Withdrawn w.e. 11/4/65

The driver of 43148 demonstrates at Melton Constable how easy it was to oil a 4MT.

43149

Built at Doncaster 24/10/51

Works number 2094
Tender 4799

Improvements and modifications
New chimney arrangement   ?
Fitting A.W.S   20/5/61

Repairs
1/6/54-7/8/54	**IH**	Stratford
16/11/56-30/11/56	**CL**	Doncaster
19/6/57-27/7/57	**Gen**	Doncaster
18/4/61-20/5/61	**Gen**	Doncaster
8/5/61-14/5/61	**CL**	Lincoln

Sheds
Melton Constable	24/10/51
Stratford	1/3/59
March	8/1/61
Cambridge	16/7/61
March	17/6/62
Lincoln	16/9/62
Colwick	5/1/64
Canklow	25/10/64
Barrow Hill	13/6/65
Langwith	3/10/65

Withdrawn 14/11/65

43149 at March on 13 July 1961 in plain black with a small BR crest; AWS had been fitted during a General repair at Doncaster completed on 20 May. After leaving the M&GN it was at Stratford for nearly two years, arriving at March in January 1961. It went to Cambridge six months later but returned for three months in mid-1962, moving on to Lincoln in September. www.rail-online.co.uk

43150

Built at Doncaster 7/11/51

Works number 2095
Tender 4800

Improvements and modifications
New chimney arrangement   5/11/54
Fitting A.W.S   ?

Repairs
13/2/52-27/2/52	**Adj**	Doncaster
7/10/54-5/11/54	**IH**	Doncaster
15/1/57-26/1/57	**CI**	Doncaster
14/8/57-19/9/57	**Gen**	Doncaster
27/10/60-30/11/60	**Gen**	Doncaster

Sheds
Melton Constable	7/11/51
Stratford	1/3/59
New England	31/1/60

Withdrawn 3/1/65

43150 at Werrington on the northern edge of Peterborough with a short freight on 21 June 1960. After a few months at Stratford after the demise of the M&GN 43150 moved to New England in January 1960, to be withdrawn there at the end of 1964.

43151

Built at Doncaster 9/11/51

Works number   2096
Tender   4801

Improvements and modifications
New chimney arrangement   ?
Fitting A.W.S   4/61

Repairs

?- p/e 19/10/57	H	Stratford
? – 4/61	H	Doncaster
Others not recorded		

Sheds

Melton Constable	9/11/51
Stratford	1/3/59
Colwick	28/2/60
New England	13/3/60
Barrow Hill	3/3/63
Crewe South	10/10/64

Withdrawn w.e. 18/2/67

43151 at Crewe South in a picture full of useful detail for the modeller. It shows the battery box of the AWS (fitted in April 1961) the curved front step on the tender, the tender cab and inward facing vents. The bolts remain in the cut-out but the tablet catcher has gone. 43151 arrived at Crewe from Barrow Hill in October 1964 and was withdrawn there in February 1967.

239

43152

Built at Doncaster 23/11/51

Works number   2097
Tender   4802

Improvements and modifications
New chimney arrangement   ?

Repairs

5/9/54-16/10/54	**HI**	Stratford
4/11/54-24/11/54	**Uncl**	Stratford
2/6/57-12/10/57	**Gen**	Stratford
15/1/61-24/2/61	**Gen**	Doncaster
13/5/61-1/6/61	**CL**	Doncaster

Sheds

Melton Constable	23/11/51
Colchester	1/3/59
Stratford	6/12/59
Colwick	21/2/60

Withdrawn 5/1/64

43152 at Breadsall on 25 May 1960 with the 4.15pm Grantham-Derby Friargate local. When it left the M&GN 43152 went initially to Colchester, then Stratford in December 1959, moving to Colwick three months later; it was withdrawn there at the end of 1963. R.J. Buckley, Initial Photographics.

43153

Built at Doncaster 4/12/51

Works number 2098
Tender 4803

Improvements and modifications
New chimney arrangement   ?

Repairs
18/11/52-4/12/52	**CL**	Doncaster
6/12/54-22/1/55	**IH**	Stratford
16/1/56-24/1/57	**CL**	Doncaster
28/8/57-4/10/57	**Gen**	Doncaster
15/4/58-25/4/58	**CL**	Stratford
22/2/62-31/3/62	**Gen**	Doncaster

Sheds
Melton Constable	4/12/51
Stratford	1/3/59
Lincoln	18/9/60
New England	20/11/60
Barrow Hill	22/9/63

Withdrawn 20/6/65

Melton Constable's 43153 at Stratford on 28 April 1958 after completion of a Light Classified repair. It was re-allocated there after the M&GN closed in February 1959, moving to Lincoln in late 1960. J. Robertson, transporttreasury.co.uk

43154

Built at Doncaster 14/12/51

Works number 2099
Tender 4804

Improvements and modifications
New chimney arrangement   18/9/54
Fitting A.W.S   ?

Repairs
10/8/54-18/9/54	**IH**	Stratford
5/9/57-12/10/57	**Gen**	Doncaster
20/7/59-22/7/59	**NC**	Stratford
7/6/61-14/7/61	**Gen**	Doncaster
6/8/62-13/9/62	**LC**	Horwich

Sheds
Melton Constable	14/12/51
Boston	1/3/59
Colwick	15/3/59
Lincoln	18/11/59
Colwick	23/9/62

Withdrawn 26/12/64

43154 at Cromer Beach on Saturday 23 August 1958 with the 9.35am from Birmingham. 4MT on bufferbeam. F. Hornby.

43155

Built at Doncaster 28/12/51

Works number   2100
Tender   4805

Improvements and modifications
New chimney arrangement   ?
Fitting A.W.S   6/61

Repairs
6/58 – 8/58   ?   Stratford
? – 6/61   **H**   Doncaster
Others not recorded

Sheds
Melton Constable   28/12/51
Boston   1/3/59
Colwick   15/3/59

Withdrawn 10/1/65

43155 in unlined livery at Colwick on 24 June 1962; it had been fitted with AWS in June 1961. It arrived at the Nottingham shed ex-M&GN in March 1959, after two weeks at Boston and was withdrawn from there in January 1965.

43156

Built at Doncaster 7/1/52

Works number 2101
Tender 4806

Improvements and modifications
New chimney arrangement   ?
Fitting A.W.S   ?

Repairs
1/11/54-18/12/54	**IH**	Stratford
21/10/57-21/12/57	**Gen**	Stratford
15/3/60-22/3/60	**NC**	Doncaster
28/3/61-29/4/61	**Gen**	Doncaster

Sheds
Melton Constable	7/1/52
Yarmouth Beach	27/1/52
Melton Constable	28/9/52
Norwich	1/3/59
Colwick	7/2/60

Withdrawn 10/1/65

43156 at Norwich Thorpe Junction on a very short freight with two SR designed Parcels Vans at the front. It was shedded at 32A from March 1959 until February 1960 when it moved to Colwick, lasting until January 1965. Dr Ian C. Allen, www.transporttreasury.co.uk

43157

Built at Doncaster 3/7/52

Works number 2102
Tender 4807

Improvements and modifications
New chimney arrangement   ?

Repairs
5/1/55-23/2/55	**IH**	Stratford
19/8/55-1/9/55	**NC**	Doncaster
10/7/57-13/8/57	**Gen**	Doncaster
26/4/60-4/6/60	**Gen**	Doncaster
19/8/60-26/8/60	**NC**	Doncaster
31/10/63-12/12/63	**LC**	Horwich

Sheds
Yarmouth Beach	3/7/52
Norwich	1/3/59
Boston	12/4/59
Retford	9/4/61
Barrow Hill	4/5/63

Withdrawn w.e. 10/1/65

43157 at Retford on 17 March 1963 still has its tablet catcher. When it left Yarmouth Beach in March 1959 it went to Norwich for a few weeks, then to Boston, arriving at Retford in April 1961 and staying until May 1963 when it was transferred to Barrow Hill.

43158

Built at Doncaster 16/7/52

Works number   2103
Tender   4808

Improvements and modifications
New chimney arrangement   ?
Fitting A.W.S   10/61

Repairs
? - 3/55	?	Stratford
6/58 - ?	?	Stratford
? – 10/61	**H**	Doncaster
Others not recorded		

Sheds
Yarmouth Beach	16/7/52
Boston	1/3/59
Colwick	15/3/59
Lincoln	8/11/59
Retford	26/2/61
Boston	9/4/61
New England	5/1/64

Withdrawn w.e. 3/1/65

43158 at its home shed Boston after fitting with AWS in October 1961. It went there direct from the M&GN but left after two weeks for Colwick. www.rail-online.co.uk

43159

Built at Doncaster 1/8/52

Works number 2104
Tender 4809

Improvements and modifications
New chimney arrangement   ?

Repairs
? - 3/58	H	Stratford
10/61-11/61	H	Doncaster
Others not recorded		

Sheds
Yarmouth Beach	1/8/52
Norwich	1/3/59
Boston	12/4/59
Colwick	26/7/59
Grimesthorpe	1/11/59
Barrow Hill	23/4/61
Grantham	4/11/62
Barrow Hill	18/5/63

Withdrawn 20/6/65

43159 at Yarmouth on 18 May 1958 after a General repair at Stratford when it emerged in plain black with centrally positioned RA4 and small BR crest. N.E. Preedy.

43160

Built at Doncaster 14/8/52

Works number 2105
Tender 4810

Improvements and modifications
New chimney arrangement   ?

Repairs

?-w/e 16/8/52	?	Doncaster
21/2/55-7/4/55	**IH**	Stratford
3/1/57-9/1/57	**CL**	Doncaster
1/2/57-5/2/57	**Adj**	Doncaster
14/4/58-23/5/58	**Gen**	Stratford
13/10/61-2/12/61	**Gen**	Doncaster

Sheds

Yarmouth Beach	14/8/52
Norwich	1/3/59
Staveley	27/11/60
Grimesthorpe	29/1/61
Colwick	10/9/61

Withdrawn 10/1/65

43160 at Melton West on the 9.35am Derby-Yarmouth on a summer Saturday in 1958. Another 4MT is waiting on the up main to cross over and work the Cromer portion of the following 9.55am Derby-Yarmouth. These were just two of nine such trains which would arrive from the Midlands that day.

43161

Built at Doncaster 3/9/52

Works number 2106
Tender 4811

Improvements and modifications
New chimney arrangement   26/6/54
Fitting A.W.S   ?

Repairs

17/11/52-27/11/52	**NC**	Doncaster
26/4/54-26/6/54	**CH**	Stratford
16/9/55-22/10/55	**IH**	Doncaster
21/2/57-28/2/57	**NC**	Doncaster
5/7/57-3/8/57	**Gen**	Doncaster
27/1/60-26/3/60	**Gen**	Doncaster
11/11/60-25/11/60	**NC**	Doncaster
16/5/63-19/6/63	**LI**	Horwich

Sheds

Yarmouth Beach	3/9/52
Neasden	1/3/53
Yarmouth Beach	27/6/54
Norwich	1/3/59
Staveley	27/11/60
Grimesthorpe	P/E 3/4/61
Colwick	P/E 7/10/61
Barrow Hill	9/3/63

Withdrawn 20/6/65

Last of the class 43161 delivered September 1952 in front of its home shed Yarmouth Beach. It is in plain black ex-Doncaster following a General overhaul completed in August 1957. 43161 was one of the engines transferred to Neasden in 1953, returning to Yarmouth in June 1954. After closure of the M&GN it went to Norwich, moving on to Staveley, Grimesthorpe, Colwick and finally Barrow Hill in March 1963. www.rail-online.co.uk

Endpiece

An Ivatt 4 at Carlisle, 43023, on pilot duty. It didn't matter by now, in the 1960s of course, but at first the authorities were concerned that such engines, for reasons of crew comfort, were put on pilot jobs which were by nature very low mileage. Old 2Fs and 3Fs were there for this sort of job! An edict went out; strangely it went unnoticed. Colour-Rail.co.uk